Workbook for DIESEL MECHANICS
Second Edition

Erich J. Schulz

Gregg Division/McGraw-Hill Book Company
New York Atlanta Dallas St. Louis San Francisco Auckland Bogotá
Guatemala Hamburg Johannesburg Lisbon London Madrid Mexico Montreal New Delhi
Panama Paris San Juan São Paulo Singapore Sydney Tokyo Toronto

Workbook for DIESEL MECHANICS, Second Edition

Copyright © 1983, 1977 by McGraw-Hill, Inc. All rights reserved. Printed in the United States of America. Except as permitted under the United States Copyright Act of 1976, no part of this publication may be reproduced or distributed in any form or by any means, or stored in a data base or retrieval system, without the prior written permission of the publisher.

3 4 5 6 7 8 9 0 SEMSEM 8 9 0 9 8 7 6

ISBN 0-07-055640-7

CONTENTS

TO THE STUDENT v

INTRODUCTORY ASSIGNMENT: SAFETY RULES AND PRECAUTIONS 1

ASSIGNMENTS

	1	BASIC COMPONENTS 5
2 and 3		ENGINE PERFORMANCE AND CYCLE OPERATION 7
	4	COMBUSTION CHAMBERS 9
	5	ENGINE DISASSEMBLY 11
	6	CYLINDER BLOCK 15
	7	CAMSHAFT 17
	8	CYLINDER SLEEVE 19
	9	CRANKSHAFT 21
	10	CONNECTING ROD 23
	11	PISTONS AND RINGS 25
12 and 13		ENGINE OIL, LUBRICATION PUMP, AND OIL COOLER 27
	14	CYLINDER HEAD AND VALVES 29
	15	VALVE-TRAIN OPERATING MECHANISM 33
	16	FLYWHEEL HOUSING, FLYWHEEL, TIMING-GEAR COVER, CRANKSHAFT PULLEY, AND VIBRATION DAMPER 35
	17	BEARINGS 37
	18	AIR-INTAKE SYSTEM 39
	19	EXHAUST SYSTEM 41
	20	COOLING SYSTEM 43
	21	HYDRAULIC LINES AND FITTINGS 47
	22	FILTERS 49
	23	SEALS AND GASKETS 51
	24	DIESEL FUEL 53
	25	GOVERNORS 55
	26	ANTIPOLLUTION CONTROL DEVICES 59
	27	FUEL-INJECTION NOZZLES AND HOLDERS 61
	28	FUEL-INJECTION SYSTEMS 65
	29	AMERICAN BOSCH, ROBERT BOSCH, AND CAV PORT AND HELIX FUEL-INJECTION PUMPS 67
	30	CATERPILLAR PORT AND HELIX FUEL-INJECTION PUMPS 73
	31	DETROIT DIESEL FUEL-INJECTION SYSTEM 77
	32	CATERPILLAR UNIT-INJECTOR FUEL-INJECTION SYSTEM 83
	33	CUMMINS FUEL-INJECTION SYSTEM AND PT FUEL PUMPS 85
	33A	CUMMINS PTB, PTC, PTD, AND TOP STOP INJECTORS 89
	34	DPA AND STANADYNE DISTRIBUTOR-TYPE FUEL-INJECTION PUMPS 91
	35	AMERICAN BOSCH DISTRIBUTOR-TYPE FUEL-INJECTION PUMPS 95
	36	CATERPILLAR SLEEVE-METERING FUEL-INJECTION PUMPS 97
	37	ELECTRICITY AND MAGNETISM 99
38 and 39		ELECTRIC CIRCUITS AND TEST INSTRUMENTS 101
	40	RELAYS, MAGNETIC SWITCHES, SOLENOIDS, AND SOLENOID SWITCHES 103
	41	BATTERIES 105
	42	ELECTRIC STARTING (CRANKING) MOTORS 107
	43	AIR AND HYDRAULIC STARTING SYSTEMS 111
	44	COLD-WEATHER STARTING AIDS 113
	45	CHARGING SYSTEM 115
	46	REGULATORS 117
	47	INSTRUMENTS AND THEIR CIRCUITS 119
	48	HAND TOOLS 121
	49	SHOP TOOLS 123
	50	MEASURING TOOLS 125
	51	FASTENERS, TAPS, AND DIES 129
	52	CHECKS AND ADJUSTMENTS BEFORE STARTING THE ENGINE 131
	53	TROUBLESHOOTING, TESTING, AND ADJUSTING 133

TO THE STUDENT

With the ever-increasing use of diesel engine equipment, innovations are needed in the training methods used for the education of diesel mechanics. In answer to this need, the workbook you are about to use supplies a new approach that will permit you, through the programmed learning technique, to augment your knowledge of theoretical fundamentals.

This workbook contains both written exercises and shop assignments. The completion of the written exercises will serve to reinforce your textbook reading assignments. The performance of the shop assignments will reinforce the procedures described in the textbook or outlined in service manuals. Every unit of the textbook is also covered in this workbook. To help you locate quickly parts of the textbook that apply to particular workbook exercises, the abbreviation DM2, for *Diesel Mechanics,* Second Edition, has been used to indicate textbook units, illustrations, and pages. Together, the textbook and workbook provide you with knowledge in the areas of analyzing component failure, in servicing components, in using testing procedures, in troubleshooting, and above all, in recognizing the care required to prevent repeated failure.

Although additional classroom instruction, guidance, and careful shop supervision are always necessary, it is you who must feel that each question has been answered and each practical job has been performed to your own satisfaction. Competence goes hand in hand with pride in seeing a job well done.

Erich J. Schulz

INTRODUCTORY ASSIGNMENT SAFETY RULES AND PRECAUTIONS

Accidents do not *happen;* they are caused! Although both you and your employer must take part in preventing on-the-job injuries, the responsibility for safety *in daily routine* is on your shoulders alone (Fig. 1).

The equipment, the tools, and the shop in which you work are designed to ensure maximum safety. In addition, the Workers' Compensation Board has laid down safety rules which it strictly enforces. The final responsibility rests upon you and your employer to keep a clean shop, and to maintain the equipment and tools at peak efficiency. Notwithstanding, you must always remember that there are no such things as foolproof tools, machines, or equipment.

Accidents are usually the result of unsafe working conditions or unsafe working habits, or both. However, another contributor may be you, the mechanic, if your mind is not on the task at hand. It may be that you are not in your usual good health or are simply tired. Either case can lead to small mistakes which may result in injury to yourself or to one of your fellow workers (Fig. 2). Another potential cause of accidents is wearing inappropriate working clothes.

1. Very briefly discuss correct working clothes for a diesel mechanic.
2. Why should you remove jewelry or a necktie before working around machinery?
3. If you wear shoulder-length hair, why should you use a hairnet or a cap when working around machinery?

Explosions and Fire Most explosions and fires are the result of carelessness. Such negligence can bring about your dismissal, or worse, cost a human life. It is the responsibility of you and your fellow workers to maintain the shop in a safe condition by observing all fire-prevention rules. Remember that it is easier to prevent a fire than to extinguish one. Here are some rules which must always be obeyed:

1. Keep all inflammable fluid and material in a safe container and whenever possible store them in a separate area.
2. Always keep your workshop clean, and immediately discard all rubbish and combustibles. Dispose of oily rags as soon as you are finished with them by placing them in a covered steel container.
3. Use solvent as a cleaning fluid. Do not use gasoline or carbon tetrachloride.
4. Keep the lids on all solvent tanks when they are not being used.
5. Make certain that all electrical equipment is properly connected and grounded.
6. When using power tools, avoid using an octopus connection, which could overload the extension cable.
7. When using an extension light, make certain that the lamp guard is in place.
8. When using a torch of any kind, make certain that you have a fire extinguisher within reach and always keep your attention on the flame.
9. Never point the flame toward yourself or others, and never rest a flaming torch on an object. Shut the torch off immediately after using it.

Fig. 1 Accidents do not pay. Ask the person who had one!

Fig. 2 Operate that vehicle as though it were your own—with your family in it. Think first!

CAPACITY	PROTECT FROM FREEZING	EXTINGUISHING EFFECT	APPROXIMATE STREAM RANGE	METHOD OF DISCHARGE
Soda-Acid				
2½ gal	Yes	Cooling	45-55 ft	Chemically generated gas pressure
20 gal			65-75 ft	
40 gal			65-75 ft	
Clear Water, Pressurized Type				
2½ gal	Yes	Cooling	40-45 ft	Stored air pressure
Clear Water, Cartridge Type				
2½ gal	Yes	Cooling	40-45 ft	Gas pressure from carbon dioxide cartridge
Antifreeze, Cartridge Type				
2½ gal	No	Cooling	40-45 ft	Gas pressure from carbon dioxide cartridge
Pump Tank (Antifreeze or Plain Water)				
2½ gal	Where clear water is used — Yes Antifreeze Solution — No	Cooling	45–50 ft	Hand pump action
5 gal				
Loaded Stream, Pressurized Type				
2½ gal	No	Cooling	45-60 ft	Stored air pressure
Foam				
2½ gal	Yes	Blanketing	30-40 ft	Chemically generated gas pressure
20 gal			55-65 ft	
40 gal			55-65 ft	
VL Pressurized Type				
1 qt	No	Smothering	25-30 ft	Internally stored air pressure
2 qt			25-30 ft	
1 gal			25-30 ft	
VL Hand Pump Type				
1 qt	No	Smothering	25-30 ft	Hand pump action
1½ qt			25-30 ft	
Dry Chemical				
2½ lb	No	Smothering	10-12 ft	Stored air pressure
5 lb			10-12 ft	
10 lb			10-12 ft	
10 lb			10-12 ft	Gas pressure from carbon dioxide cartridge
20 lb			15-20 ft	
30 lb			15-20 ft	
75 lb			18 ft	Gas pressure from nitrogen cylinder
150 lb			18 ft	
Carbon Dioxide				
2½ lb	No	Smothering	Approx. 8 ft	Carbon dioxide under pressure in extinguisher
5 lb				
10 lb				
15 lb				
20 lb				
50 lb				
75 lb				
100 lb				

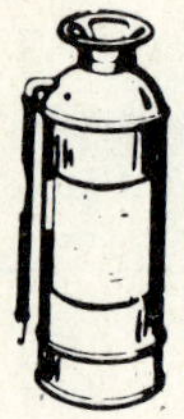

Fig. 3 Fire extinguishers.

Name _____ Date _____ Class _____

10. Do not enter a room marked "NO SMOKING" with an open flame light or a smoldering cigarette.
11. Do not flip a match or cigarette in any direction before you are certain it is extinguished. Do use an ashtray.
12. Do not block fire doors with any object.
13. Do not attempt to first fight the fire, and then sound the alarm.
14. Regularly check that all firefighting equipment and extinguishers are in operating condition and in the proper place.

Fire Extinguishers Inflammable materials, when heated to their specific kindling temperature and mixed with oxygen, will ignite. However, these materials do not have the same atomic structure, and therefore their thresholds for ignition differ. Correspondingly, the methods by which they can be extinguished also differ. Fires may be classified into three categories (A, B, and C). Fire extinguishers may be classified into six categories (Nos. 1 to 6 in Fig. 3).

Class A fires are so categorized where the combustible material is wood, fiber, paper, fabric, rubber, etc. Subdue these fires by cooling and quenching, using a fire hose or No. 1 to No. 3 fire extinguishers.

Class B fires are so categorized where the combustible material is a liquid, such as gasoline, fuel, or paint. Subdue these fires by smothering, using No. 2 to No. 6 fire extinguishers.

Class C fires are so categorized where the combustible materials are electrical components, such as motors, alternators, or switch panels. Subdue by smothering or by using No. 4 to No. 6 fire extinguishers. These have a nonconducting extinguisher agent.

4. Why should you place discarded oily rags into a steel container (preferably with a lid) and store the container in a cool place?
5. List at least four reasons why only solvent, and not gasoline, should be used for cleaning.
6. Why is it extremely important that you ground all electrical power tools and motors?

7. Explain why an overloaded electrical circuit can cause a fire.
8. How could a lamp without a lamp-guard perhaps create a fire?
9. Why must you never rest a flaming torch on any surface?
10. Why should you sound the fire alarm *before* starting to fight a fire?
11. What type of materials can you use as substitutes if no fire extinguisher or water is available?
12. Draw a sketch of your shop and outside work area, indicating the (a) location of the fire alarm, (b) location of the fire-hose outlet and hose length, (c) types of fire extinguishers.
13. List the telephone numbers of (a) the emergency hospital nearest your shop, (b) the police department, (c) your first-aid attendant.

Safety Rules There are certain basic safety rules (applicable to most tasks) which can prevent injury to the attending mechanic or to others in the work area.

14. Why should you obey the following safety rules: (a) When lifting components, start lifting from a squatting position. (b) Never try to reach and lift at the same time. (c) Always push heavy objects, never pull them. (d) Keep the floor clean and clear away any objects which could obstruct you in your work. (e) When using compressed air for cleaning, do not point the jetstream toward others and do not try to use it to clean your clothes. (f) When using power tools make certain they are properly grounded. (g) Get first-aid treatment for even a small cut, and report all injuries to the first-aid attendant. (h) Wear eye-protective shields or goggles when working underneath equipment, or when using a hammer to perform such jobs as driving, punching, or chiseling. (i) Make certain that your work area is well ventilated and adequately illuminated. (j) Disconnect the battery ground cable before performing any type of work on an engine or on connected components.

Name __Frank Stockman Jr__ Date _____ Class _____

ASSIGNMENT 1
BASIC COMPONENTS

1. List at least six differences between a gasoline engine and a diesel engine.

2. (a) Why is the compression ratio of a gasoline engine limited? (b) Why is the compression ratio of a diesel engine almost unlimited?

3. Why is it that a diesel engine with the same horsepower as a gasoline engine is nevertheless heavier?

4. Why is the engine speed of a gasoline engine limited to, for example, 5200 rpm (revolutions per minute), and how is it controlled? (See Fig. 1-1.)

5. What factor governs the engine speed limit of a diesel engine, and how is the engine speed controlled?

6. Why does a diesel engine accelerate more quickly [about 2000 rps (revolutions per second)] than a gasoline engine?

7. Check each diesel engine in your workshop. How many of these engines differ in regard to the number of cylinders and to the cylinder arrangement?

8. List the visible differences among the diesel engines in your workshop.

The cylinder block and the crankcase comprise the frame of a liquid-cooled engine. The frame design differs among manufacturers and even among engines manufactured by an individual company.

9. Inspect the engines in your shop. List the major differences in (a) cylinder-block design, (b) construction.

10. What is the purpose or function of the (a) piston, (b) piston rings, (c) connecting rod, (d) cylinder sleeves?

11. List the obvious differences between a wet and a dry sleeve.

12. One of the many differences between a 60-hp (horsepower) and a 600-hp diesel engine is found in the crankshaft. Refer to Fig. 1-2. In what ways do diesel engine crankshafts differ?

Examine the engines in your shop and then answer the next 13 questions.

13. How many of the engines in your shop use vibration dampers?

14. How many use a viscous-element vibration damper?

15. How many use a rubber-element vibration damper?

16. How many use only one cylinder head for all the cylinders?

17. How many use one cylinder head for two cylinders?

18. How many use one cylinder head for each individual cylinder?

19. How many have the timing gears in the front of the engine, and how many have the timing gears in the rear?

20. How many use an overhead camshaft instead of the conventional valve mechanism?

21. How many engines have the cooling fan bolted directly to the coolant pump?

22. How many have the oil pump mounted externally?

23. If the oil pump is externally mounted, how is the oil supply connected to the oil pump and to the main oil gallery?

24. Record the name of the fuel-injection-pump manufacturer of each engine in your shop, so that you become familiar with the various fuel-injection pumps.

25. What is the average number of fuel filters used on each engine in your shop? _two_

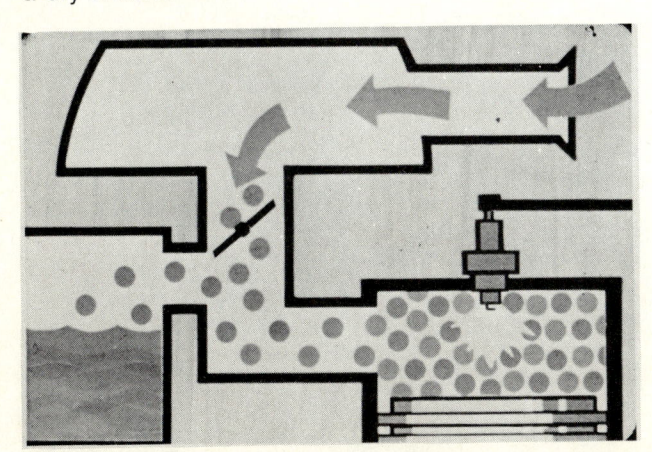

Fig. 1-1 Gasoline engine speed control.

Fig. 1-2 Diesel engine crankshaft.

Roaches is ball of diameter.

Name _____ Date _____ Class _____

ASSIGNMENTS 2 AND 3
ENGINE PERFORMANCE AND CYCLE OPERATION

1. Briefly explain the following terms: (a) cycle (in regard to four-cycle and two-cycle engines), (b) bore and stroke, (c) cylinder, (d) force, (e) pressure, (f) ratio, (g) work, (h) torque, (i) power, (j) heat.

2. Convert 150 lb (pounds) of force into metric units of measurement (kilograms). 68.4 Kg

3. When an applied force of 100 lb [45.36 kg (kilograms)] is placed on a cylinder having a diameter of 1 in (inch) [25.4 mm (millimeters)], how much is the pressure in pounds per square inch (psi) and in kilopascals? 127.34   878.24 KPA

4. What is the ratio between a pulley having a diameter of 6 in and one having a diameter of 4 in? 1.5

5. Convert the torque of a cylinder-head bolt tightened to 100 lb·ft (pound-feet) into metric units of measurement [newton-meters (N·m)]. 1.33 NM

6. What is the work done by an engine which produces an output of 300 hp on the dynamometer in 1 second, in foot-pounds and in kilogram-meters per second (kg·m/s)? 50.000 KDMS

7. In one working cycle, how many degrees would a crankshaft rotate in a (a) two-cycle engine, (b) four-cycle engine? A 360 — B 720

8. Relate the following in mechanic's terminology: (a) square, (b) undersquare, (c) oversquare.

9. Calculate the engine displacement of an eight-cylinder engine having a bore of 5 in and a stroke of 6 in (a) in in³, (b) in liters (L).

To calculate the compresssion ratio, you must know the clearance value of the cylinder.

10. What is meant by *clearance value*?
11. How do you compute (determine) clearance value?
12. Assume that a four-cycle diesel engine has the following valve and injection specifications:

(a) Intake valve open _____ 28° BTDC
(b) Intake valve closed _____ 48°
(c) Duration _____ 256°
(d) Exhaust valve open ___ BBDC ___ 53° BDC
(e) Exhaust valve closed _____ 23°
(f) Start of injection _____ 28°
(g) End of injection _____ 5°

Record (using the recognized abbreviations) the appropriate piston locations when No. 1 piston is at the valve and injection specifications.

13. Using different-colored pencils, indicate on Fig. 2-1 the point at which the valves are open and the point at which they are closed. Label each point. Also show the points at which injection begins and ends.

14. What is the percentage of volumetric efficiency when the inhaled volume of air of one cylinder equals 87 percent of the calculated piston displacement and clearance volume?

15. List at least three major factors which create a reduction in the volumetric efficiency of an engine. worn Piston rings   Rotated   BAD VALVES

All internal-combustion engines use the same method of scavenging; that is, when the piston is at TDC, exhaust stroke, the intake and exhaust valves are open. This allows the atmospheric air to force the exhaust gases from the combustion chamber. The main difference among these engines is that the valve overlap varies with engine design.

16. List the three main reasons why the valve overlap varies from engine to engine. Speed, Compression Ratio

17. Explain (a) why the intake valves close after bottom dead center (ABDC), and (b) why the moment of valve closure varies among engines (sometimes as late as 68° ABDC).

18. List at least three reasons why the actual values of compression pressure and temperature are lower than the calculated values.

19. List six factors which affect the delay period.

20. List four factors which could lengthen the second period of combustion.

21. Briefly outline at least three circumstances

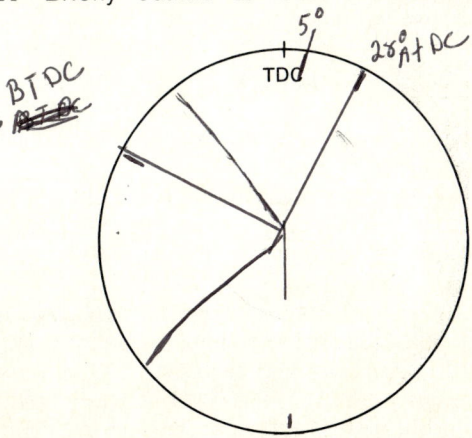

Fig. 2-1

7

which could cause some engines to have the fourth period of combustion.

22. At what point ATDC does the combustion pressure become effective? 10°-15°

23. Why, on the power stroke, does the torque on the crank remain nearly constant during the first 60° of crankshaft rotation?

24. Assume that you have an engine that operates in the following manner: 2400 rpm, intake stroke 240°, compression stroke 150°, power stroke 145°, exhaust stroke 235°, injection period 21°. Calculate the time for each stroke and for the injection period.

25. Why does the piston momentarily stand still when it is at TDC or BDC?

26. At what degree and at which stroke has the piston reached maximum speed? 63° after and 63° before

27. List three reasons why a two-cycle engine has about 30 percent more horsepower than a four-cycle engine that operates at the same rpm and has the same bore, stroke, and displacement.

28. Why is the timing (beginning of injection) more critical on two-cycle engines than on four-cycle engines?

29. Give three reasons why a two-cycle diesel engine requires an air pump. Also, explain why the air pump must have up to 40 times greater displacement capacity than a one-cylinder diesel engine.

30. Why are Roots-type blowers favored over other types of air pumps such as centrifugal pumps?

31. What are the main factors governing the power output of a (a) two-cycle engine, (b) four-cycle engine?

32. Why must the exhaust valves of a two-cycle engine open a few degrees before the inlet ports are opened by the piston?

33. How would the performance of a two-cycle engine be affected if the exhaust-valve clearance was adjusted (a) more than specified, (b) less than specified?

34. There are five major ways in which engine manufacturers are continuously trying to improve their engines: by gaining power and efficiency, and by reducing maintenance costs, exhaust emission, and noise. List at least five factors which can contribute to achieving these engine improvements.

Supercharging is by far the most effective means of gaining power output.

35. How would you describe a "supercharged engine?"

36. Which types of air pumps are used to supercharge an engine?

37. Which type of air pump is the most efficient?

38. Give seven reasons why the brake horsepower (bhp) of any engine is lower than the indicated horsepower (ihp).

39. Assume that you have a four-cycle six-cylinder engine that operates in the following manner: governed at 2200 rpm, bore and stroke 5 by 6 in, mean effective pressure (mep) 170 psi [1172.1 kPa]. What is the indicated horsepower of the engine in English and in metric units of measurement? 67.428

40. Assume that you have a dynamometer calibrated to measure torque in pound-feet. When testing the engine under maximum load, it develops a torque scale reading of 1000 lb·ft. What would be the engine horsepower (a) in English measurements, (b) in metric units of measurement?

41. Assume that you are testing the same engine, but that you are using an alternator set and the power output at maximum torque is 255.7 kW (kilowatts). Calculate this horsepower in English units of measurement.

42. Briefly explain the meaning of *thermal efficiency*.

43. Assume that the continuous horsepower per hour of an engine is 215 hp and the fuel used is 8.3 gal (U.S.). Assume also that one gal (U.S.) of fuel weighs 6.8 lb and that the heat value of the fuel is 135000 Btu. What is the (a) thermal efficiency of the engine, (b) fuel consumption in pounds per brake horsepower?

44. Calculate the fuel consumption in miles per hour (mph) when a truck has used 108.6 gal (U.S.) and has traveled 500 mi. 4.6

The operating temperature of a diesel engine is vital to the total efficiency and the life expectancy of an engine. Engine manufacturers try to ensure that as much heat as possible is converted from combustion into usable power; however, some excess must be transferred by (1) conduction, (2) convection, and (3) radiation. (See Fig. 2-2.)

45. List the major components which transfer heat through (a) conduction, (b) convection, (c) radiation.

46. Briefly explain the main difference between a liquid thermometer and a thermocoupling.

47. Assume that the engine temperature gauge of the cooling system shows 190°F and the temperature gauge of the pyrometer shows 1050°F. What are the temperatures of the cooling system and the exhaust gases in degrees centigrade (°C)?

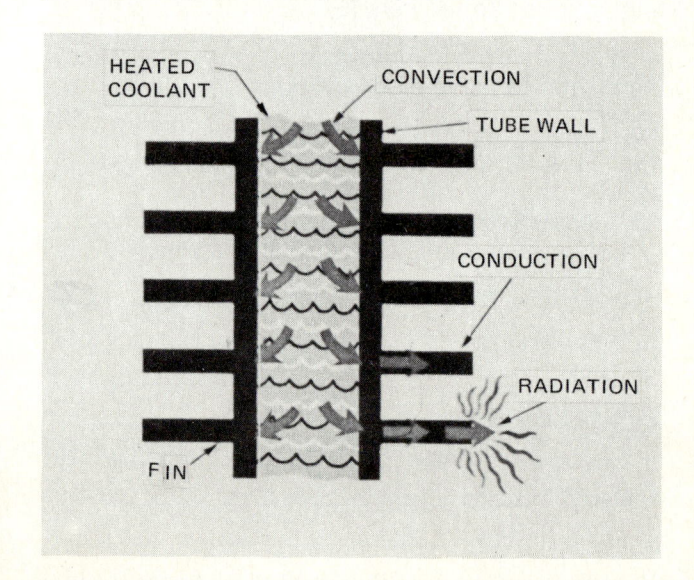

Fig. 2-2 Heat transfer. *(Detroit Diesel Allison, Division of General Motors Corporation.)*

ASSIGNMENT 4
COMBUSTION CHAMBERS

1. List the different types of combustion chambers.
2. Discuss the action in the open combustion chamber shown in Fig. 4-1, from the beginning of the intake stroke until the beginning of the power stroke.
3. List the advantages and disadvantages of direct injection.
4. Explain the action within a Caterpillar precombustion chamber from the beginning of the intake stroke to the beginning of the power stroke.

Energy cells vary to some extent, particularly in the location and the direction of the opening of the energy cell.

5. Explain the action within the energy cell shown in Fig. 4-2 from the beginning of the intake stroke to the beginning of the power stroke.
6. List the advantages and disadvantages of the special combustion chamber with regard to (a) engine efficiency, (b) power, (c) torque, (d) fuel economy, (e) timing, (f) engine speed, (g) scavenging, (h) wear.

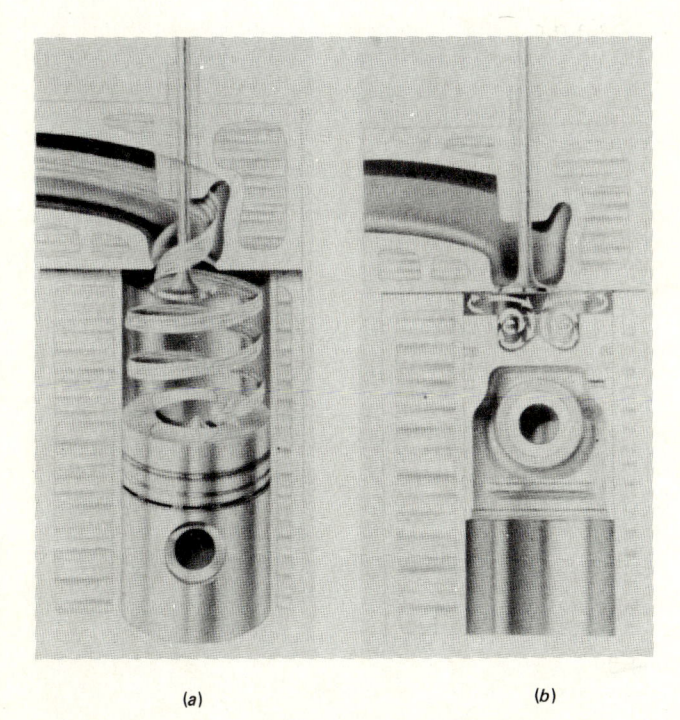

Fig. 4-1 Airflow during the (a) intake stroke and (b) compression stroke. [*J. I. Case Agricultural Equipment Division (TENNECO).*]

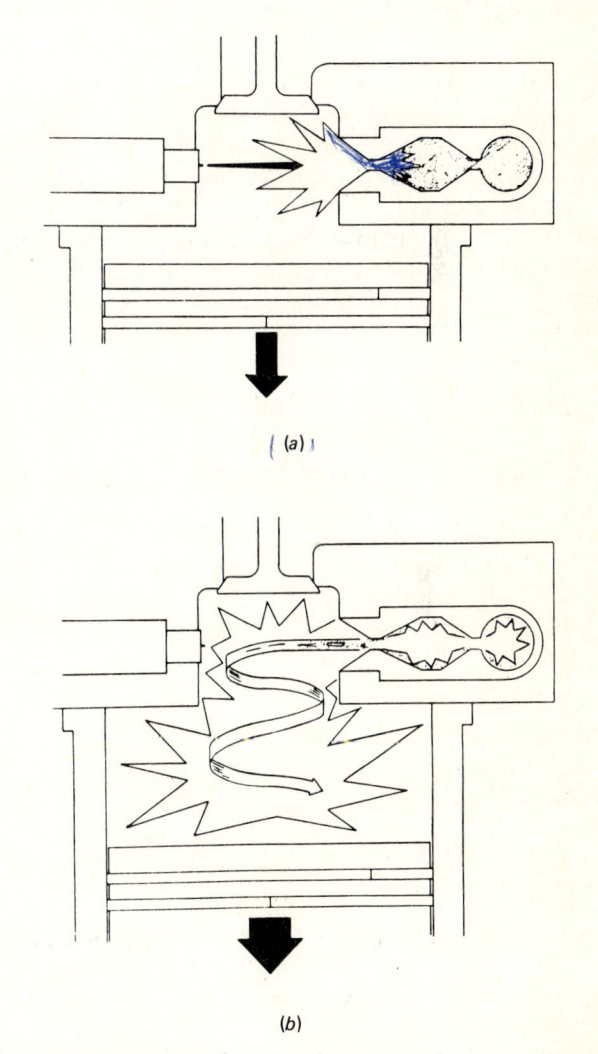

Fig. 4-2 Action within an energy cell during (a) injection and (b) combustion. [*J. I. Case Agricultural Equipment Division (TENNECO).*]

9

Name _____ Date _____ Class _____

ASSIGNMENT 5
ENGINE DISASSEMBLY

1. List the most common safety checks which you should make before climbing into the driver's seat.

Once you are in the driver's seat, familiarize yourself with the instruments, the valves, and the components.

2. Under what circumstances would you consider the vehicle safe to drive into your shop?

3. List the shutdown and parking procedures to prepare a motor vehicle for service.

4. Why is it wise to inspect and record the findings of the overall engine condition *before* steam-cleaning it?

5. Assume that you notice a very clean area at the rear of the cylinder block and a brownish color at one side of the cylinder block. *(a)* What warning or indication would this give you? *(b)* Why should you identify all electrical connections? *(c)* When is the earliest time you may drain the coolant system (radiator and cylinder block)?

A common lift application is shown in Fig. 5-1. Notice that the power-steering hoses and the power-steering ram are held between the frame and the tire. Notice, also, that there is an item which could be damaged since it is not wired up. This figure emphasizes inadvertent disregard for safety rules.

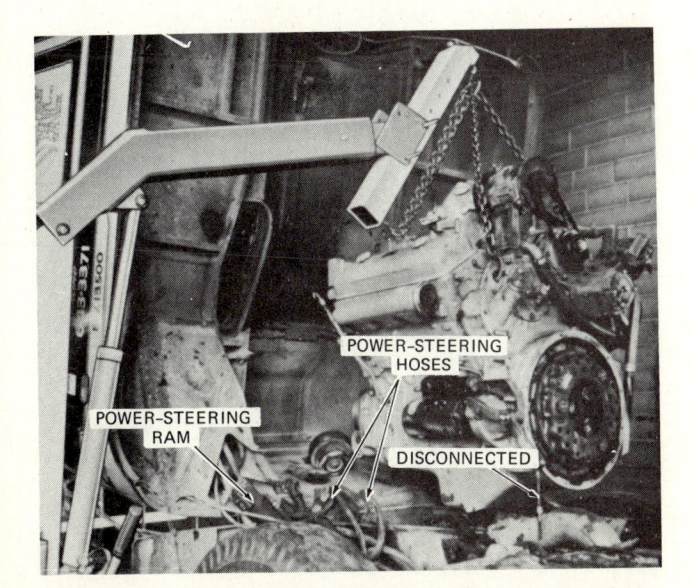

Fig. 5-1 Lifting an engine out. (Owatonna Tool Co., Tools and Equipment Div.)

6. Outline two safety rules which appear to have been ignored in Fig. 5-1.

7. An engine should be mounted to an engine stand to ensure its safety and your own. Give two other advantages of mounting the engine to an engine stand.

8. Why, upon removal of the components, should you cover the openings of the turbocharger, fuel-injection pump, and injectors?

9. Why must subcomponents be stored as a unit?

10. Explain why a turbocharger has the highest designed speed and the highest boost pressure when the engine operates at maximum torque speed.

11. What is the purpose of *(a)* a diffuser in the compression section, *(b)* the volute design of the turbine housing?

12. Explain why turbochargers use a bushing instead of a roller or tapered roller bearing.

Coolant Pump All coolant pumps, except those on marine engines, use nonpositive displacement centrifugal pumps.

13. What is meant by a *nonpositive displacement pump*?

14. Discuss the pumping action of the centrifugal pump shown in DM2 Fig. 5-4.

15. Outline three reasons why coolant pumps use mechanical seals instead of lip-type seals.

16. The valve mechanism (including the camshaft) may serve three major functions. What are these three major functions?

17. Explain why the ratio of the rocker arm is *not* 1:1.

18. List the various methods used to bring a lubricant to the *(a)* rocker-arm shaft, *(b)* pushrod end of the rocker arm, *(c)* valve end of the rocker arm. (Refer to Fig. 5-2.)

19. When removing the rocker-arm assembly, why should you identify and mark the relationship of the rocker arms, washers, and springs?

20. What factors govern the *(a)* size of the cylinder head, *(b)* size of the internal cooling passages, *(c)* location of the injector, *(d)* size and number of the intake and exhaust valves, *(e)* size and design of the valve ports? See Fig. 5-3.

21. Why should the cylinder-head bolts or nuts be loosened in the same order in which they were tightened?

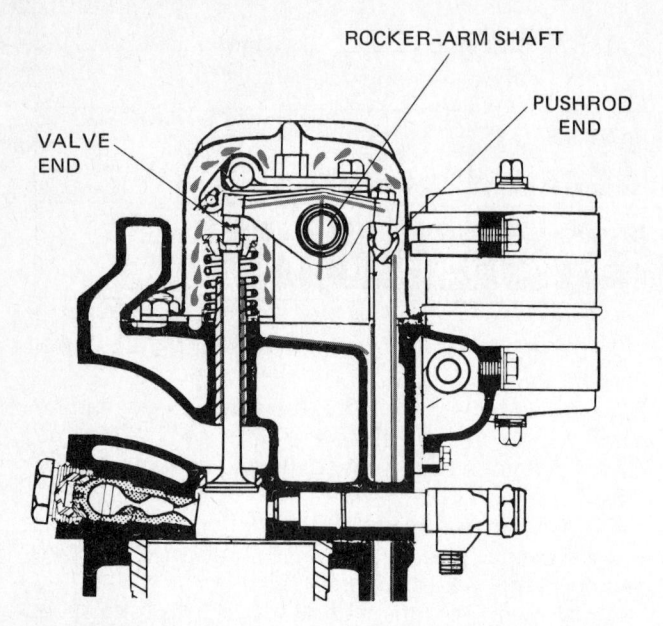

Fig. 5-2 Valve-train lubrication. *(Allis-Chalmers Corp. Engine Division.)*

22. Why must the cylinder head, upon its removal, be placed on a flat surface or stood upright?

23. Which method would you use to separate such components as the cylinder head, the coolant pump, and the timing-gear cover, when they are seized with the corresponding adjacent component?

24. Why should you place the valves and injectors in a holding fixture, and number them in sequence?

25. Explain why, in some cases, a slide hammer with an attachment is used to remove an injector from the cylinder-head bore.

26. What is the purpose of the (a) flywheel housing, (b) flywheel, (c) vibration damper?

27. Why are flywheels different in size, diameter, height, depth, and friction surface area?

28. Outline the procedure for removing the vibration damper from the crankshaft shown in DM2 Fig. 5-15.

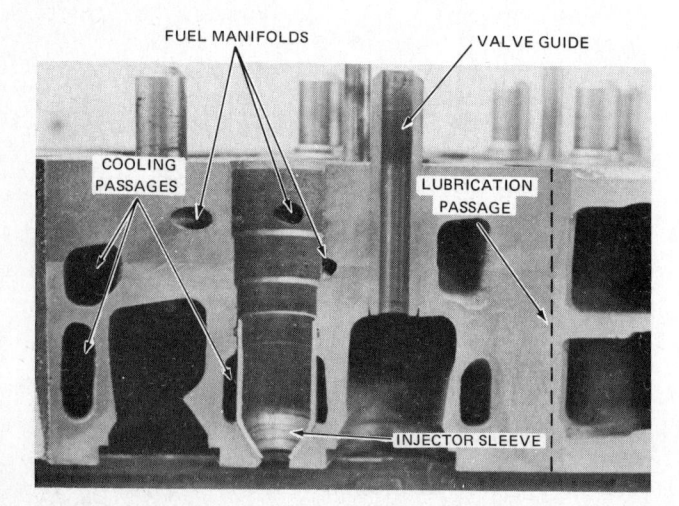

Fig. 5-3 Sectional view of a cylinder-head fuel manifold.

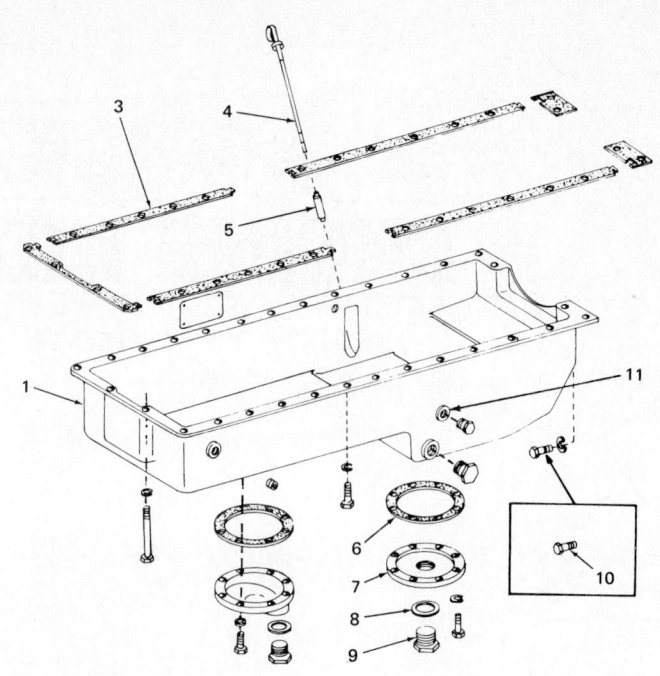

1. Oil pan
2. Oil seal
3. Gasket set
4. Oil-level gauge (dipstick)
5. Dipstick adapter
6. Cover gaskets
7. Cleanout covers
8. Gaskets
9. Drain plugs
10. Capscrew and lockwasher or Nylock capscrew
11. Oil-level plug

Fig. 5-4 Conventional oil pan. *(Allis-Chalmers Corp. Engine Division.)*

29. What two factors must be considered when selecting an engine oil pan?

30. Outline two functions of the oil pan's internal reinforcement structure, other than to strengthen the oil pan (Fig. 5-4).

31. Why do most diesel engines use an oil cooler?

32. What is the difference between (a) an oil cooler which is classified as water-to-oil and (b) one which is referred to as oil-to-water?

33. Why, in most oil coolers, is the coolant flow in opposite direction to the oil flow?

34. What is a positive displacement pump?

35. Basically, what are the design differences between an external gear pump and an internal gear pump?

36. List the advantages of a gerotor pump over an internal or external gear pump.

37. Why do some engines use two oil pumps?

38. Explain the purpose of a camshaft and why some camshafts have only one function while others have two or three.

39. What is the drive ratio between the camshaft gear and the crankshaft gear of a (a) four-cycle engine, (b) two-cycle engine?

40. Why are some camshafts driven through one or more idler gears? (See Fig. 5-5.)

Name _____ Date _____ Class _____

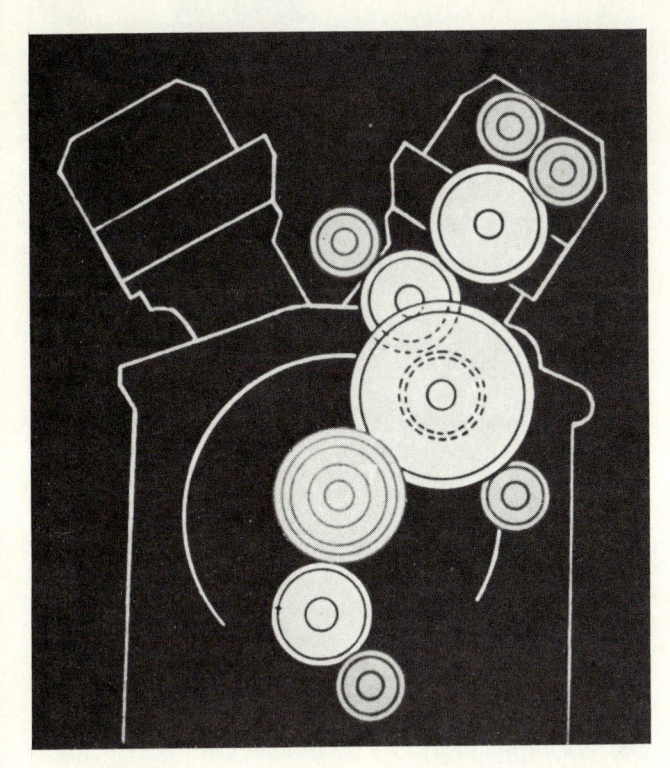

Fig. 5-5 Schematic view of a timing gear train. *(Caterpillar Tractor Co.)*

41. Why should the backlash and the end play be measured before removing the timing gears?
42. Outline the method you would use to measure the camshaft end play.
43. Removing the camshaft or the crankshaft gear requires a suitable puller. State three points which you must take into account when selecting the puller.
44. Why is it advisable to keep the followers in numerical sequence when placing them in a holding fixture?
45. List the major differences among connecting rods using a trunk-type piston.
46. Outline three methods of lubricating the piston pin and bushing.
47. Why are connecting-rod bolts of a special design and special grade?
48. Refer to Fig. 5-6. Why is this connecting rod so unusually designed?
49. List the obvious differences between a connecting rod using trunk-type pistons and one using crosshead-type pistons.
50. What is the visible difference between the trunk and crosshead pistons?
51. List a number of externally visible differences among trunk-type pistons.
52. Why is the skirt surface of most pistons somewhat rough?
53. Why is the length of the Detroit Diesel pistons greater than the length of the stroke of the engine?

54. Why do most pistons have three different diameters?
55. Give three basic reasons why piston pins are hollow.
56. Why are some pistons cam-ground?
57. Why are holes drilled in the oil-ring groove (and sometimes also just below the oil-ring groove)?
58. Before removing a piston and connecting-rod assembly from the cylinder bore, you must make two checks. What are these two checks?
59. What precautionary steps would you take when pushing the assembly from the cylinder sleeve?
60. Why should you tape the bearing half-shells together and also indicate the cylinder from which they were removed?
61. Why should you remove piston rings from the piston only with a piston-ring installing tool?
62. List some differences which exist among wet-type cylinder sleeves.
63. Outline the removal procedure for a wet-type cylinder sleeve, using a pulling arrangement similar to that shown in Fig. 5-7.
64. Why will reverse flushing of the cylinder block speed up the servicing time?
65. What is the function of a crankshaft?
66. What factors govern the *(a)* surface area of the main-bearing journals, *(b)* number of main-bearing journals, *(c)* number of connecting-rod journals?
67. Before removing the main-bearing caps, what check must you make?
68. One method of removing the main-bearing cap is shown in Fig. 5-8. Outline another safe way to remove the main-bearing cap.
69. Outline how to store the crankshaft once it has been removed from the cylinder block.

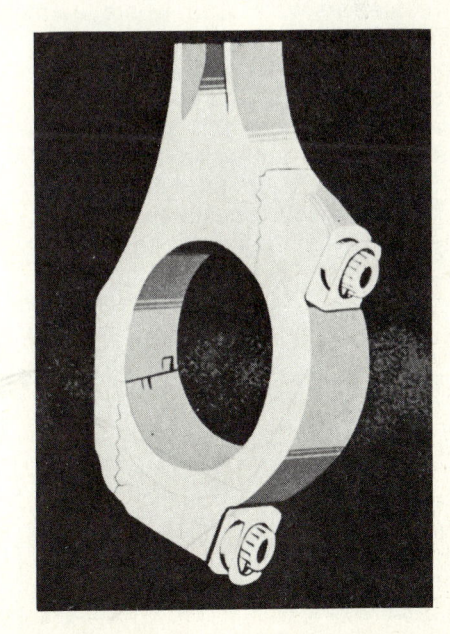

Fig. 5-6 Specially designed connecting rod. *(Caterpillar Tractor Co.)*

13

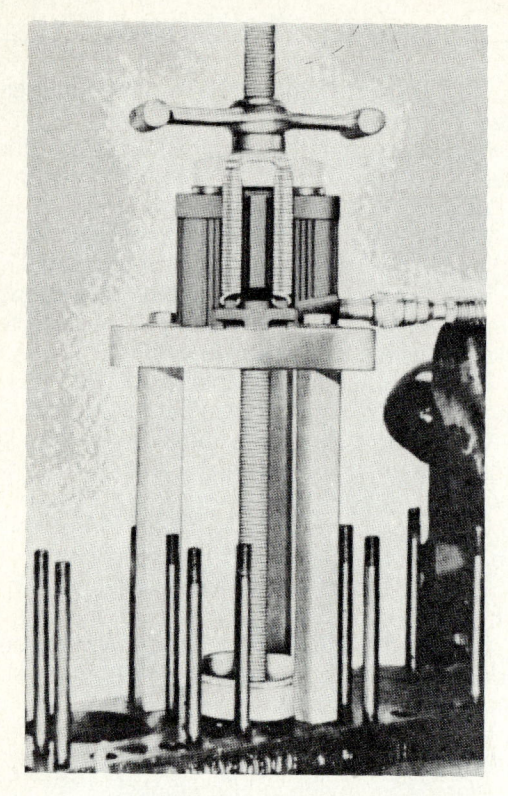

Fig. 5-7 Removing a cylinder sleeve. (Owatonna Tool Company, Tools and Equipment Div.)

Fig. 5-8 Removing a main bearing cap. (Cummins Engine Company, Inc.)

After all components have been removed, only the main structure, that is, the cylinder block and crankcase, remains. Examine a cylinder block in your shop from which the components have been removed and then answer the following questions.

70. Were wet or dry sleeves used?
71. If wet sleeves were used, where are the sleeve seals located?
72. If dry sleeves were used, are the sleeves press-fitted or slide-fitted?
73. How many vertical and horizontal transverse members were used in the cylinder block? On Fig. 5-9, draw in all this information to conform with the answers to the previous questions.
74. How many main bearings and connecting-rod bearings are used?
75. Are all crankshaft and camshaft bearings of the same width?
76. Trace the main oil galleries and draw in this information on Fig. 5-9.
77. How many lubrication openings are used to transfer lubricants to the (a) cylinder head, (b) timing gears, (c) flywheel housing?
78. Complete Fig. 5-9 by drawing in the horizontal and vertical cooling passages.
79. Why should you steam-clean oily components as soon as possible once they have been removed?
80. List four precautions to be taken when immersing and removing parts from a hot tank.
81. What is your next step after removing the components from the hot tank?

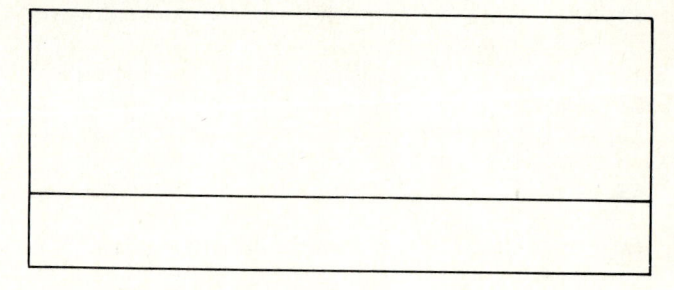

Fig. 5-9 Cylinder block.

14 Copyright © 1983 by McGraw-Hill, Inc. All rights reserved. Not to be reproduced.

Name _____ Date _____ Class _____

ASSIGNMENT 6
CYLINDER BLOCK

1. List the main checkpoints which could reveal the need for a cylinder-block replacement.
2. Where would you find the cracks on a cylinder block that has been overheated one or more times?
3. Why is it mandatory to tighten the main-bearing cap screws to specification before pressure-testing or performing any measurement or service on the cylinder block?
4. At which locations could you expect to find leaks when pressure-testing a cylinder block?
5. Which method would you use to (a) measure flat mounting surfaces, (b) refinish these surfaces?

Dry-type and wet-type cylinder sleeves require somewhat different methods of approach. Assuming that dry-type cylinder sleeves are used (Detroit Diesel), you can then start to service the cylinder bore. Your first step is to clean and measure the cylinder bore and compare this measurement with the specification given in your service manual. An example of the service manual specifications are shown in Tables 6-1 and 6-2.

6. How would you "clean a bore?"

7. Assume that, after measuring the cylinder bore, you find the out-of-roundness to be 0.003 in, the taper to be 0.0015 in, and the maximum bore diameter to be 4.6295 in. From the indication of these measurements (a) what service would the cylinder bore require, (b) how would you select a cylinder sleeve?
8. Explain how to use a taper gauge to measure the results of your honing. (Refer to Fig. 6-1.)
9. What is the importance of the contact shown in Fig. 6-2a?
10. Why should you mark (identify) the position of the bore and the cylinder number?

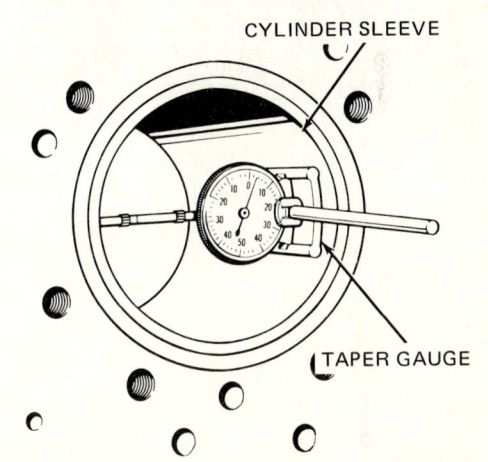

Fig. 6-1 Measuring the cylinder sleeve. (Allis-Chalmers Corp. Engine Division.)

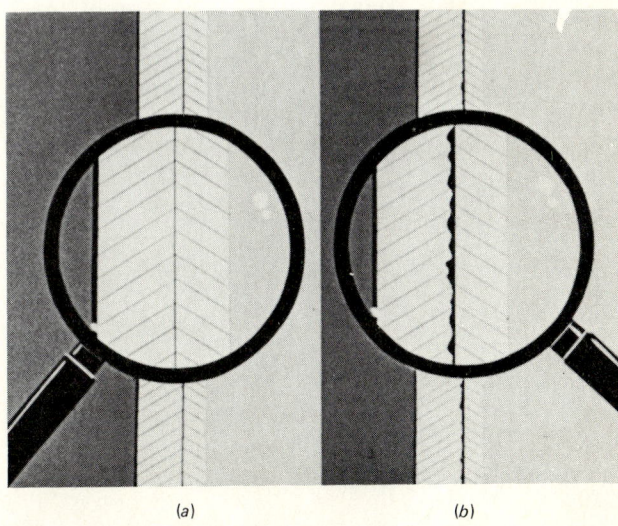

Fig. 6-2 (a) Proper, and (b) improper sleeve-to-bore fit. (Detroit Diesel Allison, Division of General Motors Corporation.)

TABLE 6-1

For average block-bore ID size, in	Use liner OD size, in	To give a liner-to-block clearance of, in
4.6260 / 4.6275	Standard	0.000–0.0025
4.6270 / 4.6285	0.001 Oversize	0.000–0.0025

TABLE 6-2

Block boring dimensions, in	Liner OD size, in	Maximum block-bore ID on a used block, in
4.631 / 4.632	0.005 Oversize	4.6325
4.636 / 4.637	0.010 Oversize	4.6375
4.646 / 4.647	0.020 Oversize	4.6475
4.656 / 4.657	0.030 Oversize	4.6575

11. Explain how to measure the counterbore of a Detroit Diesel cylinder block and how to adjust the cylinder sleeve so that it is within the specifications previously given. (See Fig. 6-3.)

Fig. 6-3 Measuring the depth of the counterbore. *(Detroit Diesel Allison, Division of General Motors Corporation.)*

12. Assume that you have measured the lower cylinder-sleeve bore and your measurement is above specification. How would you correct the bore diameter to bring it to service manual specification?

13. Explain how to measure one main-bearing bore, using an "out-of round" gauge. Give an example from your training engine.

14. How would you set this gauge to zero, using the following cylinder-block specifications?

Main-bearing bore	Inside diameter	
Worn limit	New minimum	New maximum
4.7505 in 120.663 mm	4.7485 in 120.612 mm	4.750 in 120.650 mm

15. Outline the procedure to check the alignment of the main-bearing bores (using a master-alignment bar).

16. Which measuring tool would you use to measure the diameter of the camshaft bore?

If an in-frame overhaul is made, measure *each* of the camshaft bushings for wear, taper, and out-of-roundness.

17. List the precautions to be taken before installing the camshaft bushings.

ASSIGNMENT 7
CAMSHAFT

1. When examining the camshaft lobes, where would you expect to find the greatest wear?

2. Where would bearing surface wear first be noticeable?

3. Visually inspect the camshaft of an engine in your workshop. If it passes your inspection, measure the camshaft runout and the camshaft journals. Record the service manual specification and the measurements you have just taken. (Fig. 7-1.)

SERVICE MANUAL SPECIFICATIONS

Diameter front and rear bearing journals _____ in, _____ mm; _____ in, _____ mm

Runout _____ in, _____ mm

Diameter front and intermediate bearing journals _____ in, _____ mm; _____ in, _____ mm

YOUR MEASUREMENTS

Diameter front and rear bearing journals _____ in, _____ mm; _____ in, _____ mm

Runout _____ in, _____ mm

Diameter front and intermediate bearing journals _____ in, _____ mm; _____ in, _____ mm

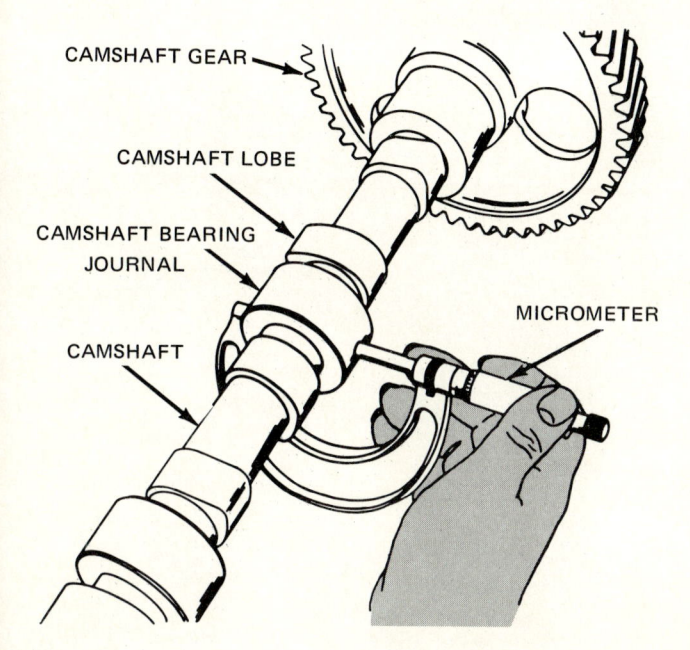

Fig. 7-1 Measuring the camshaft bearing journal. [*J. I. Case Agricultural Equipment Division (TENNECO).*]

4. What are the advantages in heating the camshaft gear to a specified temperature before installing the gear to the camshaft?

5. Why do idler gears have an odd number of teeth?

6. List two essential checks before installing an idler gear (having bushings) to an independent shaft?

ASSIGNMENT 8
CYLINDER SLEEVE

1. Name the two main groups of cylinder-sleeve failure and describe the external and internal wear patterns you may find in each group.

2. On what would you base a decision that a cylinder sleeve requires only to be deglazed?

3. List the most important points in the task of honing a cylinder sleeve. (Refer to Fig. 8-1.)

4. List the steps which must be taken after the cylinder sleeve has been honed or deglazed, but before the sleeve is installed into the cylinder bore.

5. List the precautions you must take when installing the sealing rings either onto the cylinder sleeve or into the lower cylinder-bore grooves.

6. What is the difference between a clearance fit and an interference fit in regard to dry sleeves?

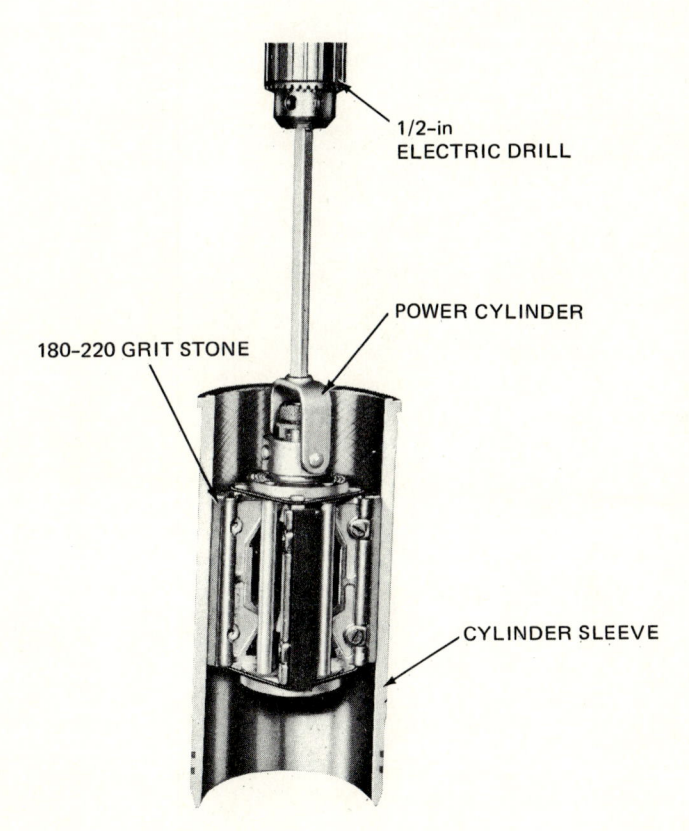

Fig. 8-1 Honing a cylinder sleeve. [*Case J. I. Agricultural Equipment Division (TENNECO).*]

19

Name _____ Date _____ Class _____

ASSIGNMENT 9
CRANKSHAFT

1. List a number of conditions which promote early crankshaft failure, but over which you have little or no control.

2. Assume that the crankshaft must be cleaned with a solvent because no other cleaning method is available. Outline the steps to clean the crankshaft using cleaning solvent.

3. On Fig. 9-1, draw all the surface conditions you find on the main and connecting-rod journals of a crankshaft in your workshop.

4. Where could you expect hidden cracks or flaws in the crankshaft?

5. Measure each journal of the crankshaft and record the service manual specifications as well as the measurements you have just taken.

SERVICE MANUAL SPECIFICATIONS

Main-bearing journals _____ in, _____ mm

Connecting-rod journals _____ in, _____ mm

YOUR MEASUREMENTS

Main-bearing journals (a) _____ in, _____ mm; (b) _____ in, _____ mm; (c) _____ in, _____ mm; (d) _____ in, _____ mm; (e) _____ in, _____ mm; (f) _____ in, _____ mm

Connecting-rod journals (a) _____ in, _____ mm; (b) _____ in, _____ mm; (c) _____ in, _____ mm; (d) _____ in, _____ mm; (e) _____ in, _____ mm; (f) _____ in, _____ mm

6. What is the importance of polishing the bearing journals and the seal contact surfaces when the shaft requires no regrinding?

NOTE: Clean the crankshaft thoroughly after it is polished, and follow the manufacturer's recommendations when installing the crankshaft plugs. Afterwards, lubricate the bearings and seal surfaces.

7. Why should the bearings remain in their packings until you are actually ready to install them?

8. Explain how to determine the size of a half-bearing shell.

9. List a number of precautions you must take before and while installing the main-bearing shells.

10. Assume that a half-shell drops rather than snaps into place. What would you do to increase its spread?

11. Outline the procedure (and precautions you must take) for installing and tightening the main-bearing caps. (Do not include measuring the end play.)

12. What problem could develop when the crankshaft end play is greater than the maximum specification given in the service manual?

13. What two instruments can be used to measure the crankshaft end play?

14. Outline the procedure to determine the taper, the out-of-roundness, and the wear limit of one main crankshaft journal while performing an in-frame overhaul without a bearing measuring tool.

15. Why is it necessary to force the crankshaft against the upper-bearing shell when measuring the wear, taper, and out-of-roundness?

16. Explain how to remove one upper-bearing shell from its bore.

17. When an engine is equipped with an inertia counterbalance, why must the drive and driven gear be timed?

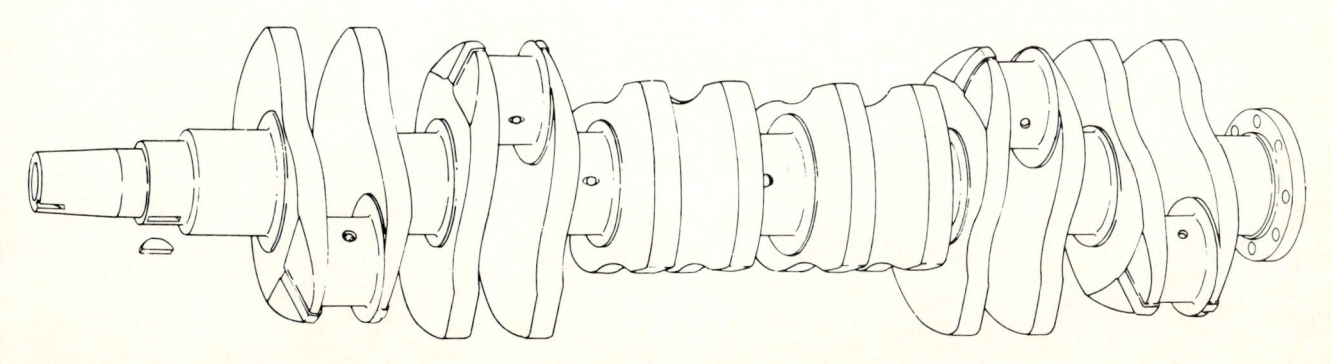

Fig. 9-1 Crankshaft.

ASSIGNMENT 10
CONNECTING ROD

1. What factors over which you have no control can cause a connecting rod to fail?

2. On Fig. 10-1, indicate where flaws or cracks would most likely appear during testing.

3. Why is it important to check that the *(a)* connecting rod is properly aligned, *(b)* bolts or nuts do not interfere with the rod cap fillet, *(c)* mating surfaces between the cap and rod fit flat upon each other?

4. On an engine in your shop, measure one connecting rod at the points recommended in your service manual. Record these measurements.

SERVICE MANUAL SPECIFICATIONS

Connecting-rod alignment with bushing _____ in, _____ mm

Connecting-rod twist with bushing _____ in, _____ mm

Connecting-rod crankpin bore _____ in, _____ mm

Connecting-rod piston-pin bore _____ in, _____ mm

Connecting-rod piston-pin bushing inside diameter _____ in, _____ mm

Connecting-rod center-to-center length _____ in, _____ mm

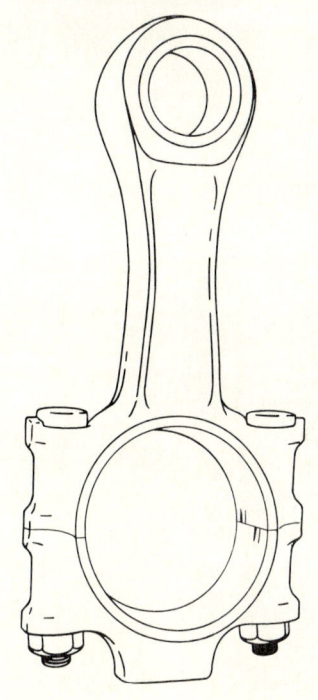

Fig. 10-1 Connecting rod.

5. Explain how to replace a piston-pin bushing.

6. Why is a specific type of tool, such as the one shown in Fig. 10-2, needed to ream the piston-pin bushing?

YOUR MEASUREMENTS

Connecting-rod alignment with bushing _____ in, _____ mm

Connecting-rod twist with bushing _____ in, _____ mm

Connecting-rod crankpin bore _____ in, _____ mm

Connecting-rod piston-pin bore _____ in, _____ mm

Connecting-rod piston-pin bushing inside diameter _____ in, _____ mm

Connecting-rod center-to-center length _____ in, _____ mm

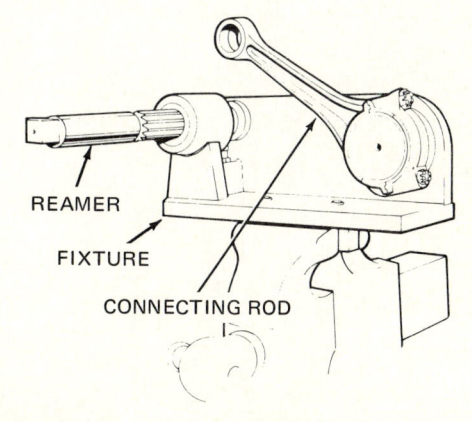

Fig. 10-2 Reaming the connecting-rod pin bushing. [*J. I. Case Agricultural Equipment Division (TENNECO).*]

ASSIGNMENT 11
PISTONS AND RINGS

1. Explain why the following actions can cause premature piston or piston-ring failure: *(a)* shutting off the engine before the engine temperature has stabilized, *(b)* allowing the exhaust back pressure to exceed that specified, *(c)* neglecting to repair minor coolant and oil leaks, *(d)* operating the engine with a restricted air cleaner.

2. List four careless work habits which would promote piston-ring failure (Fig. 11-1).

3. Explain how to clean the top compression-ring groove using the tool shown in Fig. 11-2.

4. Why is a glass-bead cleaner an ideal tool for cleaning a piston?

5. Obtain a piston from an engine in your workshop. Using your service manual as a guide, measure the piston and record the measurements.

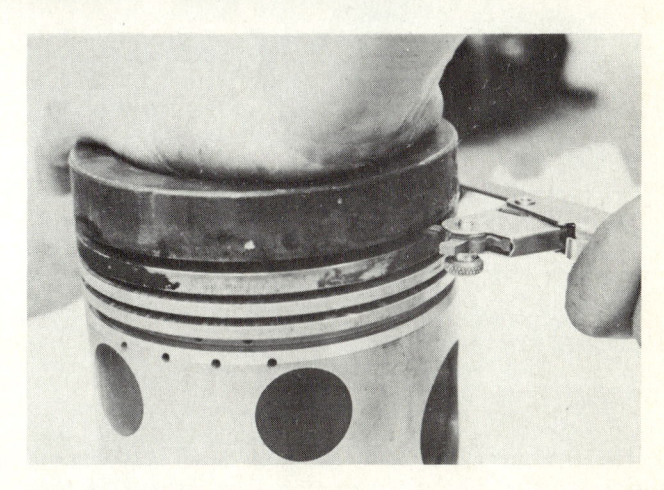

Fig. 11-2 Cleaning the top piston-ring grooves.

SERVICE MANUAL SPECIFICATIONS

Piston-skirt diameter _____ in, _____ mm

Piston-pin bore diameter _____ in, _____ mm

Ring-cap compression ring (1) _____ in, _____ mm

Ring-cap compression ring (2) _____ in, _____ mm

Ring-cap oil-control ring _____ in, _____ mm

Clearance top ring groove _____ in, _____ mm

YOUR MEASUREMENTS

Piston-skirt diameter _____ in, _____ mm

Piston-pin bore diameter _____ in, _____ mm

Ring-cap compression ring (1) _____ in, _____ mm

Ring-cap compression ring (2) _____ in, _____ mm

Ring-cap oil-control ring _____ in, _____ mm

Clearance top ring groove _____ in, _____ mm

6. Explain how to check the wear of a keystone ring groove.

7. At which point must you measure a cam-ground piston?

8. When a piston requires piston-pin bushing(s) and new bushing(s) must be installed, why is it improper to ream or hone the piston-pin bushing freehand?

9. Why is it sometimes necessary to heat the piston in order to install the piston pin?

10. What precaution must you take when assembling the piston to the connecting rod?

11. What is the function of *(a)* a compression ring, *(b)* an oil-control ring?

12. State why *(a)* a compression ring with an inside groove must be installed toward the top of the piston, *(b)* a compression ring with an outside groove must be installed with the groove facing downward.

13. Why do all types of oil-control rings have large openings?

14. Why are most pistons slightly tapered just below the oil-ring groove?

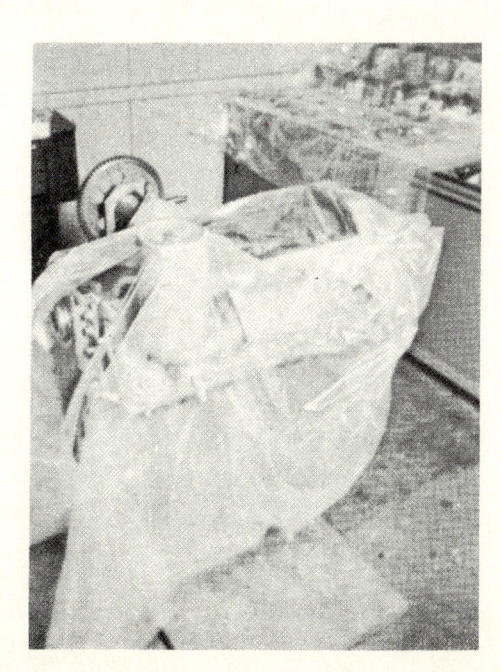

Fig. 11-1 Correctly protected component. *(Cummins Engine Company, Inc.)*

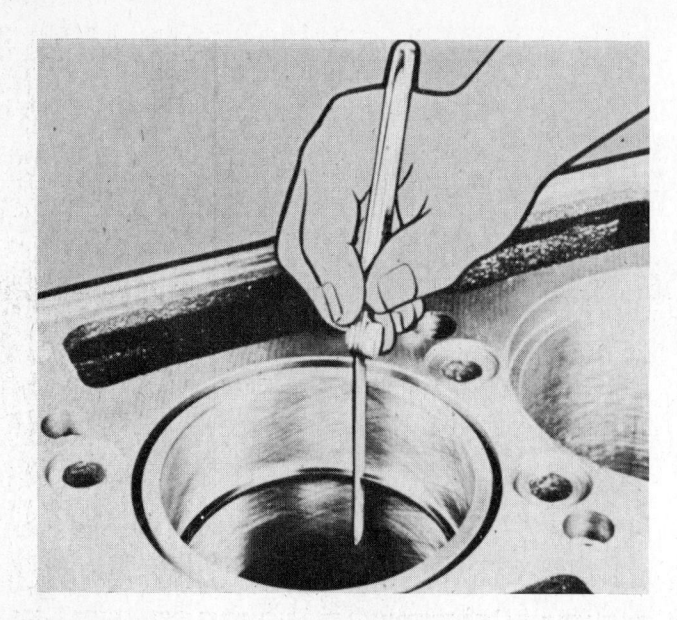

Fig. 11-3 Measuring ring gap. *(Detroit Diesel Allison, Division of General Motors Corporation.)*

15. Briefly outline how to check and measure the ring gap of one compression ring. (Refer to Fig. 11-3.)

16. When installing piston rings, why must you use a proper piston-ring installation tool rather than just your hands?

17. Why is it always necessary to check your service manual for proper ring spacing before installing the ring compressor?

18. List the steps you must take before installing the connecting rod and piston assembly into the cylinder sleeve.

When the connecting rod is aligned (see Fig. 11-4), gently force the assembly into its bore until the piston crown is flush with the cylinder head.

19. What problems can necessitate excessive force on the assembly in order to place it into its bore?

20. Outline the procedure for tightening the connecting-rod bolts and the correct method to install the cotter keys.

21. Which two checks must you make before installing the cylinder sleeve, the connecting rod, and the piston assembly (Detroit Diesel)?

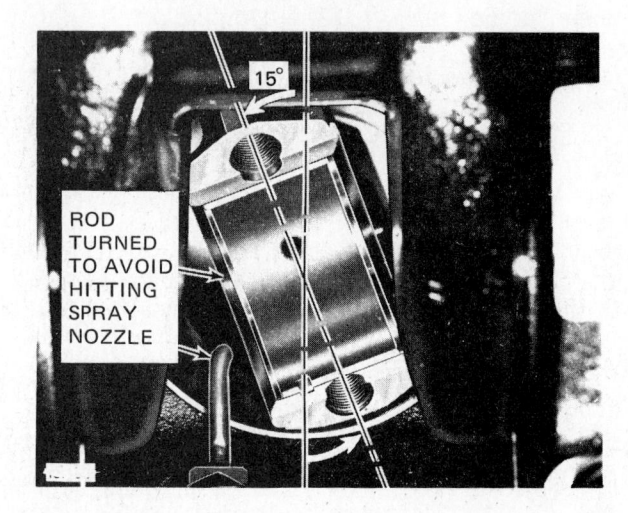

Fig. 11-4 Installing the connecting-rod assembly. *(Mack Trucks Canada Ltd.)*

Name _____ Date _____ Class _____

ASSIGNMENTS 12 AND 13
ENGINE OIL, LUBRICATION PUMP, AND OIL COOLER

1. List the three main purposes of an engine oil.
2. Which type of *crude* oil is most suitable for refining into a high-grade engine oil?
3. Explain the difference between *viscosity* and *viscosity index*.
4. List four reasons why so many different types of inhibitors and additives are blended into engine oils.
5. List all the precautions that would prevent oil from becoming contaminated *(a)* during storage, *(b)* during handling, *(c)* when filling the crankcase.
6. What, in your opinion, could cause an oil pump, under operating conditions, to *(a)* reduce its designed volume output, *(b)* fail entirely?
7. Why is it good practice to mark the meshing teeth before lifting the gears out of the center section of the pump housing?
8. Explain how to press a new bushing into the gear or, when applicable, into the housing.
9. Why, in most cases, are dowel pins used to hold the gear cover to the gear-pump housing or body?
10. When examining the oil pan, what malfunctions or damage would you look for?
11. List the checks you would make before installing the oil pan.
12. What special precautions must you take when installing an oil pan which covers the timing-gear cover (housing) and perhaps part of the flywheel housing?
13. Assume that you have cleaned and reassembled the oil cooler. Explain how to pressure-test the oil cooler shown in Fig. 12-1 so that there are no internal-external leaks.
14. What special precautions must you take when installing the oil cooler and when connecting the oil and cooling lines to the cooler?

Fig. 12-1 Oil cooler.

Name _____ Date _____ Class _____

ASSIGNMENT 14
CYLINDER HEAD AND VALVES

1. List five inadequacies or poor maintenance procedures which could cause cylinder-head failure.

2. List five improper adjustments which could cause cylinder-head failure.

3. What cylinder-head parts could fail as a result of improper service and why could they fail?

4. What types of improper maintenance, or incorrect adjustments, could cause valve or valve-insert failure?

5. What improper service could cause valve or valve-insert failure?

6. List two types of cylinder-head damage which would require it to be replaced.

7. Why must you replace a cylinder head when its height is below specification?

8. List three reasons why it is necessary to cut or ream the injector seat of a newly installed Cummins or Detroit Diesel injector sleeve. (Refer to Fig. 14-1.)

9. Why is it so important *(a)* not to overroll a newly installed (Cummins) injector sleeve, *(b)* to achieve (by using a reamer or cutting tool) the specified injector protrusion?

10. Using a bore gauge, measure the wear of the valve guides from a cylinder head taken from an engine in your shop. Explain how you made your measurements, and record them (Fig. 14-2).

SERVICE MANUAL SPECIFICATIONS

New _____ in, _____ mm
Worn limit _____ in, _____ mm

Fig. 14-1 Measuring injector protrusion. *(Cummins Engine Company, Inc.)*

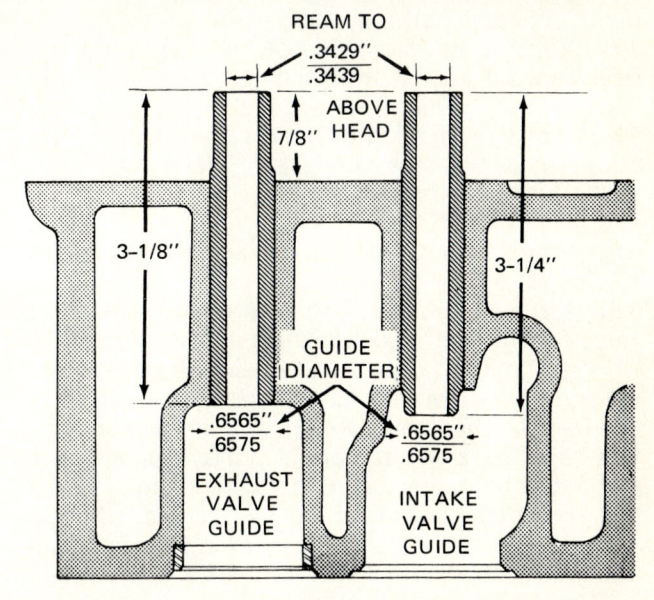

Fig. 14-2 Sectional view of a cylinder head showing measurement specifications. [*J. I. Case Agricultural Equipment Division (TENNECO).*]

YOUR MEASUREMENTS AND GUIDE CONDITIONS

(a) _____ in, _____ mm; _____
(b) _____ in, _____ mm; _____
(c) _____ in, _____ mm; _____
(d) _____ in, _____ mm; _____

11. Why should you drive or press a valve guide from the cylinder-head deck side, and not from the valve-spring side?

12. What effect will it have on the valve action, the valve, and the valve-guide wear, if you press the guide too far, for example, 6.53 mm, into the valve throat?

13. Check and measure one exhaust valve and one intake valve. Record your measurements.

SERVICE MANUAL SPECIFICATIONS

Valve-stem diameter: intake _____ in,
_____ mm; exhaust _____ in, _____ mm
Valve-stem margin: intake _____ in,
_____ mm; exhaust _____ in, _____ mm

YOUR MEASUREMENTS

Valve-stem diameter: intake _____ in,
_____ mm; exhaust _____ in, _____ mm

Valve-stem margin: intake _____ in,
_____ mm; exhaust _____ in, _____ mm

14. Make a visual inspection of the valves and note your comments on the following: (a) keeper groove, (b) valve tip, (c) valve head, (d) seat, (e) necking, (f) burns, (g) scuff marks, (f) stem bend.

15. When a valve is reused after being reground below specification, how would this affect its (a) performance, (b) wear, (c) service life?

16. When resurfacing an intake or exhaust valve, what precautions must you take? (Refer to Fig. 14-3.)

17. Outline the procedure to service the valve-stem end.

18. What checks must you make after the valve is serviced?

19. List the mandatory checks you must make on a valve seat in order to determine if it is serviceable or whether the insert should be replaced.

20. Assume that you have a valve seat which is serviceable, that the valve guide is satisfactory, that you have selected the correct grinding stone, and that the stone is dressed to the correct angle. Under this set of circumstances, outline the procedure to resurface the valve seat to the following service manual specifications:

- Minimum seat width: 0.063 in [1.59 mm]
- Maximum seat width: 0.125 in [3.18 mm]
- Minimum valve protrusion: 0.094 in [2.387 mm]
- Maximum valve protrusion: 0.1274 in [3.235 mm]

Fig. 14-3 Resurfacing a valve.

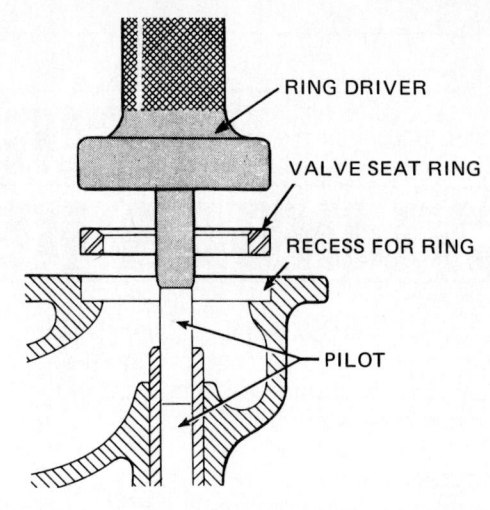

Fig. 14-4 Installing a valve insert. *(Allis-Chalmers Corp. Engine Division.)*

21. Outline the procedure to install a new valve insert after you have already cut a new valve-insert groove to the specifications given in your service manual. (See Fig. 14-4).

22. Outline how to check (a) the valve seat and seat location, (b) valve-seat concentricity.

23. If a manufacturer recommended grinding an interference angle, (a) why must the interference angle be positive rather than negative? (b) Which angle varies 1/2 to 1°, the valve angle or the valve-seat angle?

24. How would the valve action and/or the valve and valve-seat wear be affected if a valve spring (a) is below specification, (b) is above specification, (c) is bent, (d) has broken ends?

25. Measure one valve spring from a cylinder head in your shop. Record your measurements, and note your comments with regard to the straightness of the spring, appearance of the coil ends, and general condition.

SERVICE MANUAL SPECIFICATIONS

Valve-spring wire diameter _____ in, _____ mm

Valve-spring free length _____ in, _____ mm

Assembly height _____ in, _____ mm

Compressed length _____ in, _____ mm

Required load for length _____ lb, _____ kg

YOUR MEASUREMENTS

Valve-spring wire diameter _____ in, _____ mm

Valve-spring free length _____ in, _____ mm

Assembly height _____ in, _____ mm

Compressed length _____ in, _____ mm

Required load for length _____ lb, _____ kg

26. List the checks and/or measurements you must

make on the *(a)* valve-bridge guide pin, *(b)* valve bridge.

27. If the guide pin is bent, how would it affect the *(a)* valve action, *(b)* wear rate on the valve stem, *(c)* valve guide?

28. Give two reasons why some valve springs use a washer between the spring and the cylinder head?

29. When a variable-spring-rate valve spring is used, toward which component must the more tightly wound end of the valve spring be located?

30. One method of assembling the cylinder head is shown in Fig. 14-5. When using this method, what specific checks must be made before or during assembly, and also when releasing the applied force?

31. To avoid expensive service, test each valve for leakage after installation. List the three methods that you can use to check a valve seat for leakage.

32. List five checks you must make before installing the cylinder head onto the cylinder-head gasket.

33. When multicylinder heads are used, why is it necessary to align the cylinder heads before torquing the cylinder-head bolts to specification?

34. Why must you prevent oil dripping from the cylinder-head bolts into the threaded hole?

35. Why do some engine manufacturers recommend a wet torque method over a dry torque method?

36. Why must you tighten the cylinder-head bolts or nuts *(a)* in a predetermined sequence, *(b)* in at least three passes?

37. On Fig. 14-6, draw the recommended torque sequence from the cylinder head you are working on, or from one on which you have previously worked.

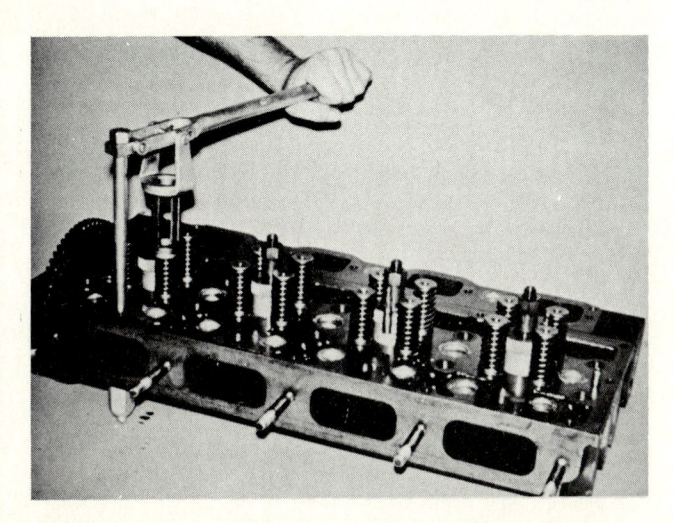

Fig 14-5 Installing a valve spring in a cylinder head. *(Detroit Diesel Allison, Division of General Motors Corporation.)*

Fig. 14-6

ASSIGNMENT 15
VALVE-TRAIN OPERATING MECHANISM

1. List four reasons why insufficient lubricant may reach the valve-train operating mechanism.
2. Why should you identify or record the location of the rocker arms, springs, and washers on the rocker-arm shaft? (Refer to Fig. 15-1.)
3. What damage or wear would you look for when inspecting the rocker arms?
4. Why must you use a special grinding attachment to resurface the rocker-arm-to-valve-bridge contact surface?
5. List the checks and measurements you must make to determine if a pushrod is reusable. (Assume service manual specification shows a maximum runout of 0.025 in [0.635 mm].)
6. Outline the procedure to adjust a (a) Cummins crosshead, (b) Detroit Diesel valve bridge (see Fig. 15-2).

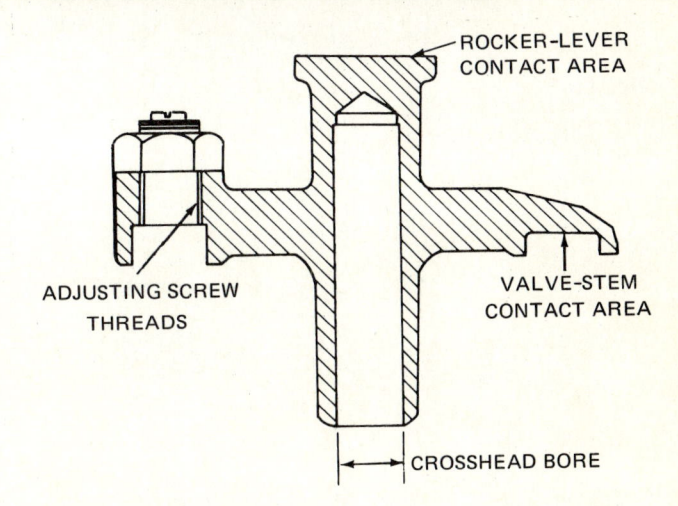

Fig. 15-2 Sectional view of a Cummins crosshead. (Cummins Engine Company, Inc.)

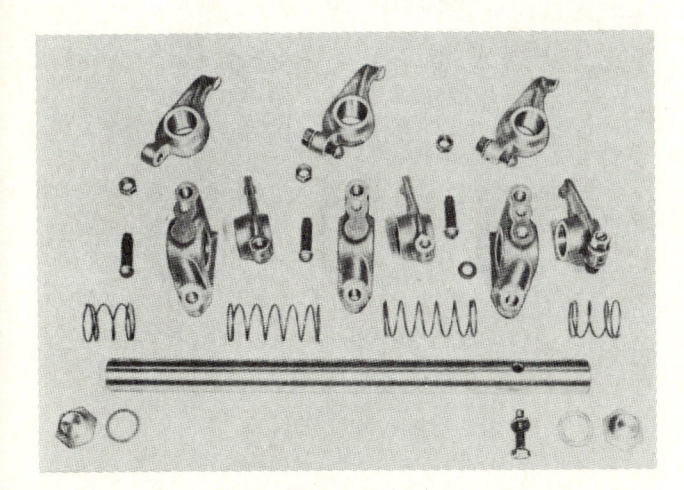

7. Outline the procedure for installing the rocker-arm assembly to the cylinder head on one of the engines in your workshop.
8. When adjusting the intake or exhaust valve, why must you adjust the clearance to within 0.001 in [0.025 mm] of specification?
9. Assume that you are adjusting the valves on an engine with a firing order of 1-8-6-4-2-7-5-3. The No. 2 piston is at TDC compression stroke. Which valves are adjustable when the No. 2 piston is in this position? (Record your answers.)

ROCKER-ARM ASSEMBLY

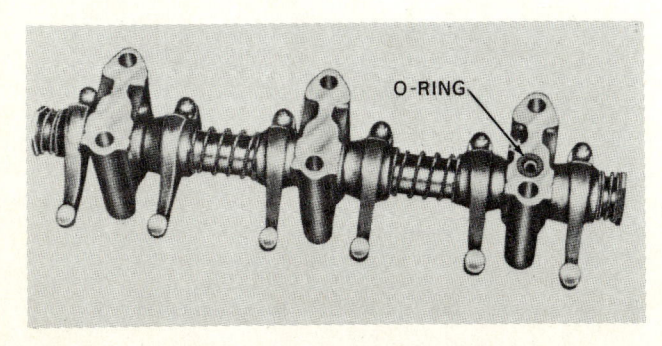

ROCKER ARM AND BRACKET O RING

Fig. 15-1 Rocker-arm assembly.

	INTAKE	EXHAUST
No. 1 cylinder		
No. 2 cylinder		
No. 3 cylinder		
No. 4 cylinder		
No. 5 cylinder		
No. 6 cylinder		
No. 7 cylinder		
No. 8 cylinder		

10. On Fig. 15-3, draw the location of each of the pistons, under the conditions mentioned in Prob. 9.

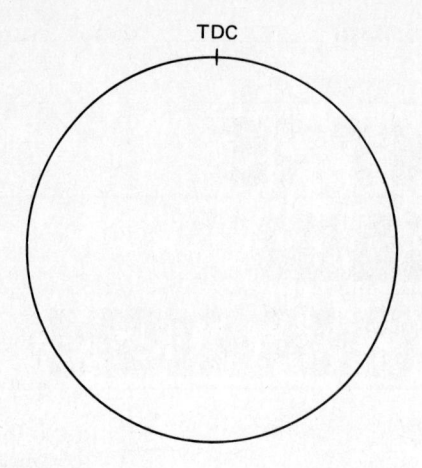

Fig. 15-3

TDC

11. Referring to Prob. 9, on which stroke is each of the following pistons?

No. 1 piston _____
No. 2 piston _____
No. 3 piston _____
No. 4 piston _____
No. 5 piston _____
No. 6 piston _____
No. 7 piston _____
No. 8 piston _____

12. Explain how to adjust the Caterpillar compression release shown in DM2 Fig. 15-6.

ASSIGNMENT 16
FLYWHEEL HOUSING, FLYWHEEL, TIMING-GEAR COVER, CRANKSHAFT PULLEY, AND VIBRATION DAMPER

1. Using a workshop engine as a guide, list the mandatory checks and measurements you must make on the flywheel housing.

2. Why do manufacturers recommend removing the dowel pins before installing a new flywheel housing, or when installing a new cylinder block?

3. Why is it necessary to align the flywheel housing and then drill and ream new dowel holes before the housing is bolted to the cylinder block?

4. Upon visually inspecting an in-service flywheel, what are the conditions which suggest to you that the flywheel must be replaced?

5. When selecting the new ring gear, what three factors must you take into consideration?

6. Why is it advisable to heat the ring gear in an oven rather than use a heating torch?

7. List the three checks you would make before installing the flywheel.

8. Whether installing a new or old flywheel to the crankshaft flange, why should you use guide studs?

9. Whether the flywheel is new or old, the flywheel-face runout and the pilot-bore runout should be measured, and the flywheel-housing concentricity rechecked. On Fig. 16-1, draw the dial-indicator position for these three measurements.

10. Assume that you have checked the flywheel-face runout, and find that the dial indicator was installed 4 in [101.6 mm] from the center of the crankshaft, and that the dial-indicator reading is 0.005 in [0.127 mm]. What would the accurate flywheel-face runout be if the flywheel-face diameter were 9 in [228.7 mm]?

11. Why must you torque the flywheel bolts in a predetermined sequence and in not less than three passes?

12. Use the timing-gear cover from an engine in your workshop and describe the wear at the following checkpoints: (a) mounting flange to cylinder block, (b) mounting flange to oil pan, (c) accessory mounting surfaces, (d) drill holes, (e) threaded holes, (f) seal bores.

13. A crankshaft pulley requires several checks to determine its serviceability. One check is to inspect the sheaves (belt grooves). List two remaining checks.

14. Discuss how you would check the belt grooves (from an engine in your workshop) in order to determine if the pulley is reusable.

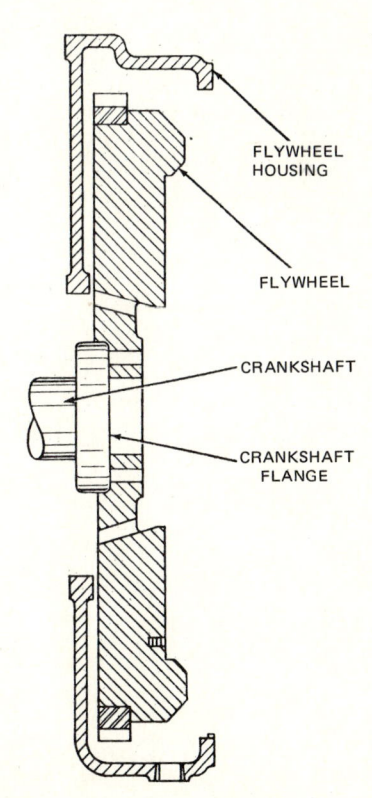

Fig. 16-1 Sectional view of an installed flywheel housing and flywheel.

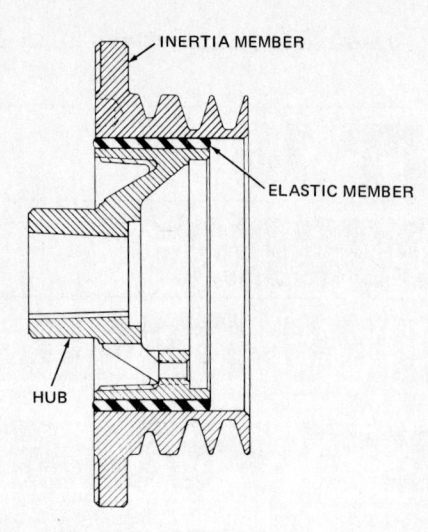

Fig. 16-2 Sectional view of a crankshaft pulley with integral vibration damper (type 1). *(Allis-Chalmers Corp. Engine Division.)*

15. Explain how to install the crankshaft pulley shown in Fig. 16-2.

16. When checking the rubber vibration damper, list two checks to be made in addition to checking the bolt holes, the mounting flange, and the deterioration of the rubber element.

17. List the essential checks you should make *(a)* before you install a vibration damper to the crankshaft pulley, *(b)* after the vibration damper is bolted to the pulley.

18. List three reasons why *(a)* an internal-combustion engine requires a crankcase ventilation system, and *(b)* three reasons why all newer engines employ a positive-crankcase ventilation system.

ASSIGNMENT 17
BEARINGS

1. List the three types of bearing friction.
2. Outline the differences between a friction bearing and an antifriction bearing.
3. Outline the function of each of the following ball-bearing designs: (a) a single-row deep-groove bearing, (b) a loading-groove bearing, (c) an (a) or (b) type with a snap-ring groove, (d) an (a) or (b) type with a shield, (e) an (a) or (b) type with a seal on one side or both sides, (f) a single-row angular-contact bearing, (g) a double-row deep-groove bearing, (h) a double-row angular-contact bearing.
4. List the main difference between a ball bearing and a roller bearing.
5. List the main differences between a cylindrical (straight) roller bearing and a self-aligning roller bearing.
6. Outline the purpose of a thrust bearing. (Refer to Fig. 17-1.)
7. Outline the main differences between needle bearings and roller bearings.
8. Explain why tapered roller bearings are used when high radial and thrust load must be carried by the bearing.
9. Explain why the bore or shaft could be damaged, or bodily injury could result, when you (a) use a hammer and punch to drive the bearing out of a bore or a shaft, (b) use a cutting torch to cut the bearing from a shaft, (c) press a bearing out of a bore or from a shaft when the component is not properly supported, (d) press a bearing out of a bore or from a shaft when the bearing is not covered with a rag.
10. Explain the procedure for removing a roller bearing from an exposed shaft (using a heating tip).
11. Explain why you should avoid using an impact wrench to turn the screw of the pulling attachment.
12. List step by step the procedure to clean a bearing which is packed with old grease.
13. What precautions must you take when cleaning a shield bearing?
14. List four conditions you might find while inspecting a bearing for serviceability that would make bearing replacement mandatory.
15. Why should you pack a bearing full of grease and wrap it in wax paper if you're not going to use it immediately?
16. Outline two checks you must make before installing a bearing.
17. Explain the procedure and precautions to install a bearing to a shaft when using a (a) heating oven to heat the bearing, (b) hydraulic press (Fig. 17-2), (c) tube-type hammer tool (see DM2 Fig. 17-38).

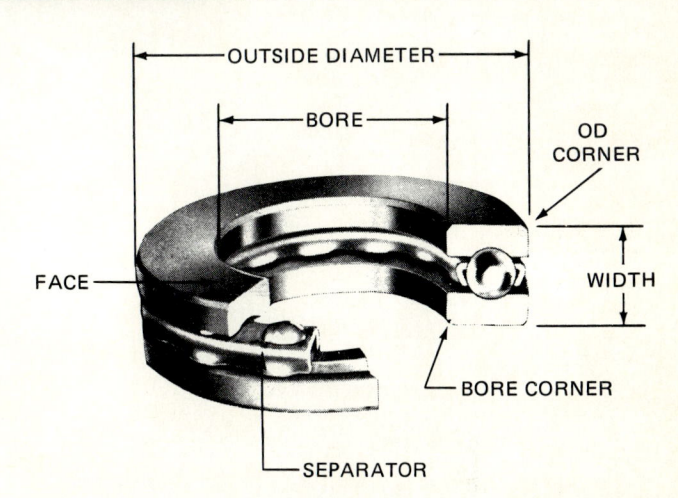

Fig. 17-1 Ball thrust bearing. *(International Harvester Co.)*

18. List the four qualities, other than fatigue strength and embedability, required of diesel engine friction bearings.
19. What methods are used to locate and to hold two half-bearings in position?

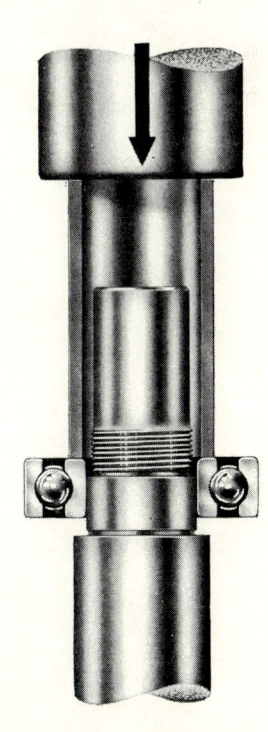

Fig. 17-2 Using a hydraulic press. *(International Harvester Co.)*

20. If an engine is operating at a constant rpm and load, in which stroke and at approximately what crankshaft position would the oil-film wedge between the connecting rod and crankshaft journal be the smallest?

21. What precautions must you take to prevent repeat bearing failure?

22. If you are presently working on an engine, and the crankshaft is removed, examine each main bearing, the connecting-rod bearings, and the thrust bearing, and give an analysis of the wear pattern on each of the bearings. *(NOTE: Do not forget to check the bores from which the bearing was removed.)*

23. How would the surface area of a bearing appear, upon removal, having had inadequate crush?

Name _____ Date _____ Class _____

ASSIGNMENT 18
AIR-INTAKE SYSTEM

1. List the major components of an air-intake system that uses a turbocharger and an aftercooler.
2. Compare the air-intake system of two engines in your workshop. List the main differences between them.
3. After you have cleaned the intake manifold, check it for cracks, and check the mounting surface for corrosion, straightness, and warpage. What two additional checks are required before mounting the manifold to the cylinder head?
4. Name the three most common types of air cleaners.
5. Outline the cleaning procedure and the service procedure for an oil-bath cleaner.
6. Why must the filter element of an oil-bath cleaner be free of any cleaning fluid before it can be installed into the filter housing?
7. List the advantages of a drip-type air cleaner over an oil-bath cleaner.
8. Explain how to service and clean a (a) Donaclone air cleaner, (b) dry-type filter-element air cleaner.
9. What is the purpose of an aftercooler?
10. Explain the air and coolant flow through the aftercooler shown in Fig. 18-1.
11. To ensure that the aftercooler does not leak after it has been serviced, it must be tested. How would you pressure-test an aftercooler using a test pressure of 15 psi [103.4 kPa]?
12. Explain why an air leak in the intake system could result in a very expensive service charge.
13. Why should you use (a) only the best-quality hoses to join two air system components, (b) two hose clamps to clamp the hose to the air-intake pipe or to the turbocharger?
14. What evidence would cause you to test the air-intake system for a leak?
15. What steps would you take (including positioning of the valves) before testing the air-intake system for a leak?
16. How would you locate a minute air leak in the air-intake system?
17. List two reasons why the air pressure could drop quickly to zero during a leakage test, even though there were no external air leaks in the air-intake system.
18. What could cause (a) excessive, though fairly clean, oil to appear on the compressor wheel or housing, (b) rough or nicked leading edges of the compressor wheel, (c) direct contact between the compressor wheel and the housing?
19. When inspecting the rotors of a Roots blower, what components (if worn) would necessitate replacement of a rotor?
20. Why should you replace both timing gears when only one gear has worn drive splines or damaged teeth?
21. What must you take into consideration (a) during the installation of the last rotor, (b) before placing the blower housing over the rotors?
22. How would you measure the clearance between each rotor and end plate, after the end-plate cover is installed and the bolts torqued to specification?
23. Why must you install the timing gear with the left-hand helical twist to the left-hand helix rotor shaft, and the timing gear with the right-hand helical twist to the right-hand helix rotor shaft?
24. Outline the procedure for installing new timing gears onto the rotor shafts.
25. Using the specifications on DM2 p. 119 and DM2 Fig. 18-16, describe how to measure the rotor clearances at point C, and at point CC.
26. Assume that your measurement at C is 0.001 in and the measurement at CC is 0.013 in. What steps must you take to bring the clearances at point C and point CC to the recommended specification?
27. What additional checks must you make to the air shutdown assembly, either during assembly or else after it has been assembled?

Fig. 18-1 Aftercooler.

39

ASSIGNMENT 19
EXHAUST SYSTEM

1. When installing a multisection exhaust manifold, as opposed to one that is unisection, what additional procedures and precautions must you follow?

2. From what source and for what reason could oil leak onto the turbocharger?

3. In order to reduce turbocharger failure, list the checks you should make (a) daily, (b) weekly.

4. When the ambient temperature is at or below the freezing level, what precautions should you take before starting an engine having a turbocharger?

5. What occurrences would cause you to suspect the turbocharger could soon fail?

6. What are the two main precautions you should take to prevent early turbocharger failure?

7. Explain why the seals of a turbocharger could leak when the (a) return oil from the turbocharger is restricted or incorrectly installed, (b) crankcase pressure is above specification.

8. What on the turbine side of the turbocharger could cause (a) damage to the turbine wheel even though no evidence of contact with the turbine housing is noticeable, (b) fine hair cracks at the volute end, or at the mounting flange of the turbine housing?

9. Outline the procedure to check the wear of a turbocharger bearing.

10. When and why should you check the return oil flow of a turbocharger?

11. When inspecting the components of a turbocharger, to what would you attribute a (a) discolored

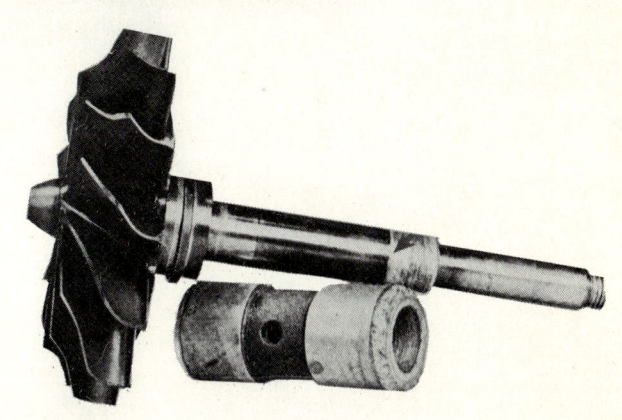

Fig. 19-1 Heat discoloration on rotor shaft. *(Cummins Engine Company, Inc.)*

turbine shaft (Fig. 19-1), (b) worn turbine thrust bearing, (c) worn compressor thrust bearing, (d) deformed bearing housing?

12. What types of damage due to inadequate service during assembly can lead to an early turbocharger failure?

13. List the checks you must make before installing a turbocharger to the engine.

14. Why is it so important to make certain that the connection to the turbocharger fits without strain?

41

ASSIGNMENT 20
COOLING SYSTEM

1. A cooling system having almost all possible temperature control devices is shown in Fig. 20-1. On Fig. 20-1, draw in the additional temperature control devices which are used on certain engines.
2. List four essential provisions which a modern diesel engine requires of its cooling system.
3. How do the following conditions relate to, or cause, coolant loss: (a) loose fan belts, (b) a shutter-stat which opens too late, (c) a restricted radiator, (d) air in the coolant, (e) a damaged radiator neck or cap?
4. Briefly describe how to pressure-test the cooling system.
5. Calculate the minimum acceptable front square area of a radiator to be used with a 350-hp engine.

6. How does a radiator dissipate excessive heat from the coolant?
7. Why are fan shrouds of various designs used?
8. Why is the design and location of the fan shroud so important?
9. Why should the air velocity not exceed 396 m/min?
10. What advantage is achieved by a radiator with a top tank divided into an upper and a lower section?
11. Describe the radiator-core design of the radiator from the engine you are presently working on.
12. Describe the condition of the same radiator and discuss its design.
13. Outline the procedure to clean trapped alien matter from the radiator core.

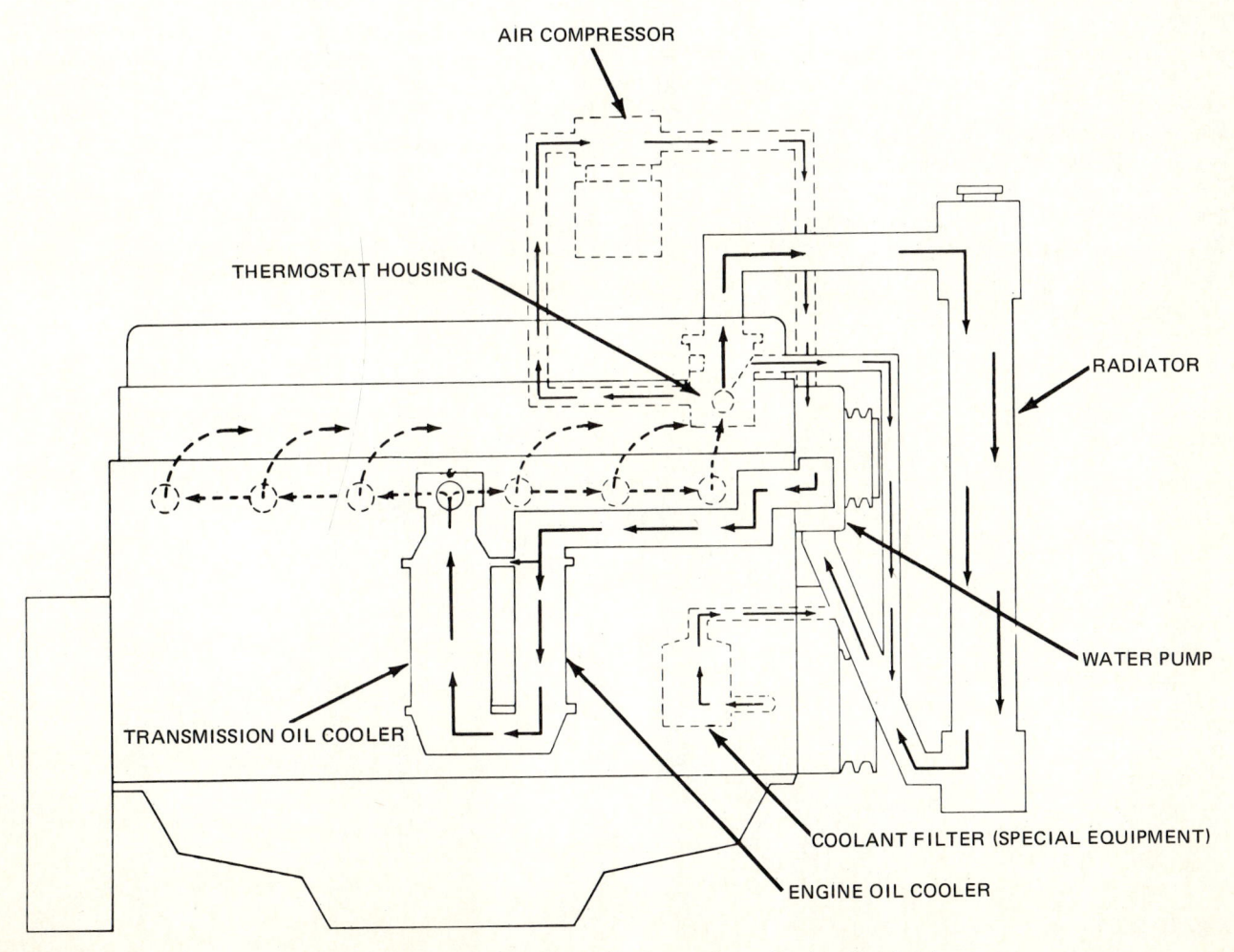

Fig. 20-1 Schematic diagram of a cooling system. *(Allis-Chalmers Corp. Engine Division.)*

14. What kind of damage to the radiator filler neck would prevent the radiator cap from sealing completely?
15. Explain how to test a radiator cap.
16. Calculate the boiling point temperature of the coolant when the pressure cap has a rating of 21 psi [144.7 kPa].
17. What is the difference and/or advantage of (a) a pusher fan over a suction fan, (b) a fiberglass fan over a steel fan?
18. What defects render a radiator fan useless?
19. Assume that you have a fan hub assembly (Fig. 20-2) which has the following service manual specifications:

- Grease   0.25 oz [7.1 g]
- Locknut torque 145 lb·ft [20.1 kg·m]
- End play   0.002 to 0.006 in [0.050 to 0.152 mm]

Assume also that the fan-hub components have been checked, and the bearing races have been pressed into the bores of the pulley. Discuss how you would (a) reassemble this fan hub, (b) change the end play of this fan-hub pulley if the end play were greater than specified.

20. List the weekly maintenance checks you should make on a thermatic fan clutch assembly (not including tests or adjustments of the thermal switch).
21. Why should you also check, weekly, the fan belt or belts, the fan-belt tightener, and the remaining pulleys?
22. Outline the procedure to check the actuation of the thermal switch when the valve opening temperature is adjusted to 190°F [88°C].
23. What is the purpose of a radiator shutter?
24. Why is air pressure used to close the shutter?
25. Why is a spring used to open the shutter?
26. List five mandatory visual maintenance checks to be made on the shutter assembly.
27. Describe how you would check the radiator shutter in order to confirm satisfactory shutter-blade closure?
28. How would the engine coolant temperature be affected when (a) the adjustment from the shutter cylinder to the shutter pull rod is incorrect (causing the shutter blades to remain slightly open), (b) there is a small air leak in the shutter cylinder, (c) the thermal switch opening is incorrectly adjusted, for example, to 160°F [71.1°C]?
29. Outline the procedure to check the opening of the shutterstat when the opening temperature is adjusted to 185°F [85°C] and the closing temperature is 177°F [80.5°C].
30. What are the differences among a full-blocking thermostat, a partial-blocking thermostat, and a non-blocking thermostat?
31. Explain how to check the operation of an installed thermostat when its opening temperature is 170°F [76.6°C].
32. What is the temperature of the thermostat mentioned previously when it is in the fully open position?
33. Explain why the thermostats used on smaller diesel engines have a small hole in the valve plate.
34. When you test the opening and closing of a thermostat which has been removed from the engine, why should it (a) not be cleaned before testing, (b) be allowed to float freely in the water?
35. Why does the closing temperature of the thermostat have to be checked?
36. At what point and for what reasons can (a) combustion gases enter the cooling system, (b) air enter the cooling system?

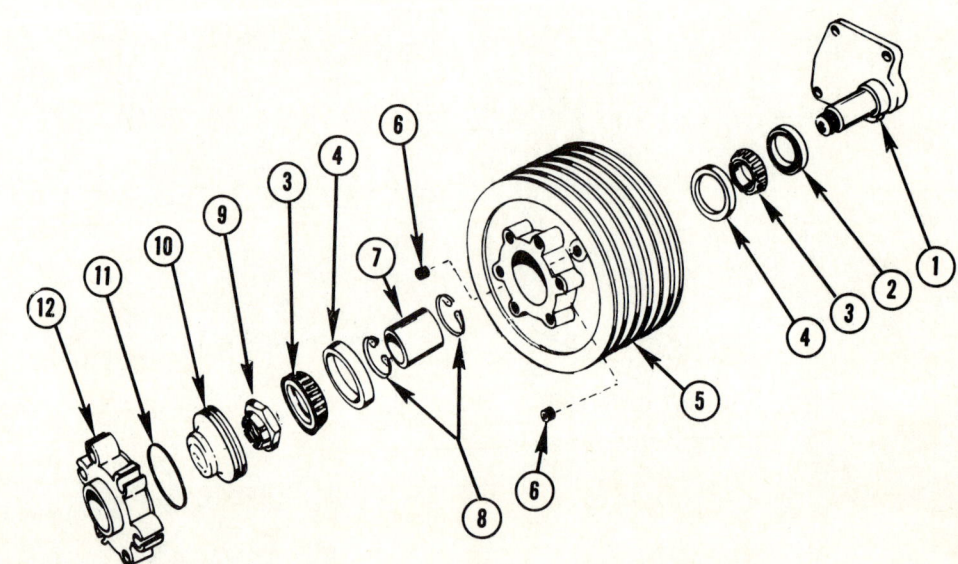

1. Shaft
2. Oil seal
3. Bearing
4. Bearing race
5. Pulley
6. Pipe plug
7. Bearing spacer
8. Snap ring
9. Locknut
10. Retainer
11. O ring
12. Spacer

Fig. 20-2 Exploded view of a fanhub assembly. *(Cummins Engine Company, Inc.)*

Name _____ Date _____ Class _____

37. Outline two methods to determine if air is in the cooling system.
38. List four causes of failure of (a) coolant-pump bearing(s), (b) a coolant-pump seal. Refer to Fig. 20-3.
39. What damage or extent of wear would render the following components unserviceable: (a) pump housing, (b) pump shaft, (c) impeller?
40. Discuss the pros and cons of the following statement: It is better in the long run to replace the bearings and the seals (including O rings) of a coolant pump when the pump is being serviced.
41. Why should the water used for an engine contain not more than 340 parts per million of dissolvable solids?
42. Why do most diesel engines use a coolant filter?
43. Describe how to fill a coolant system which has a capacity of 11.5 gal (U.S.) with a solution of 40 percent ethylene glycol antifreeze and 60 percent water, and calculate how much of this solution is needed.
44. By what means can you determine if the drive belts are in good, fair, or poor condition?
45. What drive belt problems result when (a) the sheaves (pulley grooves) are not smooth, (b) the belt is not adjusted correctly (too loose or too tight), (c) the pulleys are misaligned, (d) the belt tightener or idler causes a great reverse bend in the belt, (e) oil or grease is allowed to contaminate the belt?
46. Why should dual-drive belts be used only in matched sets?
47. Why should you not pry the belts over the pulley?

48. Why must you implicitly follow service manual recommendations in regard to belt tension?

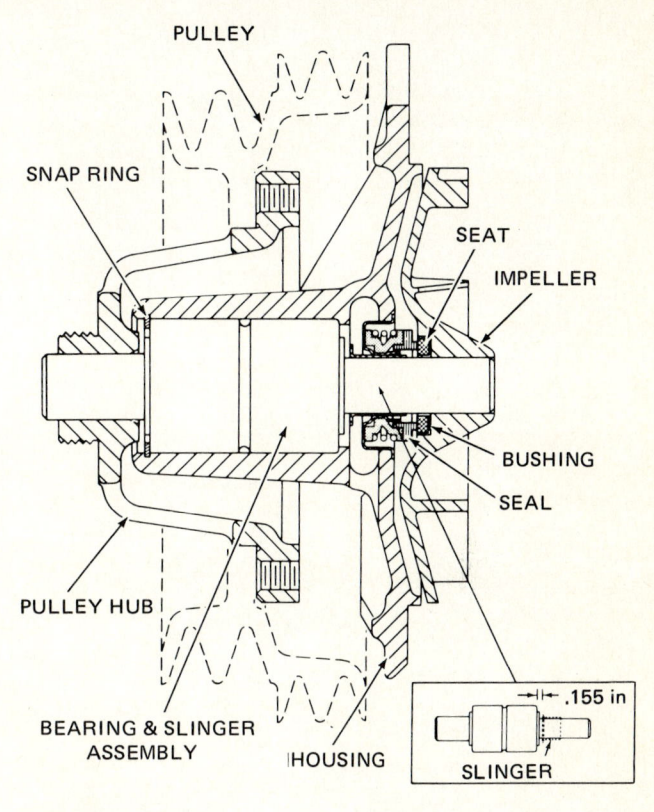

Fig. 20-3 Sectional view of a coolant pump. *(International Harvester Co.)*

ASSIGNMENT 21
HYDRAULIC LINES AND FITTINGS

1. List the reasons why you should avoid, as much as possible, using (a) a 90° elbow, (b) reducers.
2. Why should you avoid using cast-iron fittings on diesel engines?
3. If, when installing a hose or tube, you find that you must go around an object or component, how small can you make the bend radius when a No. 8 hose is used?
4. List the differences between the classifications "pipe" and "tube."
5. Interpret the standard dash number 12 in regard to (a) a tube, (b) hydraulic hose.
6. Explain the method you would use to measure the correct tube length using the safest route but without wasting tube material.
7. Why should you hold the tube coil in an upright position and hold the tube end to a flat surface when you are rolling the tube coil out to the desired tube length?
8. The most common mistake made, and one which leads to a leak, is cutting the tube incorrectly. Outline in detail how you would cut a No. 8 tube to the desired length, and then explain the remaining steps to be taken before you make a flare.
9. List the two main reasons why you should use a mechanical tube bender when bending a tube to a bend angle greater than 20°.
10. Name the six threaded-type connectors.
11. Which types of connectors are most suitable for use on diesel engines? Why?
12. To form a good double flare, you must have a straight square cut and a round tube. Also, the inside of the tube, which is folded inward as a result of cutting, must be straightened or reamed. Why are these three factors mandatory when you wish to achieve a good double flare?
13. How can you avoid making an oversize flare end?
14. List the steps you must follow and the precautions you must take when installing a double-flared fuel line.
15. When replacing a tube which uses a compression fitting, why must you make sure, when the nut is being tightened, that (a) the tube is bottomed against the adapter shoulder, (b) the tube is straight in line with the fitting, (c) the nut is not overtorqued?
16. What happens when the fitting nut is overtorqued?
17. Outline the reason why a hydraulic hose is more reliable for connecting components than a tube.
18. Explain the procedure for installing the hose end to a hose shown in Fig. 21-1.
19. Assume that you must install a new hose to connect the primary fuel filter with the fuel line from the fuel tank, which is inside the frame rail. List the factors you must consider when making up the new hose.

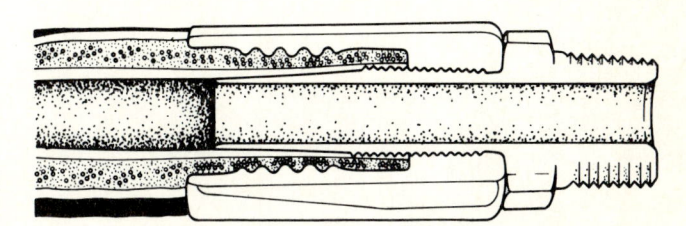

Fig. 21-1 Sectional view of a mechanical pressure-base assembly. *(Detroit Diesel Allison, Division of General Motors Corporation.)*

ASSIGNMENT 22
FILTERS

1. Which two classes of filter materials are used for filters on the diesel engine?

2. The unit of measurement used to determine the effectiveness of a filter is the micrometer (μm). What is the measurement of 1 μm (a) in inches, (b) in millimeters?

3. List the four basic types of filter designs.

4. Describe the basic difference between a surface-type filter and an edge-type filter.

5. List five types of inactive absorbent filter material used in filters.

6. Explain why a full-flow filter requires a bypass valve.

7. A common factor of all filters is that they filter liquid or air from the outside to the inside. Why is this method of flow the most effective?

8. Outline the steps which you would follow to service or replace a (a) spin-on-type oil filter, (b) replacement-element oil filter, (c) replacement-element fuel filter. (Refer to Fig. 22-1.)

9. What maintenance would you perform to extend the service life of a fuel filter?

10. Name the two devices used to indicate when the primary or secondary fuel filter is restricted, and state where they are located within the fuel-injection system.

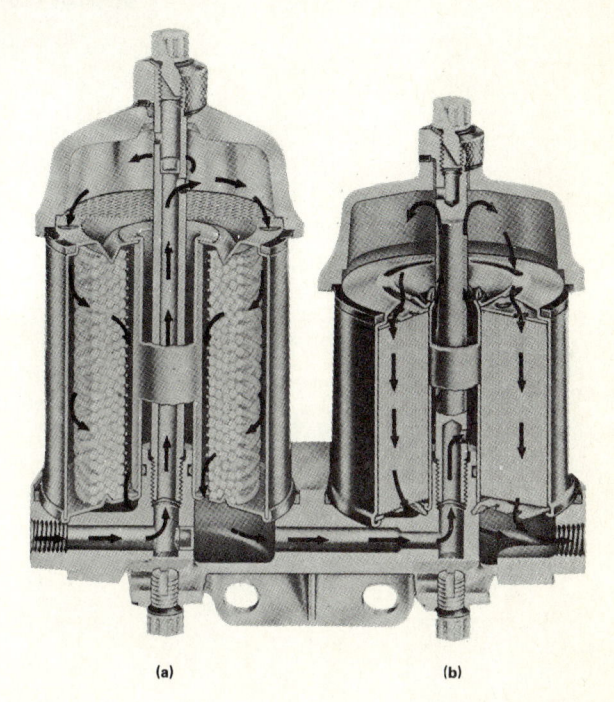

Fig. 22-1 Sectional view of fuel filters. (a) Special V-form construction (paper); (b) Deep-type woven cotton construction. *(CAV Limited.)*

ASSIGNMENT 23
SEALS AND GASKETS

1. List at least 10 points which you must do or not do to prevent an early seal or gasket failure.
2. Under what circumstances would the following seals be used: *(a)* static seal, *(b)* dynamic seal?
3. What is meant by the expression "using a gasket as a sealing medium?"
4. List the eight major types of gasket materials and state where these gaskets are primarily used.
5. Today, the O ring has, to a large extent, replaced the gasket. List at least five reasons why, in a static application, an O ring has a better sealing effect than a gasket.
6. An O ring can be effective only when it is selected and installed correctly. List nine reasons (in regard to selection of material and installation procedure) why an O ring could fail to seal.
7. Explain why *(a)* the design of the head gasket varies from engine to engine, *(b)* some head gaskets have internal and/or external grommets.
8. When or for what reason would you use *(a)* a sealant compound, *(b)* an antiseize compound, *(c)* a lock-type compound?
9. Outline the procedure to install an oil pan.
10. What additional precautions or measurements would you take when the oil pan covers part of the front cover and/or the timing-gear cover?
11. List three major differences between various lip-type seals. (Refer to Fig. 23-1.)
12. List a number of locations on the diesel engine or its components where you will find lip-type seals which *(a)* confine oil, *(b)* confine fuel, *(c)* confine coolant, *(d)* prevent air from entering the system.
13. Explain how the lip-type seal shown in Fig. 23-1 is able to stop oil from leaving the confinement whether or not the shaft is turning.
14. Again referring to Fig. 23-1, how is the atmospheric pressure prevented from entering the confinement?
15. Why should you examine the lip-type seal and the seal area before actually removing the seal?
16. List the reasons why a lip-type seal could fail to seal (other than because of improper installation, incorrect positioning, or normal wear on the seal lip).
17. Why is it important to use the lip-type seal recommended by the manufacturer?
18. List the check you should make immediately prior to pressing or driving a new seal into place.
19. Explain in detail how to install a new seal. (Refer to Fig. 23-2.)
20. When installing a lip-type seal that must have its opening side facing outward, what precaution must you take when pressing the seal into its bore?
21. Why should you use a sealing compound sparingly when sealing the bore to the seal case?
22. When must you use a seal-protection sleeve when installing a lip-type seal?

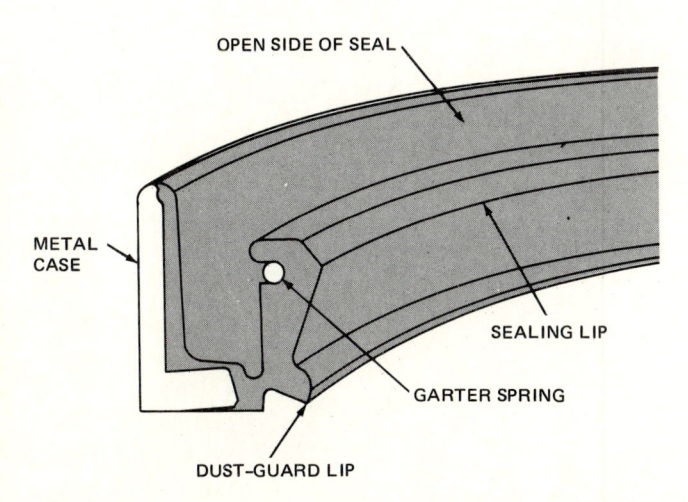

Fig. 23-1 Sectional view of a conventional lip-type seal. *(Cummins Engine Company, Inc.)*

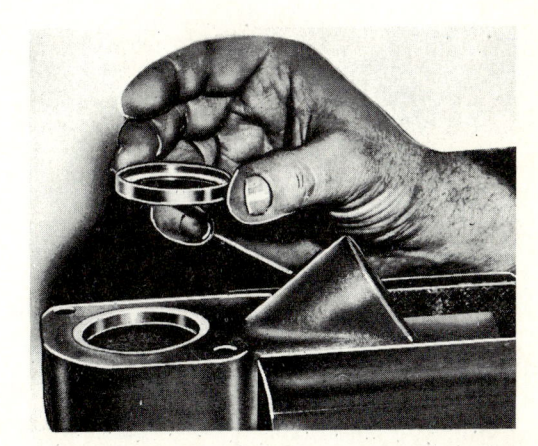

Fig. 23-2 Installing a thermostat seal. *(Mack Trucks Canada Ltd.)*

ASSIGNMENT 24
DIESEL FUEL

1. Name the three hydrocarbon groups used in the production of fuel or crankcase oil.

2. There are 13 properties listed in DM2 Table 24-2. Give a short outline of each property as it relates to engine performance, wear, and handling.

3. State the purpose of each of the four additives: (1) ignition or cetane improvers (amyl nitrate), (2) detergents or solvents, (3) oxidation inhibitors or stability improvers, and (4) corrosion inhibitors.

4. List four precautionary procedures you would follow when storing fuel in drums.

ASSIGNMENT 25
GOVERNORS

1. What controls the speed of a diesel engine and why is a diesel engine not self-speed-limiting?

2. Name the five basic types (classifications) of governors.

3. (a) What are the two main functions of all governors? (b) List the components involved in those functions (see Fig. 25-1).

4. Define the following terms: (a) low idle, (b) high idle, (c) rated speed, (d) droop speed, (e) overspeeding, (f) speed drift, (g) speed regulation, (h) speed deviation, (i) momentary speed changes, (j) sensitivity, (k) stability, (l) promptness, (m) hunting, (n) dead band, (o) governor cutoff speed.

5. Explain how the following three modifications will improve a governor: (a) increasing the rotating speed of the flyweights, (b) reducing transmission of pulsation to the flyweights, and (c) modifying the flyweight fingers and pivot points.

6. How can the following two steps be accomplished: (a) reducing friction between the opposing force of the governor spring and weight, and (b) installing a device (sliding-sleeve assembly) to increase the spring force? (See Fig. 25-2.)

7. In what way do the previous two modifications improve the governor?

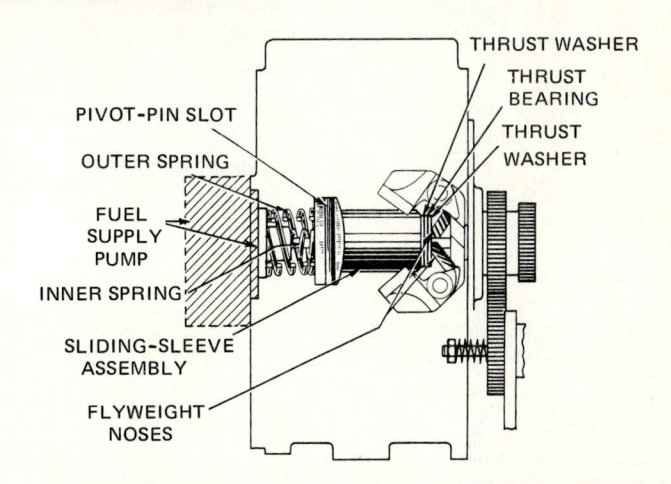

Fig. 25-2 Buildup of a mechanical governor: reducing friction and installing a device to increase the spring force. *(American Bosch, United Technologies Automotive Group.)*

The next modification would be to link the throttle shaft to the control rack and place the connecting link between the weight force and the spring force, as shown in Fig. 25-3.

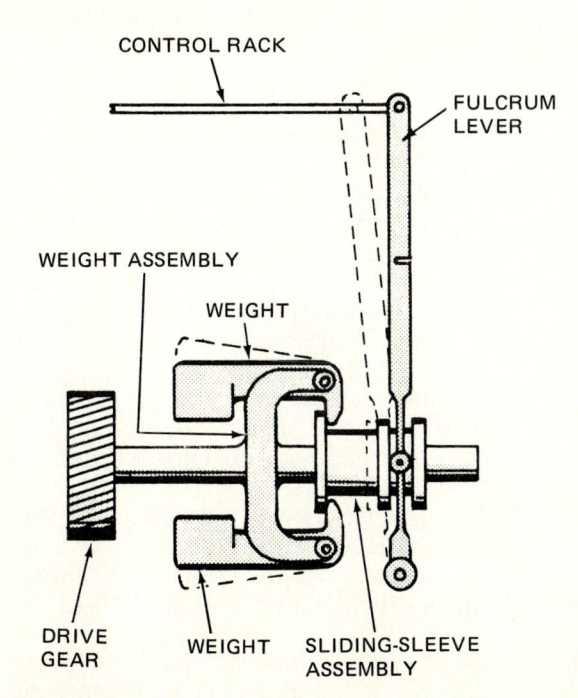

Fig. 25-1 Simplified governor.

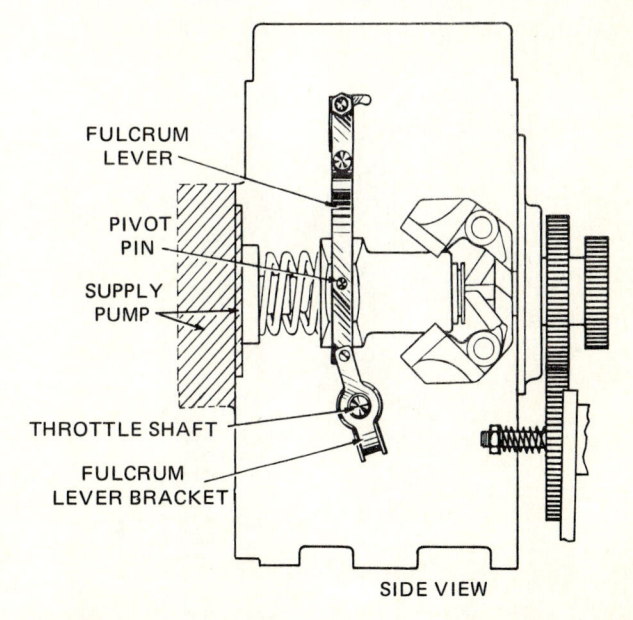

Fig. 25-3 Buildup of a mechanical governor: linking a throttle shaft to the control rack and placing a connecting link between the weight force and the spring force. *(American Bosch, United Technologies Automotive Group.)*

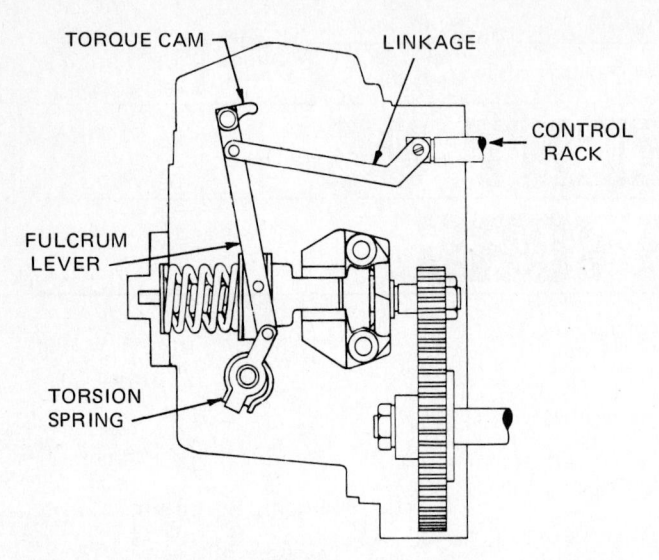

Fig. 25-4 Buildup of a mechanical governor: adding devices which limit maximum fuel and increase fuel at maximum torque. *(American Bosch, United Technologies Automotive Group.)*

A governor to this stage would be very satisfactory for a gasoline engine but would not be adequate for a diesel engine. A diesel engine requires a fuel stop. Its governor, therefore, requires one device which limits the maximum fuel and another which gives the governor the ability to move the control rack to increase fuel when the engine lugs down to maximum torque (Fig. 25-4).

8. What is the purpose of the governor spring force and what is the purpose of the flyweight force?

When the operator moves the throttle lever to the maximum-fuel position, the lever is stopped by the

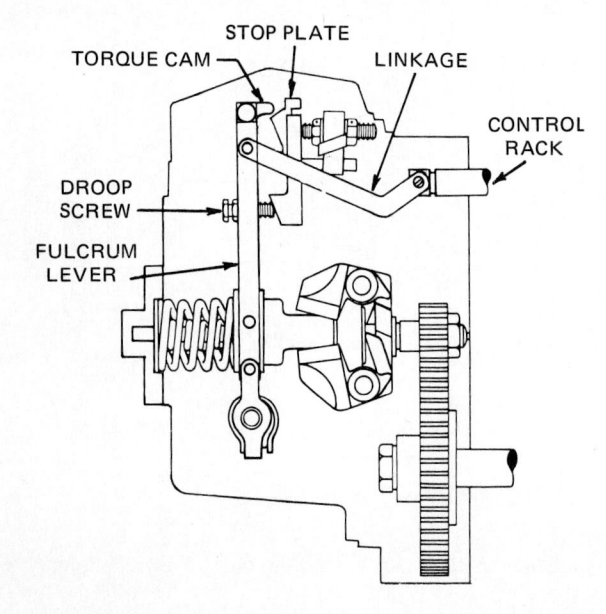

Fig. 25-5 Buildup of a mechanical governor: addition of a droop screw. *(American Bosch, United Technologies Automotive Group.)*

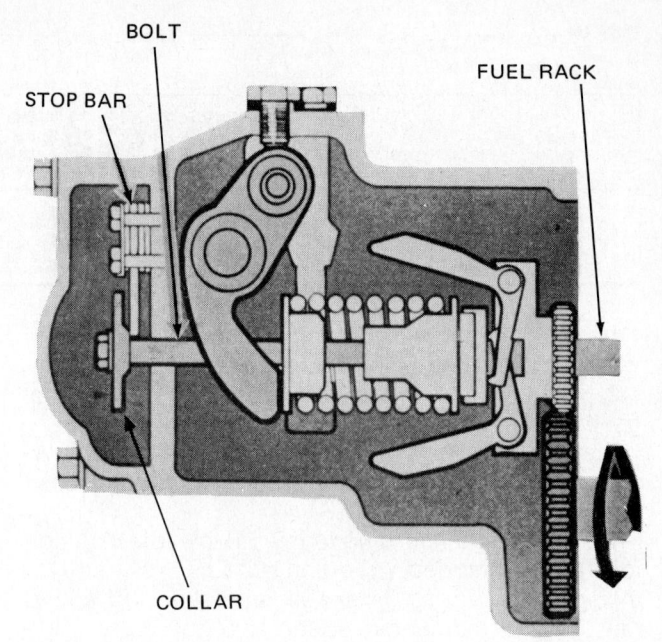

Fig. 25-6 Limiting speed governor. *(Caterpillar Tractor Co.)*

front stop screw (high-idle adjustment screw) and the fulcrum lever is repositioned. When the engine is operating at rated speed and load, the governor takes a position as shown in DM2 Fig. 25-5 and DM2 Table 25-1.

9. Explain the action within the governor when the engine load increases and the governor reacts to the position as shown in Fig. 25-5 and DM2 Table 25-1.
10. Outline how the droop screw prevents excessive fuel delivery during acceleration and at maximum speed and load until the turbocharger has reached maximum boost pressure.
11. Explain the action within the governor when the throttle has compressed the governor spring to its maximum and the engine operates at high idle and no load (Fig. 25-6).
12. Explain the action within the governor as the engine reduces in speed because of increased load and then operates at droop speed and finally at maximum torque speed.
13. Explain the action within the servo governor mechanism when the operator moves the throttle to (a) increase speed, (b) decrease speed.
14. Explain the reaction of the servo mechanism when the engine speed is reduced (owing to increased load) from high-idle to torque speed (Fig. 25-7).
15. What mechanical action will take place within the DPA hydraulic governor (assuming that the engine is *not* operating) when the throttle lever is moved to the (a) no-fuel position, (b) idle-fuel position, (c) maximum-fuel position?
16. Explain the mechanical action and the fuel flow of the governor when the engine is operating at high idle and a load is placed on the engine.
17. Discuss why this simple hydraulic governor al-

56 Copyright © 1983 by McGraw-Hill, Inc. All rights reserved. Not to be reproduced.

Name _____ Date _____ Class _____

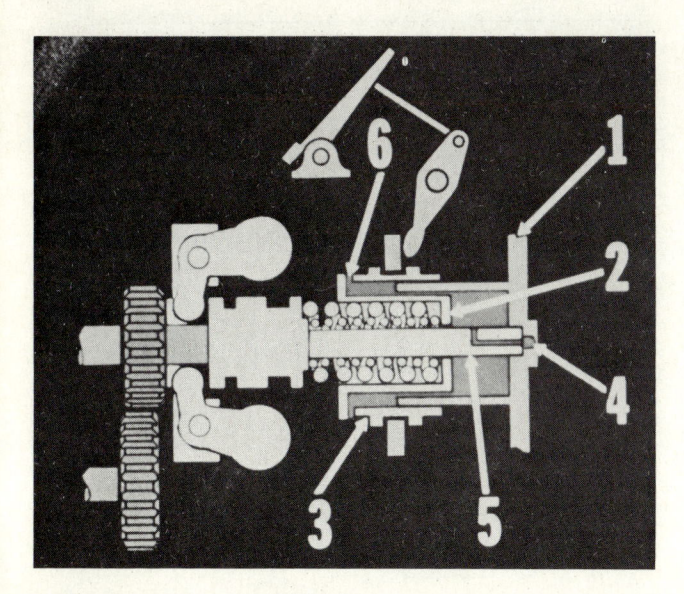

1. Cover
2. Piston
3. Cylinder
4. Oil inlet
5. Spindle
6. Oil outlet

Fig. 25-7 Servo governor. *(Caterpillar Tractor Co.)*

lows more fuel to pass through the metering port at torque speed than at high-idle speed.

A simplified direct-acting governor is shown in Fig. 25-8. Note that the fuel rack is linked to the piston, and that the control valve is fastened to the right-hand governor spring seat and to the oil inlet and oil outlet.

18. Explain how the governor reacts when the throttle is set at full fuel and the load on the engine *(a)* increases, *(b)* decreases.

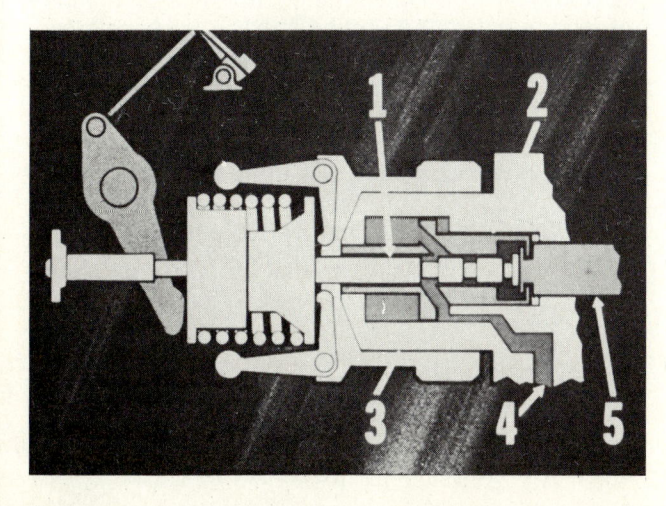

1. Valve
2. Piston
3. Cylinder
4. Oil inlet
5. Fuel rack

Fig. 25-8 Hydraulic governor. *(Caterpillar Tractor Co.)*

19. When the engine operates at a constant speed, the flyweight force and the spring force are in balance and the control valve is in a fixed position. Why is the piston also in a fixed position and what forces hold it there?

An indirect single-acting governor is shown in DM2 Fig. 25-17. The major difference between it and the direct-acting governor is that the fuel-changing mechanism is not directly linked with the servo.

Schematic and sectional views of an SG speed-droop governor are also shown in DM2 Figs. 25-16 and 25-17. Note that the activating mechanisms, that is, the speed-adjusting lever, the spring fork, and the floating lever, are different from that on a direct-acting hydraulic governor. Note also that a droop-adjusting bracket is used and is bolted to the terminal lever. The pin of the droop-adjusting bracket can slide in the slot of the floating lever.

20. *(a)* What governor adjustment is required to change the droop speed from 5 to 3 percent? *(b)* How does this mechanical change affect the governor?

Isochronous Governor Let us build an isochronous governor from a speed-droop hydraulic governor having a double-acting piston. (Refer to DM2 p. 177.) To help the governor spring adjust to speed changes, a receiving piston is linked with the control valve and with the governor spring (see Fig. 25-9).

21. How are the receiving pistons and the connecting links able to assist the governor in controlling the engine speed?

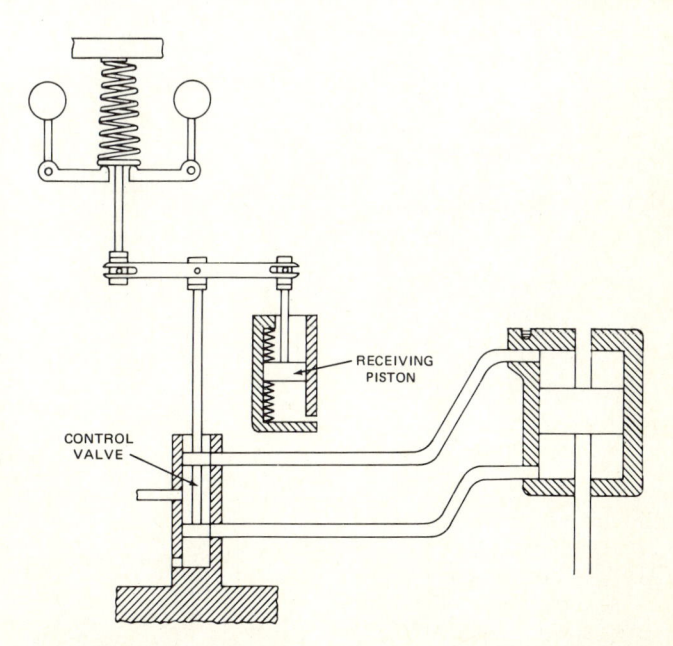

Fig. 25-9 Buildup of an isochronous governor: addition of a receiving piston.

Let us now add another piston, that is, a transmitting piston. Connect it hydraulically to the receiving piston. Use a valve to control the oil flow between the two pistons. Mechanically link the transmitting piston with the servo piston. (See Fig. 25-10.)

22. Why have the added components improved the speed control of the governor?

To help the governor even further to control the engine speed, a lever arm is placed over the governor spring. The arm is fastened on one end to the governor housing and fastened at the other end to the servo piston. (See Fig. 25-11.)

23. In what way does this final, additional mechanical arrangement improve the governor?
24. The sectional view of an isochronous governor is shown in DM2 Fig. 25-20. This governor is similar to the one you have hypothetically built. Using Figs. 25-9 to 25-11 as a guide, explain the oil flow and the action within the governor when the engine operates at a constant speed and when (a) a load is placed on the engine, (b) the load is taken off the engine.
25. State the main purpose of the following components: (a) venturi butterfly valve, (b) venturi throat, (c) auxiliary venturi, (d) governor spring, (e) diaphragm, (f) stop lever.

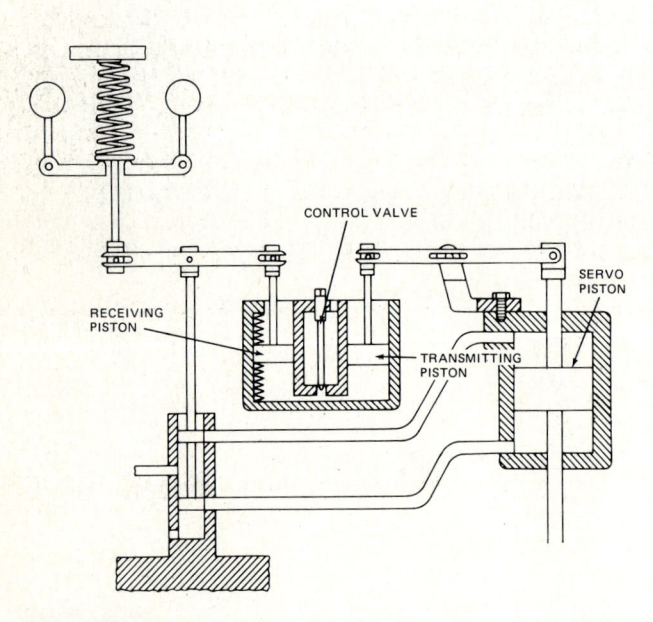

Fig. 25-10 Buildup of an isochronous governor: addition of a transmitting piston.

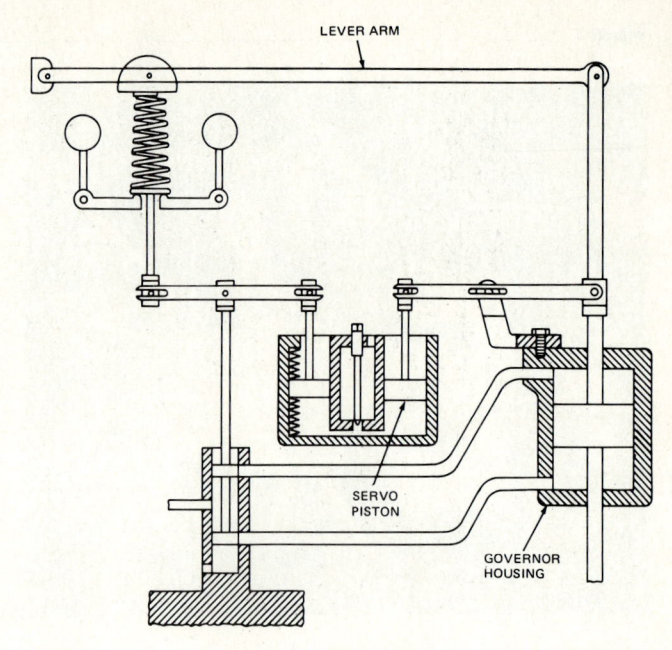

Fig. 25-11 Buildup of an isochronous governor: addition of a lever arm.

OPERATING PRINCIPLE When the engine is not operating, the governor spring moves the diaphragm against the maximum-fuel stop. For easier starting, you should floor the accelerator pedal.

26. Why does this action produce quicker starting?
27. Assume the engine is at operating temperature and the operator moves the accelerator pedal to the idle-stop position. Explain the action which reduces the engine speed to idle speed.
28. Explain the action that brings the engine to high-idle speed.
29. List the components and adjustments that limit the maximum engine speed.
30. Assume the engine is operating at high idle and the truck now starts to climb a grade. Explain how the governor moves the control rack to increase fuel and maintain the engine speed.
31. Explain why improper governor adjustment could create the following difficulties: (a) hard starting, (b) engine overspeeding, (c) poor performance or hunt, (d) surge, (e) rough idle, (f) excessive smoke, (g) high fuel consumption. (Discuss each reason separately.)
32. Why could mechanical or hydraulic failure and/or wear create the same difficulties? (Discuss each reason separately.)

ASSIGNMENT 26
ANTIPOLLUTION CONTROL DEVICES

1. Why does a turbocharged diesel engine require an antipollution control device?

2. Define *aneroid*.

3. Explain the purpose of the *(a)* starting plunger, *(b)* valve throttling rod (Fig. 26-1).

4. How would the aneroid and/or the engine (Cummins) performance be affected if the *(a)* air breather becomes plugged, *(b)* starting plunger stops in the open position, *(c)* bellows spring is broken, *(d)* bellows are punctured?

5. When the manifold fuel pressure is reduced from its maximum by 10 inHg [25.4 cmHg], what action takes place within the aneroid (PT) to reduce the exhaust emission?

6. An aneroid used with a port helix-type-metering fuel-injection pump is somewhat different from an aneroid used with a PT fuel pump. What are the main differences between these two aneroids?

7. Outline the position of the fuel-ratio control when the engine is operating at idle speed.

8. Assume that the engine is operating at its maximum torque speed and that the load is then quickly removed from the engine. Under these circumstances, how does the *(a)* governor respond to the load change, *(b)* fuel-ratio control respond to the load change?

9. Outline why an engine having a fuel-ratio or aneroid control has adequate rack travel (fuel) for starting. (Refer to Fig. 26-2.)

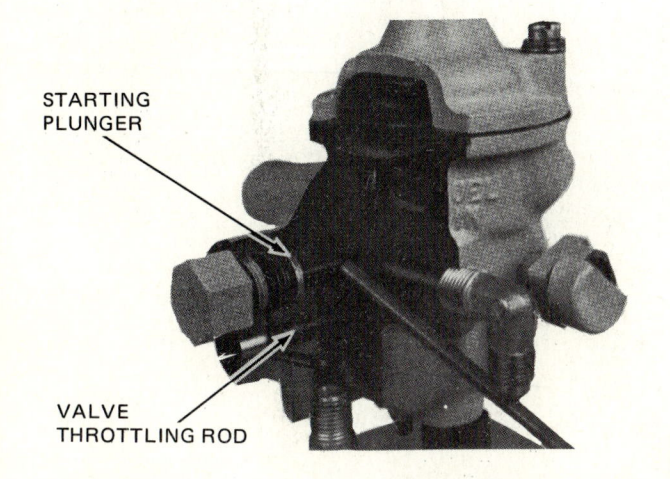

Fig. 26-1 Sectional view of an aneroid. *(Cummins Engine Company, Inc.)*

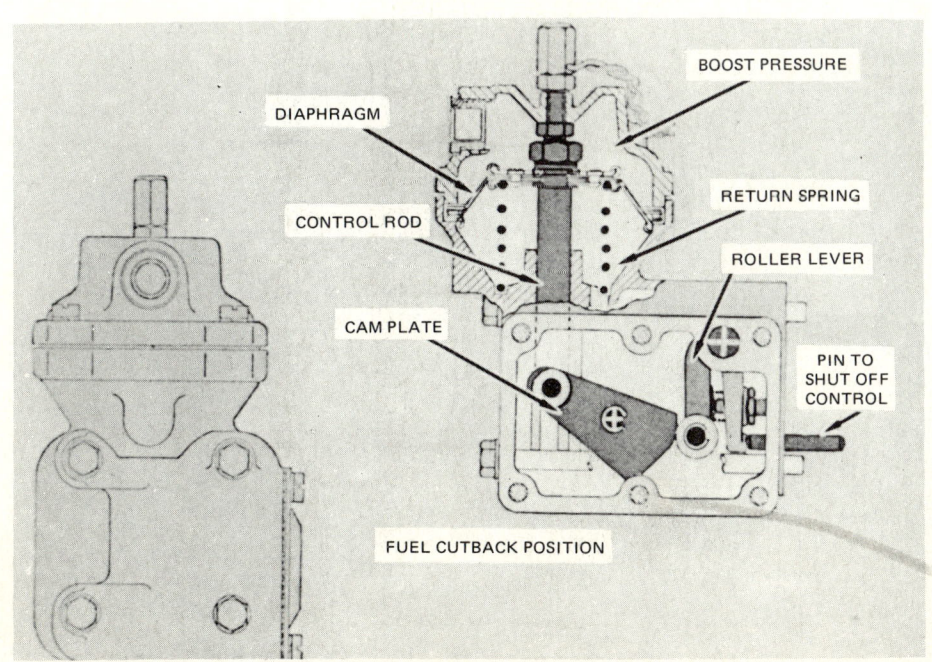

Fig. 26-2 Operation of an aneroid. *(International Harvester Co.)*

10. Explain why the governor cannot move the fuel control rack to the maximum-fuel position when *(a)* the diaphragm is damaged, *(b)* an excessively strong ratio-control spring is used, *(c)* one or more parts within the unit cause a binding or hang-up.

11. Why could the engine emit excessive exhaust smoke when *(a)* the fuel-ratio-control spring is broken, *(b)* an inadequate (weak) spring is installed, *(c)* the vent on the ratio control is restricted, *(d)* one or more parts of the ratio control cause a restricted movement of the diaphragm?

12. What dual purpose does the hydraulic air-fuel-ratio control serve (see Fig. DM 26-5)?

13. At what boost pressure does the hydraulic air-fuel-ratio-control valve commence operation?

14. What are the basic differences in operation between a fuel-ratio-control mechanism and a throttle-delay mechanism?

15. Why cannot a fuel-ratio control be used on a Detroit Diesel engine to control the exhaust emission?

16. How would the engine respond when the *(a)* check valve is stuck in a closed position, *(b)* check valve is stuck in an open position, *(c)* oil supply to the delay piston is restricted, *(d)* mechanical linkages have excessive resistance?

ASSIGNMENT 27
FUEL-INJECTION NOZZLES AND HOLDERS

1. A typical injector assembly used on engines having a special combustion-chamber design is shown in Fig. 27-1. Indentify each numbered component.

2. Refer to Fig. 27-1. What is the main purpose of *(a)* the holder assembly, *(b)* the nozzle assembly?

3. Name each of the nozzles shown in Fig. 27-2, state their intended application, and draw their predetermined spray pattern.

4. Explain the hydraulic and mechanical actions of the fuel-injector assembly from the time the fuel pressure increases above residual pressure to the time the pressure drops back to residual pressure. (Assume the opening pressure is 2700 psi [18,616.5 kPa].)

5. Explain why the *(a)* nozzle chatters during the injection period, *(b)* spray pattern and droplet size remain equal during the time of injection, *(c)* pressure chamber of a new injection-nozzle assembly has a reduced fuel area.

6. Outline the procedure to determine if an injector is defective.

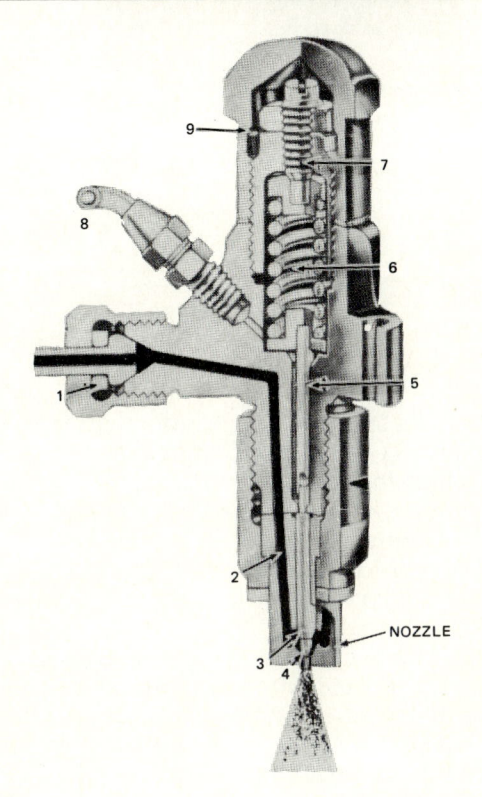

Fig. 27-1 Sectional view of a pintle-type injector. *(American Bosch, United Technologies Automotive Group.)*

A Stanadyne pencil-type injector is shown in Fig. 27-3. The assembly is very compact and, in comparison to a CAV or Bosch injector, it is small. However, it is equally effective. Because of its compactness, the Stanadyne pencil-type injector differs somewhat from a Bosch or CAV injector.

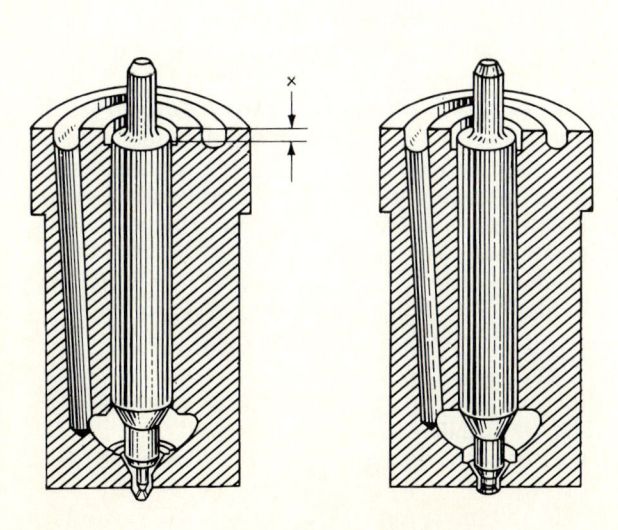

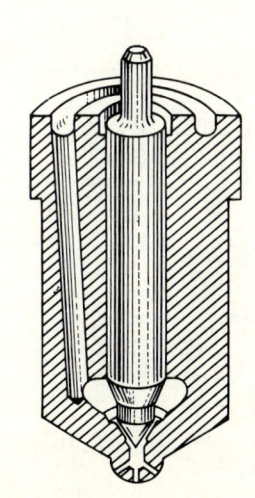

A _____ B _____ C _____ **Fig. 27-2** Nozzle designs. *(CAV Limited.)*

61

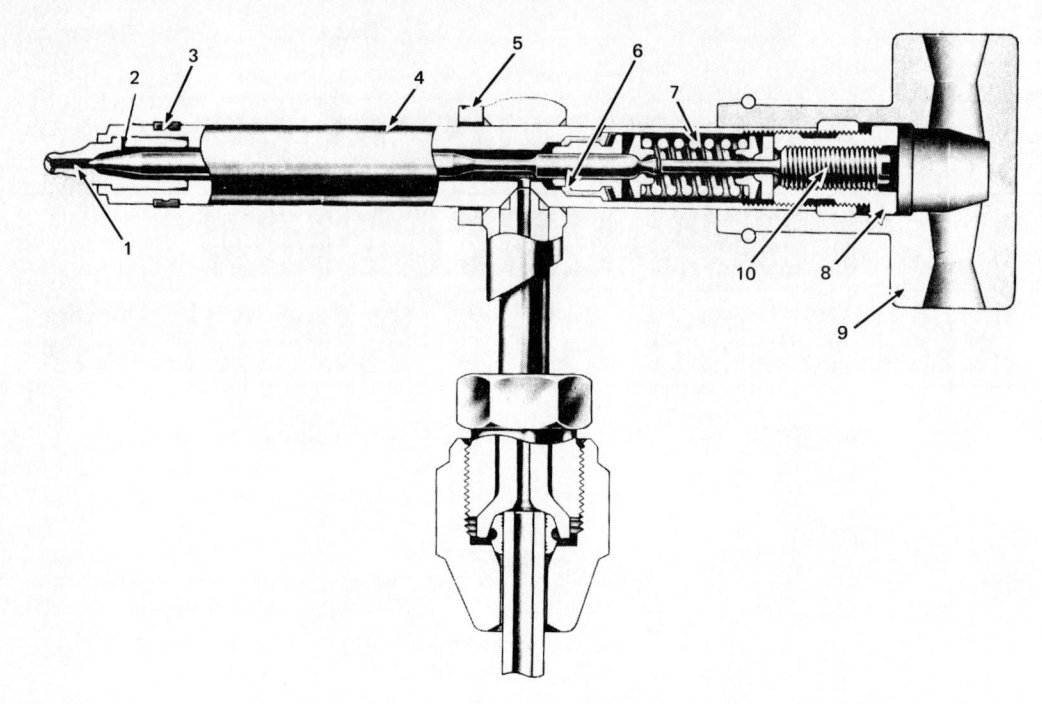

Fig. 27-3 Stanadyne pencil-type injector. *(Stanadyne Diesel Systems.)*

7. *(a)* List the major differences between a Stanadyne injector and the injector shown in Fig. 27-1. *(b)* State the purpose of the components numbered 3, 5, 6, 10, and 8 in Fig. 27-3.
8. Why is the lower part of the injector body Teflon-coated?
9. Remove an injector from a cylinder head of the engine on which you are working and then describe how you removed it.
10. Why should two wrenches be used to loosen the injection-line fittings?
11. Why should a hammer puller be used to remove an injector, particularly the pencil-type injector?
12. Refer to Fig. 27-4. Criticize this mechanic's approach.
13. Outline the step-by-step procedure to disassemble the injector shown in Fig. 27-1.
14. Outline the step-by-step procedure you used to service the nozzle assembly of an injector from an engine in your shop.
15. How would you remove a seized nozzle valve?
16. Explain how to check the freedom of the valve within the body.
17. *(a)* Why is it necessary to measure the nozzle-valve lift height? *(b)* What effect would an excessive lift have on the spray pattern and droplet size?
18. Outline the step-by-step procedure you used to service the holder assembly of an injector from an engine in your shop.
19. How would you remove the dowel pins (if used) from the holder body?
20. When reassembling the injector, certain precautions must be taken. List at least four of these precautions, and state why they must be taken.

Testing and Adjusting Injector Assembly To adjust and test an injector assembly, an injector tester is required. It may be one of any of the various testers on the market, so long as it is in good working order. The manufacturer's test specifications are, of course, also essential.

Following is the type of torque and test specifications which you will find in your service manual to which you will need to refer when you are testing or adjusting an injector assembly.

TORQUE SPECIFICATIONS
■ Holder cap nut and locknut: 60 to 80 lb·ft [81.3 to 108.4 N·m]
■ Nozzle retaining nut: 50 to 60 lb·ft [67.75 to 81.3 N·m]

Fig. 27-4 The result of poor work habits.

- Injector hold-down nut: 14 to 17 lb·ft [18.97 to 23.03 N·m]

TEST SPECIFICATIONS
- Nozzle opening pressure: 2700 psi [18,616.5 kPa]
- Closing presssure minimum: 2400 psi [16,548 kPa]
- Maximum permissible wear on lower face of holder caused by needle: 0.003 in [0.075 mm]
- Valve lift: 0.012 to 0.014 in [0.3 to 3.55 mm]
- Maximum wear limit: 0.021 in [0.525 mm]
- Nozzle leak-off time: 2000 to 1500 psi [13,790 to 10,342 kPa]
- 5-second minimum to 60-second maximum
- Nozzle seat angle: 59°50′ ± 10′
- Needle seat angle: 60°55′ ± 5′
- Four holes: 0.0128-in diameter [0.32 mm]
- Centering sleeve needed

21. Assume you have an injector with the above test specifications. Describe how you would test and adjust this injector. Alternatively, describe how to test and adjust an injector from an engine in your shop using its test specifications.

22. Explain how to test and adjust the injector to the specifications previously given to (a) adjust the opening pressure, (b) check the closing pressure.

23. If the closing pressure tests out to say, 2000 psi [13,790 kPa], which components may have caused this low closing pressure?

24. After the opening pressure has been adjusted, the next test to be made is the valve leakage test. Explain how to make the valve leakage test.

25. Next, check for leakoff (back leakage). Explain how to make the leakoff test.

26. Which part of the injector assembly or components could cause excessive leakoff?

27. Explain how to (a) make the spray-pattern test, (b) check nozzle chatter.

28. List at least three reasons why a nozzle could fail to chatter.

29. Outline the procedure to disassemble a pencil-type injector.

If during the testing and/or before disassembly, you have indications that the leakoff is too high and that the seat is leaking slightly, two recourses are open to you: (1) You may replace the injector, or (2) you may use an oversize needle valve and lap it to the valve guide and then lap the tip seat to the nozzle seat.

30. Explain how to lap (a) the needle valve seat, (b) the valve guide.

31. Explain how you would (a) adjust the valve opening pressure to 2700 psi [18,616 kPa] and valve-lift height three-quarter turns, (b) check the leakoff.

32. How would injector performance be affected if you neglected to clean the injector bore?

33. How would you clean the injector bore if no special tool were available?

34. Outline the procedure you would follow to install the injector shown in Fig. 27-5 into the cylinder head.

35. Outline the general procedure you would follow to install a pencil-type injector and to connect the fuel line.

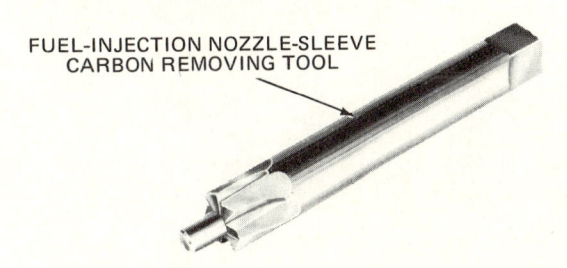

Fig. 27-5 Preparing to install an injector. *(Allis-Chalmers Corp. Engine Division.)*

ASSIGNMENT 28
FUEL-INJECTION SYSTEMS

There are as many types of fuel-injection systems as there are types of injection pumps. There are similarities in the design of some models, and yet others are totally different. Nevertheless, all fuel-injection systems must meet the following objectives: (1) to store, clean, and transfer fuel; (2) to meter the quantity of fuel required by the engine regardless of load and speed, with the quantity being metered in equal amounts to all cylinders; (3) to begin injection at the correct time within the cycle of the engine; (4) to ensure quick beginning and ending of injection; (5) to inject fuel at the rate necessary to control combustion; (6) to direct, distribute, and atomize the fuel as required by the combustion-chamber design.

1. Elaborate on the six fuel-injection system objectives previously mentioned as they relate to engine performance.

2. The basic components which make up a port- and helix-metering fuel-injection system are shown in Fig. 28-1. Name the purpose of each component.

3. When a four-cycle six-cylinder engine is operating at 1800 rpm and has a fuel consumption of 5 (U.S.) gal, how many fuel injections are made in 1 minute and how many in 1 hour?

4. How great is each individual fuel quantity (that is, the fuel injected by each pumping element per cycle) in cubic centimeters at the same 1800-rpm engine speed?

5. How many seconds would the injection pump have to (a) meter the fuel when the metering time is 650° of crankshaft revolution, (b) inject the fuel when the injection duration is 15° of crankshaft revolution?

6. Draw in the missing components on Fig. 28-2 to illustrate a modern fuel-tank design.

7. Give the purpose of each component or part you have drawn and explain how the sum of the improvements yields a good fuel-tank design.

8. Why is it a good maintenance practice to (a) fill the fuel tank after each working shift, (b) drain the sediments from the tank before putting the equipment to work?

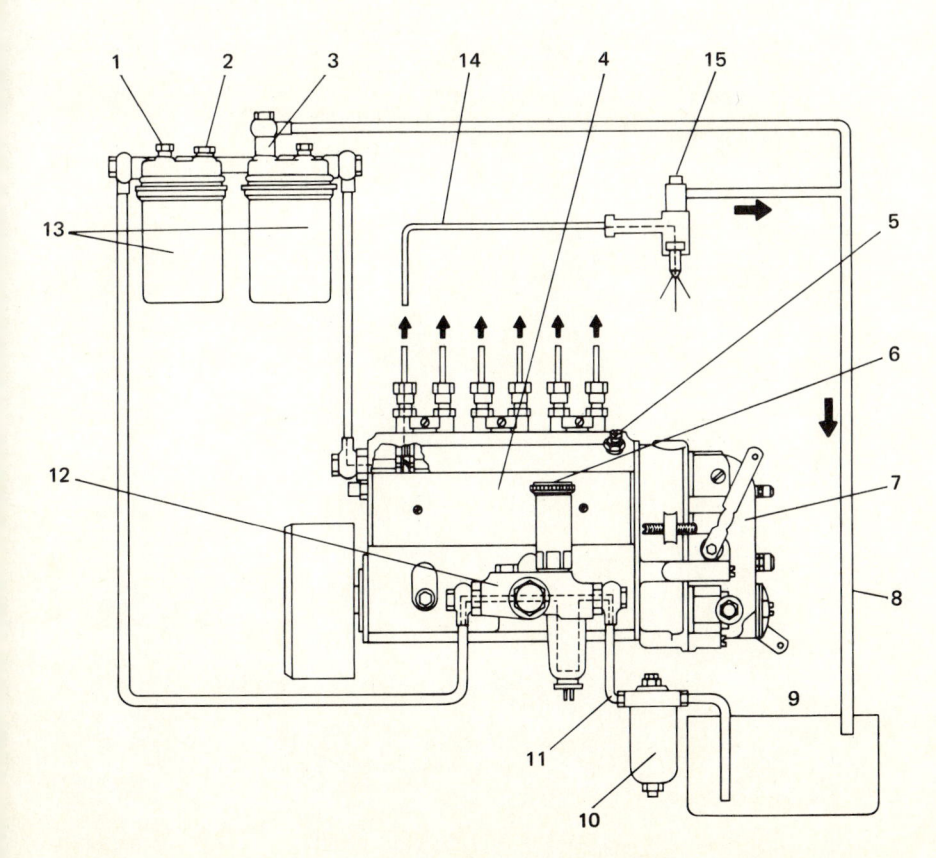

Fig. 28-1 Components of a fuel-injection system. *(Robert Bosch GmbH.)*

65

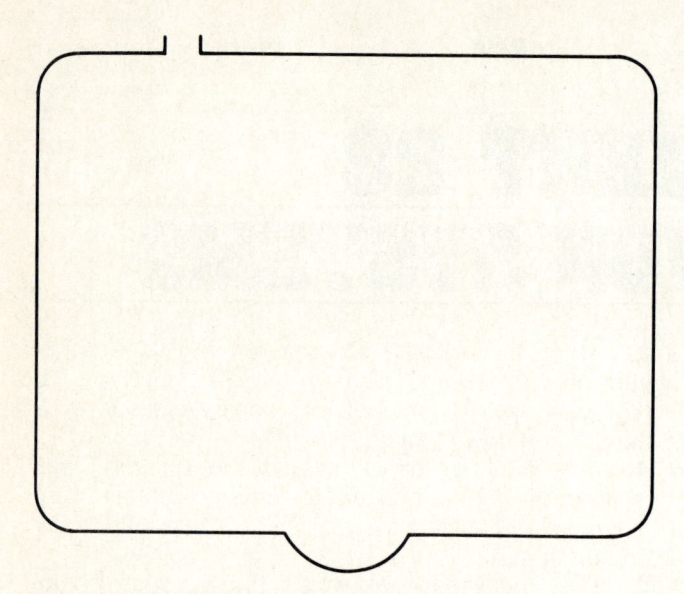

Fig. 28-2 Skeletal diagram of a fuel tank.

The fuel-injection systems that use port and helix metering—the DPA, Stanadyne, Robert Bosch, or Caterpillar sleeve-metering fuel-injection pumps—have three different pressures: (1) atmospheric pressure, (2) transfer-pump pressure, and (3) injection pressure.

9. Use different-colored pencils to indicate the presence of the three pressures in Fig. 28-1.

ASSIGNMENT 29
AMERICAN BOSCH, ROBERT BOSCH, AND CAV PORT AND HELIX FUEL-INJECTION PUMPS

1. Record the model number of the fuel-injection pump which you are working on in your shop and interpret the nameplate; that is, explain what each letter and number stands for.

2. Refer to Fig. 29-1. Write the name and purpose of each numbered component.

3. Multicylinder injection pumps from American Bosch, Robert Bosch, and CAV are shown in DM2 Figs. 29-2 and 29-4. List the noticeable differences between these injection pumps.

4. List, in the order of actuation, the components which are used for (a) pumping, (b) metering.

5. What advantage has a plunger design with an upper helix over a plunger with a lower helix?

6. Explain one pumping cycle of a pumping element having a lower helix. Start and end with the moment the camshaft lifts the follower. Assume that fuel at transfer-pump pressure is in the manifold. Omit the action of the delivery valve.

7. Refer to Fig. 29-2. (a) What movement was required to change the plunger position from zero to partial fuel delivery? (b) What actually has changed within the pumping element?

8. Explain the delivery-valve action from the point when the fuel pressure increases below the valve to the point when the plunger ends the injection.

9. How and why would it affect the beginning of injection if the retraction piston were badly worn or damaged?

10. How would you determine if it is the fuel-injection pump that is causing the trouble? (Do not, at this time, explain how to check the timing or cylinder compression pressure.)

11. Outline six common steps to remove a fuel-injection pump.

12. What checks must be made and what servicing must be done before connecting the fuel supply to the injection pump?

13. Assume you have a six-cylinder four-cycle engine, having a firing order of 1-5-3-6-2-4. Explain how you would find the No. 1 piston and position it on compression stroke so that the timing marks coincide.

14. Explain how you would install and time the injection pump to the engine after the No. 1 piston is correctly positioned. (See Fig. 29-3.)

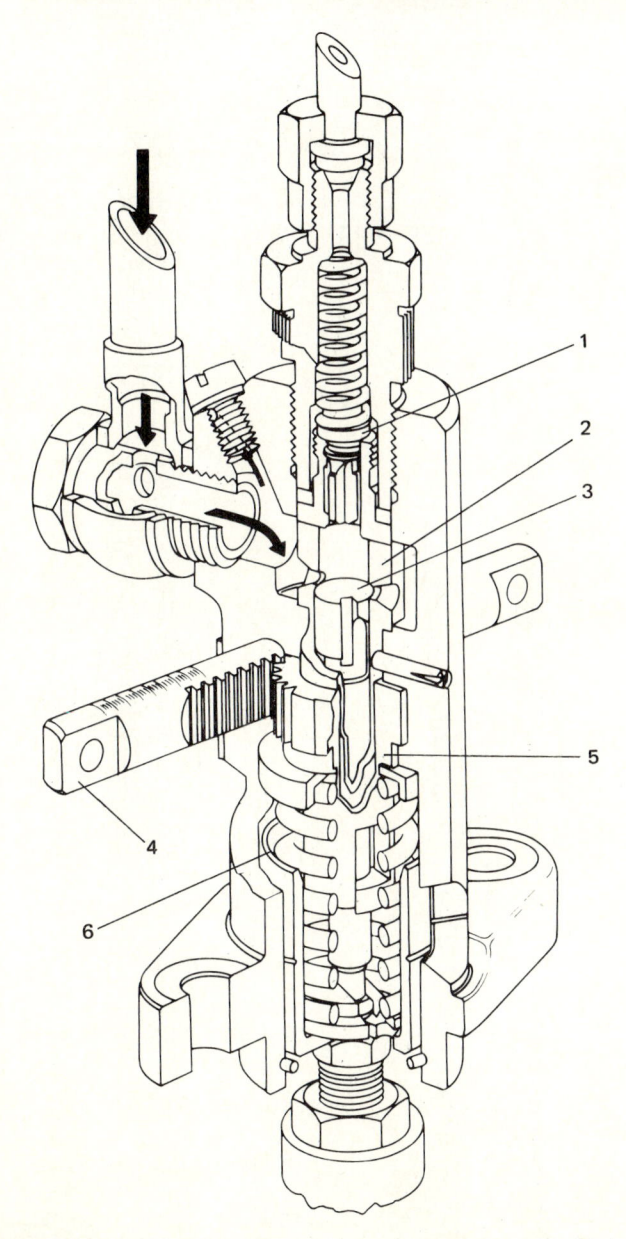

Fig. 29-1 Sectional view of a PF fuel-injection pump. *(Robert Bosch GmbH.)*

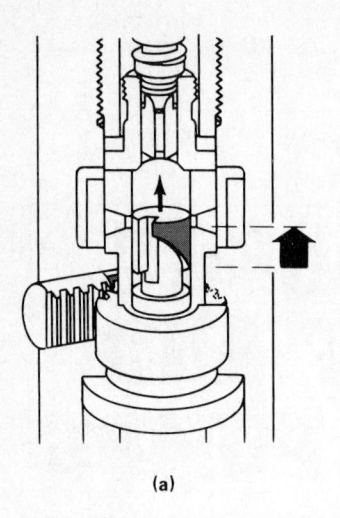

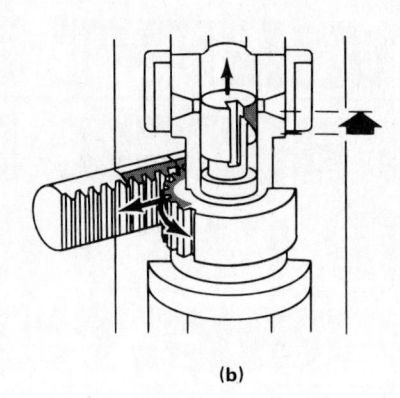

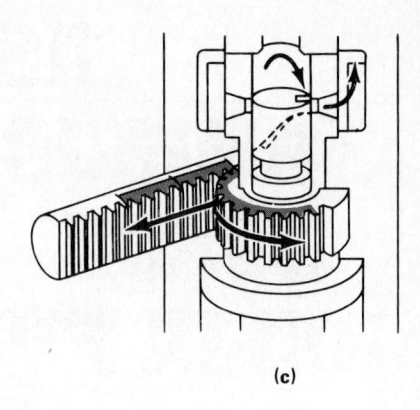

Fig. 29-2 Metering principle. Positions of pumping element at (a) maximum delivery, (b) partial delivery, and (c) zero delivery. *(Robert Bosch GmbH.)*

15. Why is it recommended at this time (referring back to Prob. 14) not to connect the fuel-injection lines to the injectors?

16. It is essential to remove all air trapped in the low-pressure side of the fuel system. This includes the air trapped in the injection-pump fuel manifold. Why is this so essential?

17. Explain how you would bleed the fuel-injection system which you just installed to the injection pump.

18. When the low-pressure side is free of air, actuate the decompressor and crank the engine over until airfree fuel flows from the high-pressure fuel lines. Then connect the injectors. List two reasons for this procedure.

19. Explain how to check the injection-pump timing using the spill method, when the plunger has (a) a lower helix, (b) an upper helix.

20. Outline the preparation procedure to time an engine and explain how to time the engine when using a diesel timing light.

21. Why are good work habits so important during disassembly procedures?

22. Explain how to remove the drive coupling from the camshaft of the fuel-injection pump you are working on.

23. Explain how to remove the governor from the fuel-injection-pump housing you are working on.

Fig. 29-3 Installing the fuel-injection pump. *(International Harvester Co.)*

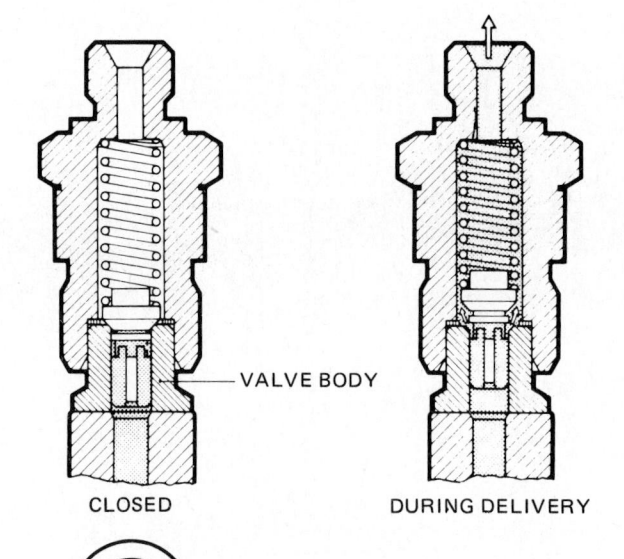

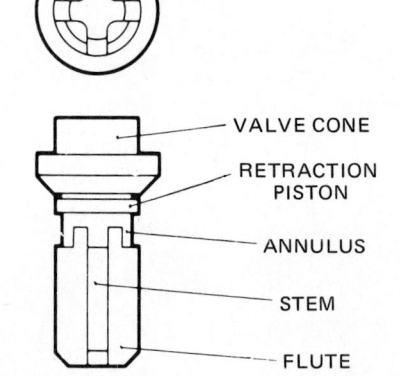

Fig. 29-4 Delivery valve action. *(Robert Bosch GmbH.)*

Name _____   Date _____ Class _____

24. Outline the procedure to remove the camshaft from an APE injection pump. (Refer to DM2 Fig. 29-17.)
25. Outline the procedure to remove the camshaft from a PEP fuel-injection pump. (Refer to DM2 Fig. 29-2.)
26. Outline the procedure to remove one complete pumping element from an APE injection pump.
27. Outline the procedure to remove one complete pumping element from a PE6P injection pump.
28. Outline the procedure to remove the pump body from a Majormec injection pump and to remove one pumping element from the pump body.
29. Explain how to remove (using a suitable puller) the inner and outer (Magneto-type) ball-bearing or tapered-roller-type races from the camshaft and bearing cap on which you are presently working.
30. List the checks and/or inspection points you must make on the pump housing and the control rack.
31. How would you determine if the control rack bushings or guides are worn?
32. Why is it necessary to line-ream control rack bushings?
33. When would it be necessary to use the hand milling cutter to service the barrel seat?
34. (a) When checking the camshaft, which area must be inspected? (b) What measurements must be taken and with what instruments?
35. Explain how to check the fit of a tapered drive coupling.
36. List the parts and the areas of the tappet roller assembly which, if worn, must be replaced.
37. When inspecting a pumping element, what damage might you find that would necessitate assembly replacement?
38. When the plunger and barrel assembly is reusable, what service must be performed?
39. Under what circumstances would you replace the plunger spring?
40. List the checkpoints which will help you to determine if the control-sleeve gear or fork should be replaced.
41. If the delivery valve shown in Fig. 29-4 is reusable, how should it be serviced?
42. Explain the basic differences between a positive displacement pump and a nonpositive displacement pump.
43. Explain why one type of pump is suitable for one fuel-injection system but not for another.
44. Describe the pumping action of the nonpositive displacement diaphragm-type transfer pump shown in Fig. 29-5.
45. Explain why a nonpositive displacement transfer pump has a constant fuel pressure, regardless of the engine rpm.
46. What would be the effect, in regard to fuel pressure, on a nonpositive displacement pump, if (a) the inlet valve or seat were damaged, (b) the outlet valve or seat were damaged?
47. List the steps you would take to test and check

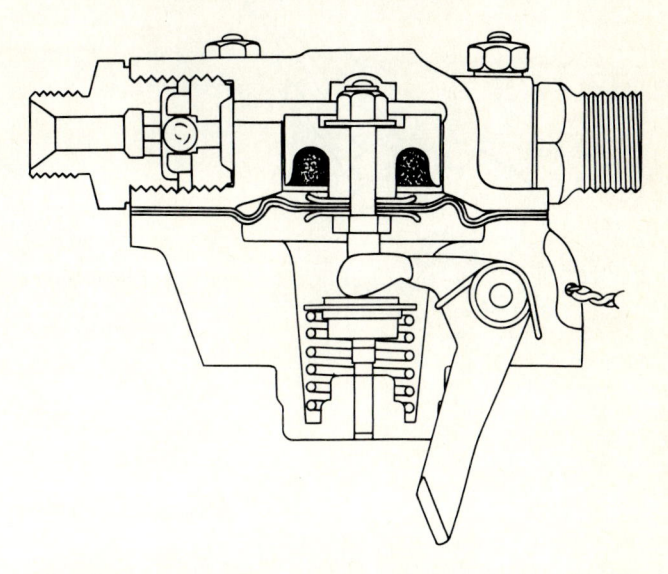

Fig. 29-5 Diaphragm-type transfer pump. *(CAV Limited.)*

the operating condition of the transfer pump, using a presssure gauge and a vacuum gauge.
48. What could cause a diaphragm-type transfer pump to lose some of its efficiency?
49. What could cause the nonpositive-displacement-type piston pump to lose some of its efficiency?
50. Explain the pumping action of the gear-type transfer pump shown in Fig. 29-6.
51. Explain the change in the fuel flow when the system pressure has reached its relief-valve setting.
52. Explain the pumping action of the hand-priming pump when it is used to bleed the fuel-injection system.
53. Why is it essential to keep the hand-priming pump locked into position when it is not being used?
54. List the checks and measurements which must be made when checking the gear-type transfer pump for its serviceability.
55. Why should the mating gears be marked before the gears are removed from the housing?
56. How do you determine which camshaft end is the drive end?
57. What precautions must be taken when tightening bearing-housing screws or bolts?
58. Explain how to measure the end play of a Majormec camshaft and how the end play can be changed if it is not within specification. (Refer to Fig. 29-7.)
59. Outline the procedure to install one pumping element into an APE fuel pump housing.
60. Outline the procedure to assemble one PEP pumping element and install it into the pump housing.
61. Outline the procedure to assemble a Majormec single pumping element into the pump body.
62. The partly assembled injection pump must be tested for leakage at the barrel seat and for pump-housing porosity. Explain how to make these two tests on an injection pump you have partly assembled.

(a)

(b)

(c)

(d)

Fig. 29-6 Gear-type transfer pump. *(American Bosch, United Technologies Automotive Group.)*

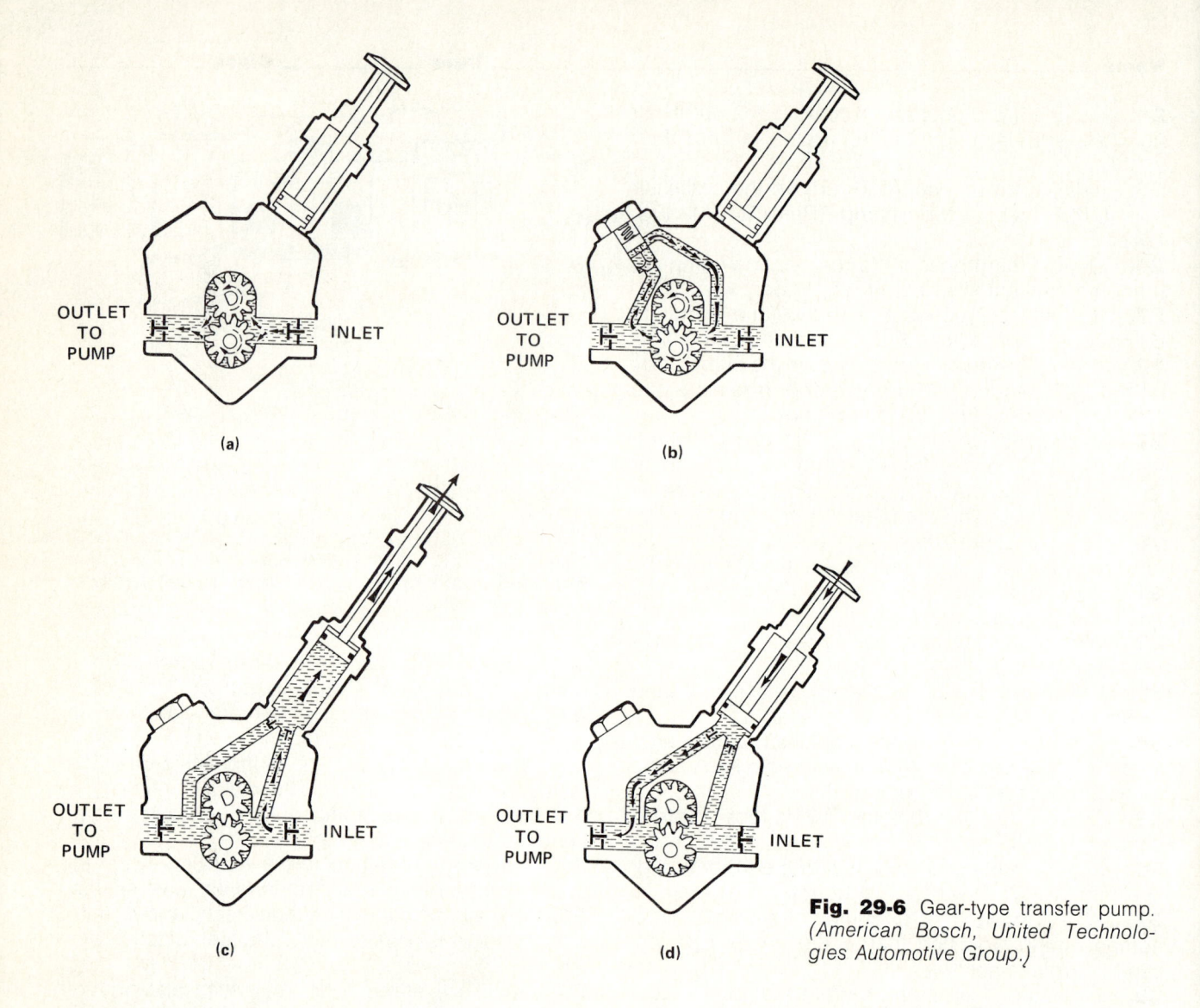

63. List the damage or wear which could occur to the following components: (1) drive, driven gear, and friction-gear assembly; (2) flyweights and shafts; (3) sliding-sleeve assembly; (4) fulcrum lever, pivot pin, torque cam, and linkage; (5) operating shaft (fulcrum lever), spring hub, and torsion spring.
64. Define *phasing*.
65. Define *calibration*.
66. Explain how the head clearance is measured on an APE fuel-injection pump and why this clearance is necessary.
67. Explain how you would spill-time the No. 1 element when the plunger has a *(a)* constant beginning and variable ending, *(b)* variable beginning and constant ending.
68. Explain how to phase a six-element injection pump.
69. Explain how to spill-time the No. 1 element of a Majormec injection pump. (Refer to Fig. 29-8.)
70. Outline the procedure (include any precautions to be taken) when installing the injection pump to the test stand and connecting the drive coupling, the fuel-inlet lines, the fuel-outlet lines, and the injection high-pressure fuel lines.
71. Explain how you adjusted the control rack (fuel rack) of an injection pump you installed to the test stand.
72. The next step before calibration is to remove

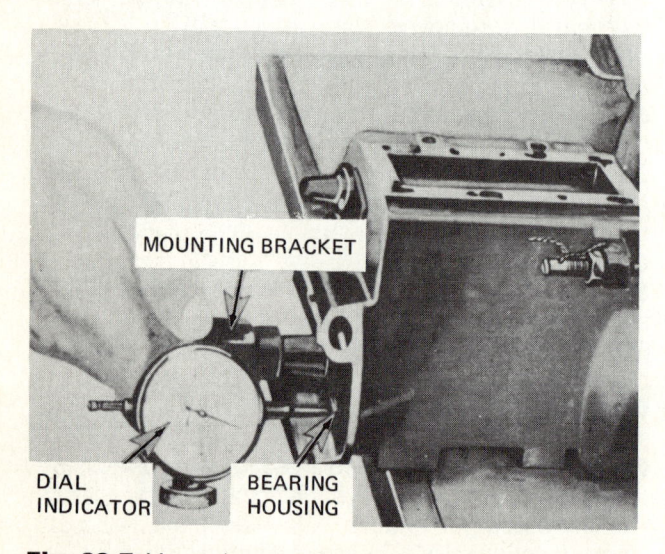

Fig. 29-7 Measuring camshaft end play. *(CAV Limited.)*

Name _____ Date _____ Class _____

Fig. 29-8 Majormec infection pump.

the air as quickly as possible from the system and warm up the fuel-injection pump and test oil. Explain how you would do this.

73. How would you determine if the transfer pump has the capacity to draw the minimum vacuum and to supply the required volume to create the maximum pressure?

74. Explain how to make the adjustments to the control rack so that the fuel delivery of the No. 1 pumping element is within specification.

75. Explain how to adjust the remaining elements to specification.

76. How would you adjust the low-idle speed to ensure that the recommended fuel will be delivered at low speed?

77. How would you adjust the high-idle speed of a Robert Bosch MW fuel-injection pump?

78. Your final step is to check the fuel delivery at cranking speed. Explain how to make this check.

Name _____ Date _____ Class _____

ASSIGNMENT 30
CATERPILLAR
PORT AND HELIX
FUEL-INJECTION PUMPS

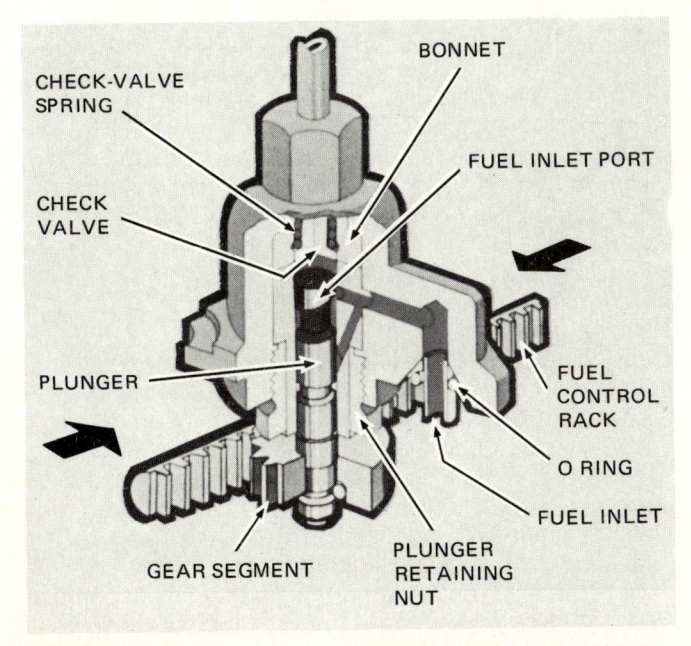

1. A sectional view of a forged-body fuel-injection pump is shown in Fig. 30-1. Compare the forged-body fuel-injection pump with an APE pumping element and list the main differences.

2. List the major differences between the construction of the Caterpillar fuel-injection-pump housing and that of an APE fuel-injection-pump housing.

3. Outline the major differences between compact-housing fuel-injection pumps, and forged-body fuel-injection pumps.

4. Outline the procedure to remove a forged-body injection pump from the pump housing and list any special precautions you must observe.

5. List the steps to remove the camshaft from a forged-body fuel-injection pump.

6. Outline the checks and measurements you must make when inspecting the (a) pump housing, (b) camshaft, (c) drive-gear assembly, (d) lifter assembly, (e) pumping element.

7. When reassembling the drive gear assembly to the drive shaft, what determines the location of the drive spring? (Refer to DM2 Fig. 30-6.)

8. Explain how to measure and to adjust one lifter to specification.

9. What are the specifications for the injection pump (forged body) you are presently adjusting?

10. Assume that the lifter settings are to be checked on a 769B engine which uses a timing bolt to position the piston at TDC. Explain how to bring the No. 4 piston into position so that the lifter height can be measured.

11. List the steps and precautions you must take when installing an injection-pump element (forged body) to the pump housing.

12. Which parts of the rack limiter require special attention?

13. Why does the rack limiter shown in Fig. 30-2 require no preadjustment?

14. Refer to the servo-type governor shown in DM2 Fig. 30-14. List the checkpoints and also the points of possible wear you would examine when inspecting the governor components.

15. List the governor specifications you might find in the service manual for (a) governor spring (color code), (b) governor group number, (c) rack setting, (d) fuel-ratio control setting.

Fig. 30-1 Sectional view of a forged-body fuel-injection pump.

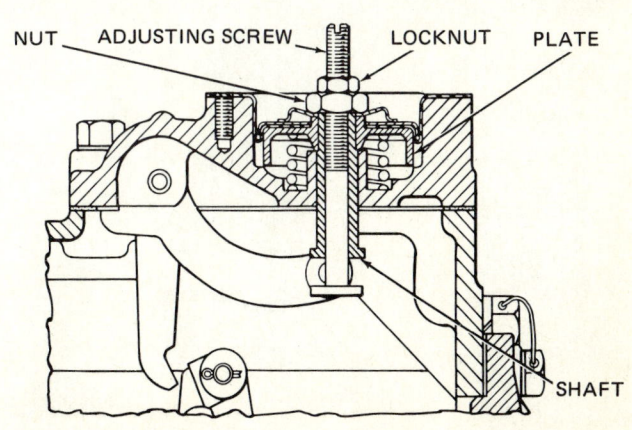

Fig. 30-2 Rack limiter adjustment. *(Caterpillar Tractor Co.)*

73

16. What check must be made to ensure that the rack setting gauge is properly installed?
17. Why is it advisable to place a feeler gauge of the same thickness as the spacer between the housing and the torque spring?
18. Why must the speed limiter be removed in order to adjust the fuel rack to specification?
19. Explain how to check and to adjust the fuel rack to a setting of 12.06 mm.

After the fuel rack is adjusted, remove the feeler gauge. Install the rack limiter and then adjust the fuel rack to the rack limiter specification given in the service manual.

20. Explain how this adjustment is made.
21. From this point on, explain how to measure and adjust the (a) fuel rack to specification, (b) rack limiter to specification.

Spill-Timing Caterpillar Fuel-Injection Pump
The spill-timing method recommended by the Caterpillar Company is slightly different from that recommended by other companies. Caterpillar Company recommends using a dial indicator to determine TDC and using a spill pressure of 15 psi [103.4 kPa]. Port closure for most injection pumps is established when 6 to 12 drops per minute leave the swan-neck pipe. The dial-indicator reading in inches or millimeters is then converted by using a chart in degrees (see DM2 Table 30-2).

22. Outline step by step the procedure to install the dial indicator.
23. Outline the procedure to precisely zero the (Cal) dial indicator.
24. Explain how to install and time the fuel pump to an engine, when the engine and fuel pump camshaft use a timing pin and the drive is over the mechanical variable timing unit.
25. Outline the procedure to remove one pumping element from a compact-housing fuel-pump.

Fig. 30-3 Sectional view of an injection pump.

26. Why is it important to keep the lifter-assembly spacer and the pumping element together as a unit?
27. List the additional checks which must be made after this type of injection pump is disassembled and cleaned.
28. What type of damage requires a replacement of the (a) barrel plunger assembly, (b) plunger spring, (c) bonnet and check valve?
29. Why should the barrel, the bonnet, and the check-valve surfaces be lapped when the plunger and barrel, the bonnet, and the check valve are reusable?
30. When is it necessary to replace the fuel rack?
31. Why is it a good work habit to reassemble each pumping element immediately after it is serviced, and to place the assembly in clean fuel?
32. List the precautions you must observe when installing the (a) camshaft, (b) lifter, (c) spacer. See Fig. 30-3.

Measuring and Adjusting Lifter Height To measure and adjust the lifter height, first mount the pointer to the pump housing and the degree wheel to the camshaft. Then turn the degree wheel in a counterclockwise rotation to the first timing-plate degree number.

NOTE: You may start with any one of the following timing-plate degree numbers (lifter numbers from front to rear): 1—0°, 2—120°, 3—240°, 4—60°, 5—300°, 6—180°.

33. From this point, explain how you would measure and change the lifter height. (Assume that the micrometer reading is 0.004 in higher than specified.)
34. List several factors which could give you a false micrometer measurement.
35. Explain the preparation you must make before a pumping element can be installed.
36. When installing an injection pump, you must proceed with caution. What type of damage could result to the pumping elements and the housing by careless installation?
37. Outline the step-by-step procedure to check and adjust the fuel rack to the specifications recommended in the service manual. (For this question use 0.130 in.)
38. List three conditions which could prevent the fuel-ratio-control valve from controlling the exhaust-smoke density.
39. Outline the checks you must make to test the fuel-ratio control for leakage. Use the specifications for testing given in the text.
40. Assume that the dial indicator is installed and that the fuel rack is adjusted. From this point on, explain how to adjust the fuel-ratio control when the specifications are minus 0.020 in.
41. What is the most significant difference between a forged-body and a flange-type fuel-injection pump?
42. When measuring the lifter height, between which surfaces is the dimension taken?
43. How is the lifter height adjusted?

Name _____ **Date** _____ **Class** _____

44. The mechanical variable-timing unit used on some Caterpillar engines is shown in DM2 Fig. 30-33. Outline how this unit senses engine speed, and changes the position of the injection-pump camshaft with respect to the engine drive as the engine speed (a) increases from low to high idle, (b) decreases from high idle to low idle.

45. List the components of the variable-timing unit which prevent or reduce the retarding of the injection-pump camshaft.

46. The hydraulic variable-timing unit used on some Caterpillar engines is shown in DM2 Fig. 30-39. Outline how this unit is able to vary the positioning of the injection-pump camshaft with respect to the drive gear when the engine speed is (a) reduced from 1900 to 1000 rpm, (b) increased from 1000 rpm to high idle.

47. List the components which could cause reduced efficiency of the hydraulic variable-timing unit.

48. After checks and adjustments have been made on the low- and high-idle speeds, and the operation of the variable-timing unit has been checked with a diesel timing light, it is still possible to have excessive exhaust smoke when the engine is accelerating. What should you do in this case to reduce the exhaust smoke?

49. Write the name and purpose of each numbered component shown in Fig. 30-4.

50. Elaborate on the design and construction differences between the capsule-type nozzles used in the precombustion chamber and those used in the adapter.

51. Outline the removal procedure of a capsule-type nozzle from the combustion chamber.

52. List the steps to remove the precombustion chamber or adapter.

53. List the checks you must make before you install a new nozzle assembly.

54. When installing a new or serviced precombustion chamber using a glow plug, what checks must you make before and after installation?

55. List the wear or damages which demand replacement of a (a) precombustion chamber or adapter, (b) capsule-type nozzle or injection valve.

56. Explain how to test a capsule-type nozzle on a nozzle tester using the following specifications: (a) used—400 to 750 psi, (b) new—685 to 750 psi.

57. What service can you perform to improve the spray pattern of a capsule-type nozzle?

58. When installing the assembly, what would happen if the (a) nut is overtorqued, (b) nut is undertorqued, (c) precombustion chamber or adapter is overtorqued, (d) precombustion chamber or adapter is undertorqued?

59. Explain how to test the injection valve using the following specifications: (a) used nozzle—2500 to 3100 psi, (b) new nozzle—2800 to 3000 psi.

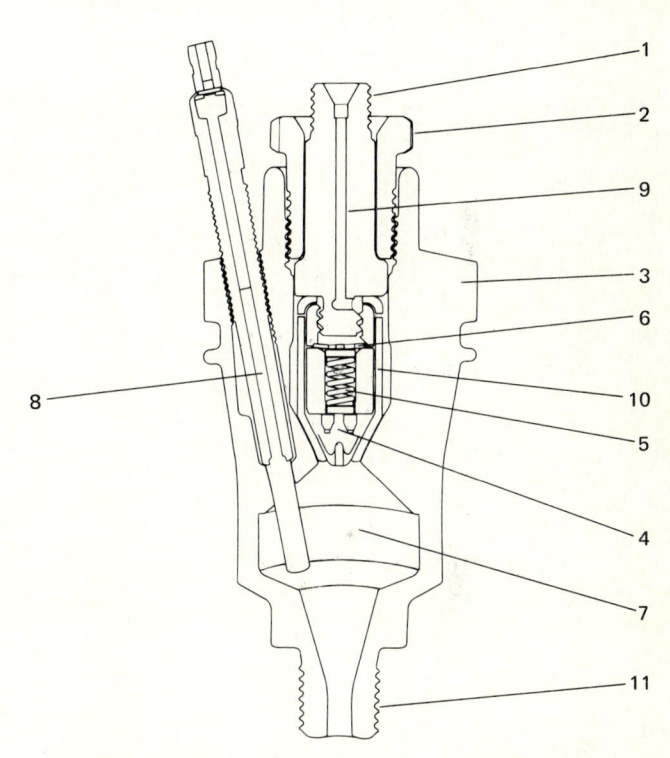

Fig. 30-4 Sectional view of a precombustion chamber.

Name _____ Date _____ Class _____

ASSIGNMENT 31
DETROIT DIESEL
FUEL-INJECTION SYSTEM

1. Write the name and purpose of each component shown in Fig. 31-1.

2. Briefly describe the fuel flow (when the engine is running), and, on Fig. 31-1, indicate the location of the various pressures, using different-colored pencils.

3. List the components by the order in which they activate each other to cause (a) rotary motion of the plunger, (b) reciprocating motion of the plunger (Fig. 31-2).

4. Identify the unit injector with regard to plunger design, fuel output, spray-hole size, number of spray

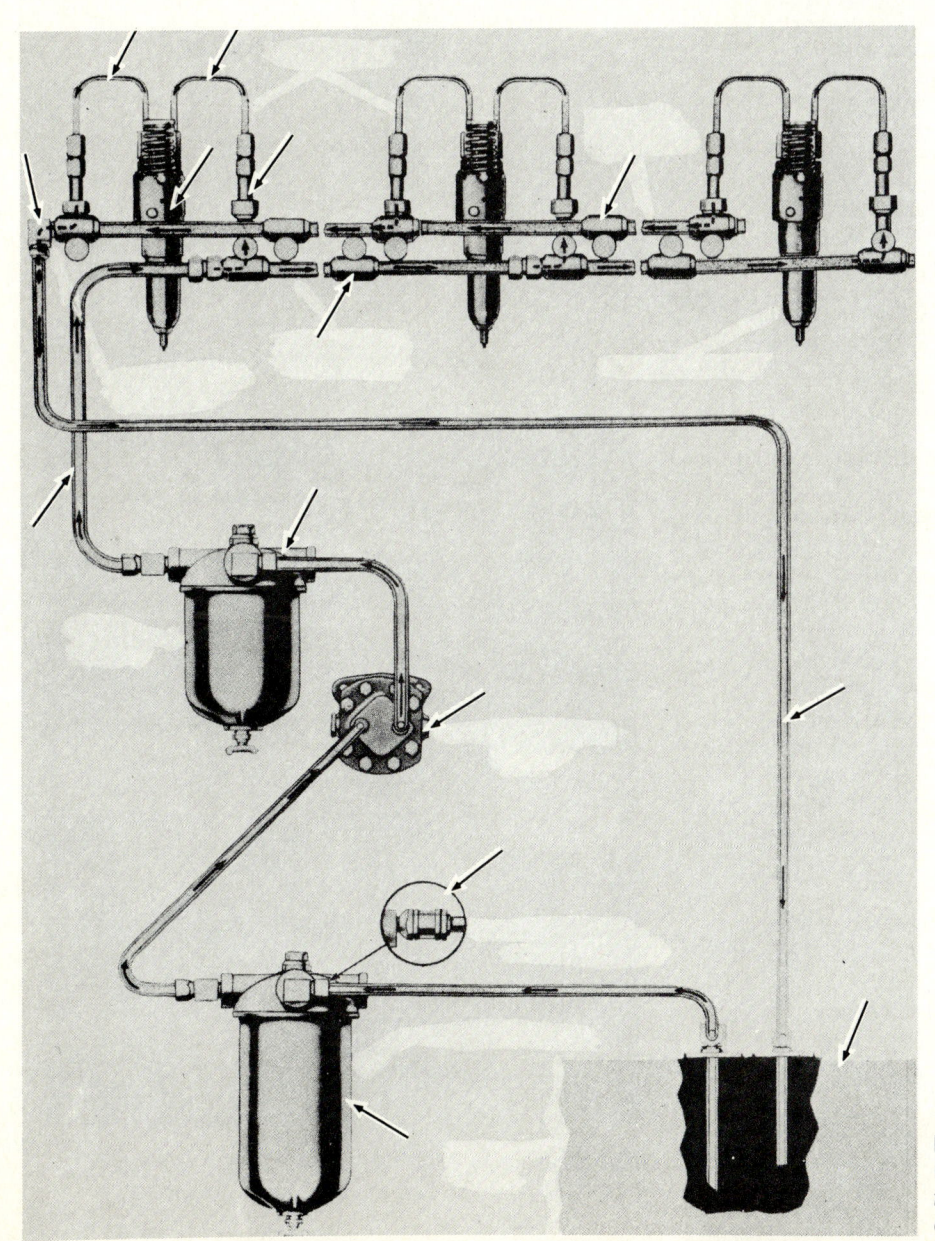

Fig. 31-1 Components of a Detroit Diesel fuel-injection system. *(Detroit Diesel Allison, Division of General Motors Corporation.)*

77

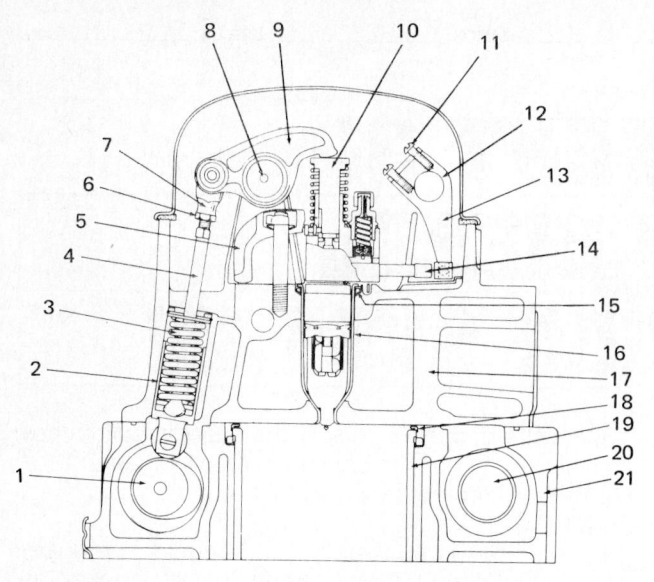

1. Camshaft
2. Cam follower
3. Spring
4. Pushrod
5. Injector clamp
6. Locknut
7. Rocker-arm clevis
8. Rocker-arm shaft
9. Rocker arm
10. Follower
11. Adjusting screw
12. Injector control tube
13. Rack control lever
14. Injector control rack
15. Gasket
16. Injector tube
17. Cylinder head
18. Gasket
19. Cylinder sleeve
20. Balance shaft
21. Cylinder block

Fig. 31-2 Sectional view of the unit-injector actuating mechanism. *(Detroit Diesel Allison, Division of General Motors Corporation.)*

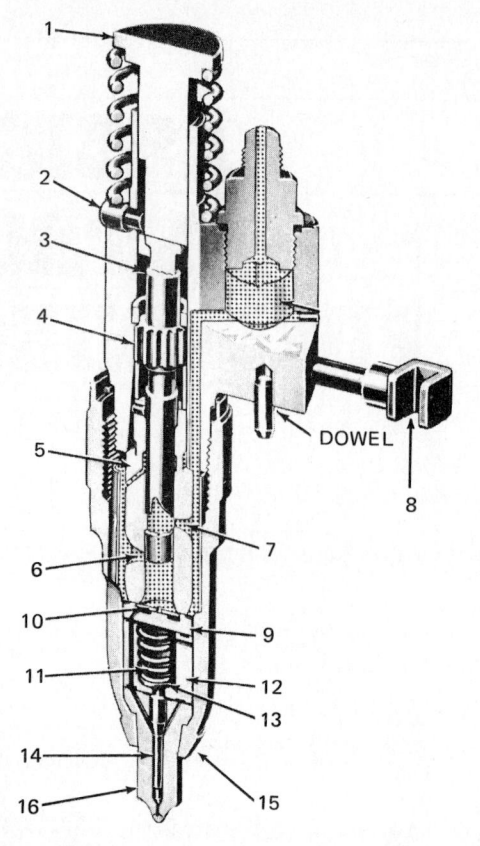

Fig. 31-3 Sectional view of the injector. *(Detroit Diesel Allison, Division of General Motors Corporation.)*

holes, and spray angle, when the identification tag is brown in color and has a lettering of C70.

5. List the four functions of a unit injector.
6. Write the name and purpose of each numbered component shown in Fig. 31-3.
7. With the assistance of DM2 Fig. 31-7, explain the effect on engine performance of an engine which uses a 50/50-type plunger design compared to one which uses a retarded-type plunger design.
8. List four differences between the metering principle of a Detroit Diesel unit injector and the Caterpillar compact-housing fuel-injection pump.
9. Explain the mechanical action within a unit Detroit Diesel injector: when the governor moves the plunger to the (a) no-fuel position, (b) full-fuel position.
10. List a number of differences between the pumping action of a unit injector and a Robert Bosch P-type fuel-injection pump.
11. Describe one injection cycle (including the fuel flow, the mechanical action, and the injection), beginning with the plunger at half-fuel position and the cam follower on its base circle.
12. List the steps you would take to locate a misfiring unit injector on a 149 series engine. (Refer to Fig. 31-4.)

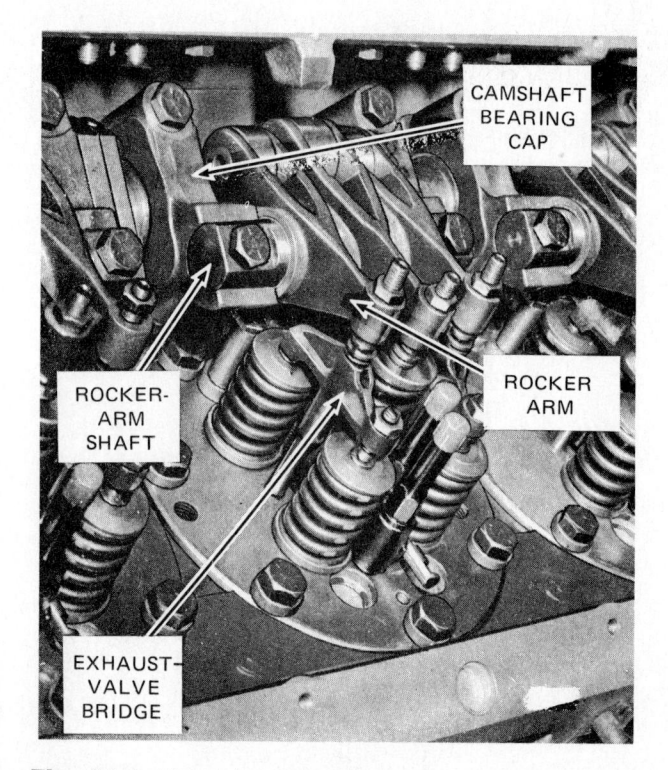

Fig. 31-4 View of a 149 cylinder head. *(Detroit Diesel Allison, Division of General Motors Corporation.)*

Name _____   Date _____ Class _____

13. Give several reasons why all injectors should be removed and tested after 5000 hours operation although only one injector may be faulty.
14. Describe how to remove one unit injector from the engine on which you are working.
15. List the steps you must take to disassemble a unit injector. (Use Fig. 31-5 and the following specifications as a guide.)

- Spray-tip shoulder   0.199 in [5.054 mm] minimum
- Cage check valve   0.163 in [4.140 mm] minimum
- Check valve   0.022 in [0.558 mm] minimum
- Spring cage   0.602 in [15.29 mm] minimum
- Needle-valve lift   0.012 to 0.08 in [0.3 to 0.2 mm]
- Follower spring   1.504 in [38 mm]; free-length spring wire 0.142 in [3.60 mm]
- Spring compressed to 1.028 in [26.11 mm] should read 70 lb [31.75 kg]
- Follower length within 0.005 in [0.125 mm] of 1.650 in [41.91 mm]
- Opening-pressure used injectors 2300 to 3300 psi [15,858.0 to 22,752.8 kPa]
- Opening-pressure rebuilt injectors 2500 psi [17,237 kPa] or 3000 psi [20,684.4 kPa]
- Injector-nut torque   85 lb·ft [115.2 N·m]
- Spray-tip runout   0.008 in [0.2 mm]; maximum fuel-output comparator 30 to 36
- Calibration stand   57 to 66 mm³

16. List all the checks you must make when inspecting the bushing and plunger assembly, and discuss what service you would render if the assembly were reusable.
17. In your opinion, what would have caused the damage to the plunger when (a) the plunger had horizontal shiny ring marks, (b) the plunger had vertical scratch marks, (c) there were pit marks on the lower helix?
18. Which test(s) would produce a negative result if the bushing or plunger were damaged or worn?
19. List the checks and service you must make on the injector body and nut.
20. Which test(s) would produce a negative result if the injector body or nut were damaged or not properly serviced?
21. List the checks and measurements you should make when servicing the (a) spring cage, (b) check valve, (c) check-valve cage.
22. Which test(s) would produce a negative result if one or all components listed in Prob. 21 were damaged or not within specified limits?
23. Describe how to clean an injector-tip assembly.
24. Outline the service procedures if the assembly were reusable.
25. Describe how to restore the valve seat, using a polishing compound.
26. List the measurements you must make on the tip assembly, and briefly describe how to make these measurements.

Fig. 31-5 Component reassembly order. *(Detroit Diesel Allison, Division of General Motors Corporation.)*

27. Which test(s) would produce negative results if the tip assembly were not up to specification or were not serviced satisfactorily?
28. List the checks and describe the measurements you must make when servicing the (a) follower, (b) follower spring.
29. How will injection performance be affected when the (a) follower is below specification, (b) follower spring is 4.5 kg below specification?
30. List the checks you would make for damage and wear to the control rack and gear.
31. Which test(s) would produce negative results if the gear or rack were damaged?
32. What forms of damage are appreciably visible on a deflector sleeve?
33. Describe how to make the (a) opening-pressure, (b) spray-pattern, and (c) chatter tests.
34. What could cause unduly light chatter during testing?
35. When reassembling a unit injector, which assembly points require special attention?
36. Describe how to check the (a) control-rack-to-plunger timing after the injector is assembled, (b) concentricity of the spray tip.
37. Explain how to check the freeness of the injector control rack and plunger.
38. Describe how to make the (a) high-pressure test, (b) valve-holding-pressure test.

39. Assume now that an N60 unit injector is to be tested and you have to use a comparator to check the fuel output. Outline the checks you must make to the tester before installing the unit injector.
40. Outline the procedure for a fuel-output test.
41. Explain how to (a) clean the injector sleeve, (b) install one unit injector to an in-line 71 series engine.
42. After the fuel pipes are connected, you should test the manifold and the injector connection for leakage. Outline how you would pressure-test the manifold to check for fuel leakage using a hand-priming pump.
43. List the checks you must make before doing a tuneup.

A tuneup on any Detroit Diesel engine must be made in a specific sequence; otherwise the results will be unsatisfactory. A typical tuneup sequence when a limited-speed governor is used is shown in Fig. 31-6. (Note that the sequence changes after No. 3 when the hydraulic governor is used.)

44. Assume you have to make a tuneup on an 8-71 engine having a limited-speed governor. The engine is at operating temperature. Elaborate on the nine tuneup steps shown in Fig. 31-6. (Use the following specifications.)

- Exhaust valves cold   0.016 in [0.406]
- Exhaust valves hot   0.014 in [0.355 mm]
- Timing gauge dimension   1.460 in [37.084 mm]
- Governor gap   0.0015 in [0.038 mm]
- Low idle   450 rpm
- High idle   2150 rpm

Test specification	1200 rpm	1800 rpm	2100 rpm
Inlet-manifold psi fuel pressure using 0.080-in restriction orifice	30–65	45–70	45–70
Fuel spill, no-load (GPM)	0.8	0.9	0.9
Maximum exhaust back pressure (inHg): full load / no load	1.5 / 1.0	3.3 / 2.1	4.0 / 2.6
Maximum crankcase pressure (inH_2O): no load	2.0	2.8	3.1
Minimum air-box pressure (inHg) at zero exhaust back pressure	1.7	4.3	6.0
Maximum exhaust back pressure (inHg)	3.2	7.6	11.1
Air-inlet restriction, dry air cleaner less pre-cleaner (inH_2O)	5.2	9.1	11.5

45. Explain how you would test or check the following (use the previously given specifications): (a) fuel spillback, (b) crankcase pressure, (c) exhaust back pressure, (d) air-intake restriction, (e) air-box pressure.
46. Assume that you have a double-weight limiting-speed governor and that the speed-control lever is in idle-speed position. What would be the position of the fuel rod or plunger?
47. Outline the mechanical action within the governor after the engine has started and is operating at idle speed.
48. Assume that the engine is operating at high idle (no load) and that the truck approaches a hill. How does the governor react as it tries to maintain engine speed?
49. Which parts of the flyweight assembly, in addition to worn fingers, could reduce governor performance?
50. What is likely to be the most common damage you will find when inspecting the operating shaft fork and thrust bearing?
51. How will governor performance be affected when the fork of the differential lever or the pin of the speed-control lever is worn?
52. What mistake can be easily made when installing the shaft bearing?

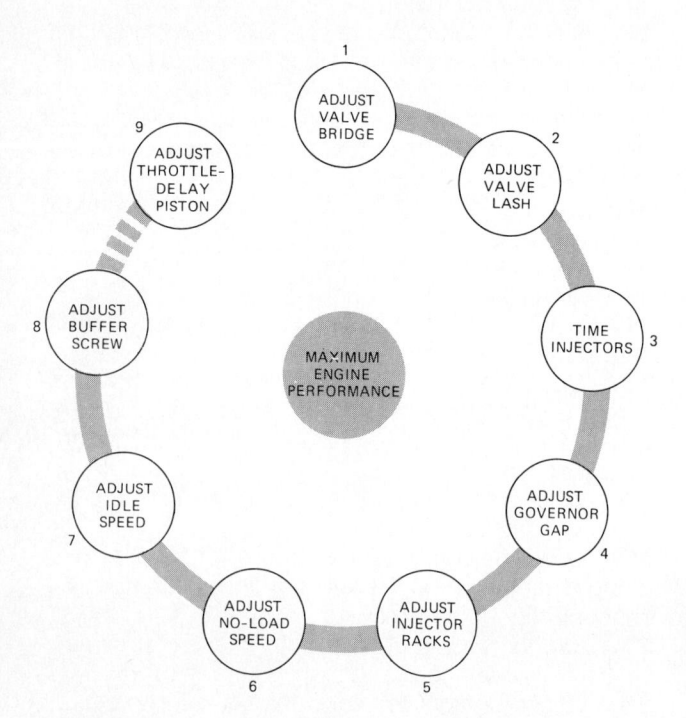

Fig. 31-6 Tuneup sequence for a limited-speed governor.

(Tuneup sequence, clockwise from top:
1. ADJUST VALVE BRIDGE
2. ADJUST VALVE LASH
3. TIME INJECTORS
4. ADJUST GOVERNOR GAP
5. ADJUST INJECTOR RACKS
6. ADJUST NO-LOAD SPEED
7. ADJUST IDLE SPEED
8. ADJUST BUFFER SCREW
9. ADJUST THROTTLE-DELAY PISTON
— center: MAXIMUM ENGINE PERFORMANCE)

53. When reassembling the governor components, which components require special attention or checks in regard to fit and location?

SG Hydraulic Governor The schematic view of an SG hydraulic governor and the drive assembly is illustrated in DM2 Figs. 25-16 to 25-17. As a general rule the drive assembly and the SG hydraulic governor are less likely to cause reduced engine performance than the mechanical governor. However, there are some components in the SG governor assembly which are susceptible to wear and could therefore reduce the governor performance.

54. List the components and the areas of the speed-measuring section which could reduce the speed response.

55. List the components and the mechanical areas wherein delay could be attributed to the fuel-changing mechanism.

56. How would engine performance be affected if the relief valve and/or the oil pump were not operating within specification?

ASSIGNMENT 32
CATERPILLAR
UNIT-INJECTOR
FUEL-INJECTION SYSTEM

1. List six differences between the low-pressure fuel system of the Caterpillar 3512 engine and the Detroit Diesel engine shown in DM2 Figs. 31-1 and 32-1.

2. How is the Caterpillar manifold pressure controlled?

3. Refer to DM2 Fig. 32-1, and then outline the differences in fuel flow: *(a)* when hand priming the system, *(b)* when the engine is operating.

4. List the four most significant differences between the Caterpillar and Detroit Unit injectors.

5. List, in sequence, the seven components which move the fuel control rack.

6. List, in sequence, the six components which move the plunger.

7. Give two methods used to locate a faulty injector.

8. What causes one cylinder exhaust temperature *(a)* to be higher than the average exhaust temperature, *(b)* to be lower than the average exhaust temperature?

9. What checks must be made before installing a new or rebuilt unit injector?

10. List four reasons why the fuel rack could be tight after the injector is installed.

11. What is meant by *injector synchronization*?

12. Where (between which parts) is the synchronizing gauge positioned when an injector is synchronized?

13. What is the purpose of the synchronizing pin?

14. What is significant about the Caterpillar startup procedure that makes it applicable to all engines?

Name _____ Date _____ Class _____

ASSIGNMENT 33
CUMMINS FUEL-INJECTION SYSTEM AND PT FUEL PUMPS

1. Name the components or actions of the PT fuel-injection system which are similar to the Detroit Diesel fuel-injection system.

2. State one hydraulic law and one hydraulic principle on which the PT fuel-injection system is based.

3. A sectional view of the PTR fuel pump having a limited-speed governor is shown in DM2 Fig. 33-5. State the general purpose of each component.

4. What is the reason for the second passage by-pass arrangement shown in DM2 Fig. 33-5?

5. Explain the position of the governor and throttle and their involvement in controlling idle speed and high idle speed.

Minor adjustments in regard to fuel pump pressure can be made on the test stand or on the engine by adjusting the restriction plunger and/or rear throttle screw.

6. Explain how this minor adjustment is made, using the restriction plunger to increase the fuel pressure, say, by 10 psi [68.9 kPa] (See DM2 Fig. 33-3.)

7. Explain how the pressure regulator: controls (a) idle fuel pressure, (b) maximum fuel pressure.

8. Explain the action within the pressure regulator when the engine operates at high idle with the throttle at idle position.

9. All PT fuel pumps use a pulsation damper plus a combination electrical and mechanical shutdown device. Describe the purpose of these two components.

10. What additional components do you find on the PTG pump that you don't find on the PTR fuel pump?

11. Explain the fuel flow within the PTG fuel pump (without pressure regulation) when the engine is operating at idle speed. (Refer to Fig. 33-1.)

1. Tachometer shaft
2. Filter screen
3. Fuel to injectors
4. Shutdown valve
5. Gear pump
6. Check-valve elbow
7. Fuel from tank
8. Pulsation damper
9. Throttle shaft
10. Idle adjusting screw
11. High-speed spring
12. Idle spring
13. Gear-pump pressure
14. Fuel-manifold pressure
15. Idle pressure
16. Governor plunger
17. Governor weights
18. Torque spring
19. Weight-assist plunger
20. Weight-assist spring
21. Main shaft
22. Bleed line

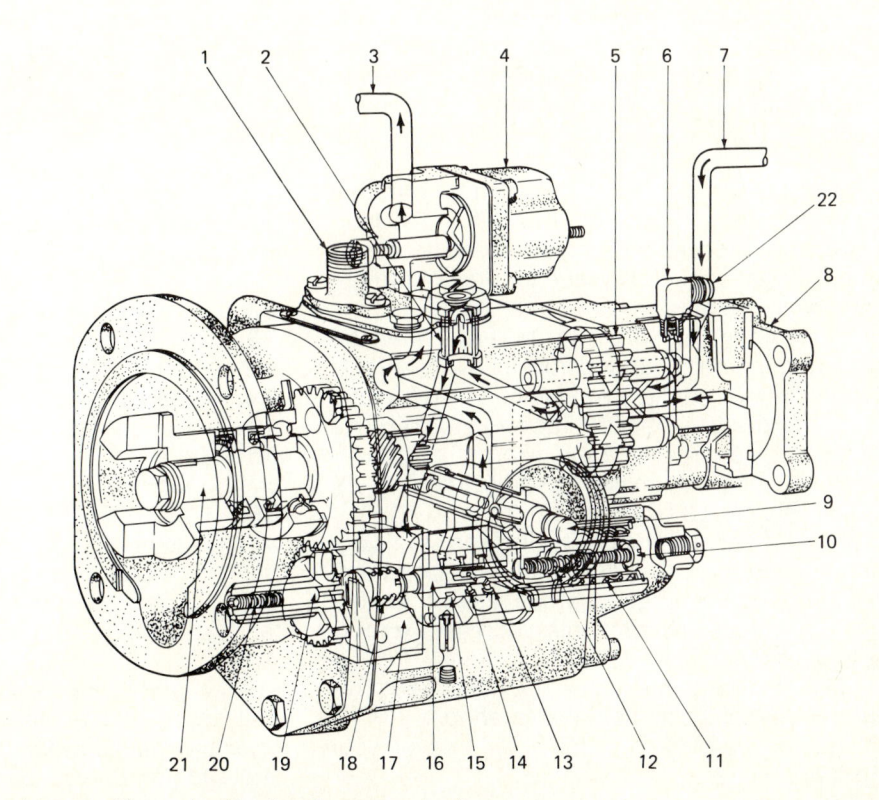

Fig. 33-1 Fuel flow in a PTG fuel pump. *(Cummins Engine Company, Inc.)*

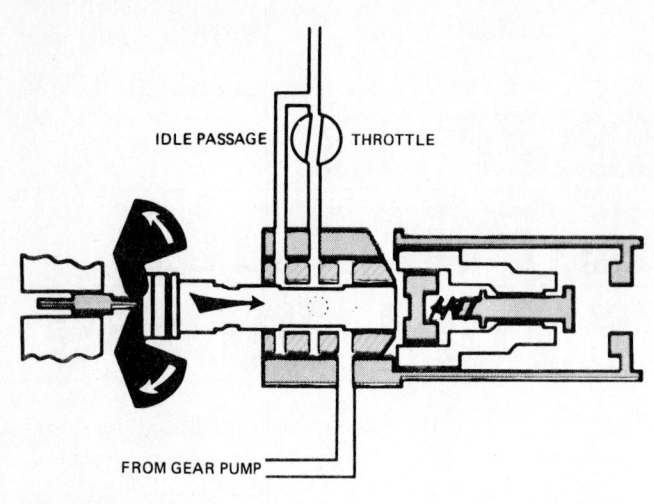

Fig. 33-2 Simplified illustration of governor components. *(Cummins Engine Company, Inc.)*

The components which control the fuel pressure are shown in Fig. 33-2. These components can be changed to accommodate different fuel pressures and torque rise according to the engine model.

12. When the engine is cranked, fuel from the fuel tank enters the gear pump. Outline the route that the fuel takes from this point until it reaches the injector.
13. Assuming that the throttle is set at idle speed and the idle fuel pressure is adjusted to 30 psi [206.8 kPa], explain the mechanical action within the governor to maintain a 30-psi [206.8-kPa] inlet manifold pressure.
14. When the throttle opening is increased so that the engine operates, say at three-quarters speed (manifold pressure of 150 psi [1034.2 kPa]), what action takes place within the fuel pump to maintain a fuel pressure of 150 psi [1034.2 kPa]? (Refer to Fig. 33-2.)
15. Assume that the throttle is wide open and that the engine is operating at high idle. When the load of the vehicle increases the engine speed to above high idle, what action takes place to prevent the engine from overspeeding?
16. Why would the fuel pressure increase when the idler-spring plunger is changed from size 125 to 100?
17. The governor spring and weight assembly is a matched set. However, high idle (governor cutoff) can be increased or decreased by making shim adjustments. How would you make the adjustment to increase low-idle speed by 50 rpm?
18. The weight-assist plunger spring and shims are used to increase the fuel pressure at idle speed and thereby increase the engine torque at this speed. Explain how these components increase engine torque at low speed.
19. Outline the steps that you would take to remove the fuel pump from an engine in your shop.
20. Write the nameplate number for one of your training fuel pumps.
21. List the steps to disassemble a PT fuel pump.
22. List the checks you must make of the main housing to determine if it can be reused. Do not, at this time, explain the checks for the governor barrel or throttle sleeve.
23. Explain how you would lap a larger (class) plunger to the barrel. How would you check its fit?
24. If the governor barrel is worn beyond a class 7 governor plunger, the assembly must be replaced. Explain how to replace the thrust washer. What measurement must you make after replacing the washer?
25. What wear or indication of damage would necessitate lapping a new throttle shaft into the throttle-shaft sleeve?
26. After the disassembly of the gear pump, you must make several checks and measurements to determine if the gears and/or body are reusable. Outline the checks and measurements you must make to the gear-pump assembly.
27. Generally speaking, the fuel-pressure damper causes very little trouble but nevertheless it should be checked. Which (a) points of the fuel-pressure damper should be inspected and (b) components can be serviced?
28. How would you check the fuel pump shutoff valve coil using an ohmmeter?
29. When inspecting the remaining shutoff valve components, what defects might you find, and how would you service the defective components?

The components which make up the tachometer drive assembly are shown in DM2 Fig. 33-16.

30. Explain how to assemble and install the tachometer drive assembly.
31. Explain how you would replace the (a) governor weight-shaft bushing, (b) drive-shaft bearing and seals.

Make certain that if a replacement of the governor assembly (weight carrier and shaft) is necessary, you replace it with the same assembly number and (when pressing the gear on the shaft) that you do not support the assembly by its weights.

32. What are the reasons for these precautions?
33. Explain how to measure and adjust the governor weight-assist protrusion.
34. In which direction must the number of the idle-spring plunger face when assembled?
35. By what method do you change the throttle-shaft opening?
36. Outline the steps to install the throttle shaft.
37. Outline the procedure for installing the fuel pump to the engine.
38. Outline the procedure to install a fuel pump to the test stand.

Now fill the fuel pump housing with test oil. Manually open the fuel shutoff valve, switch on the heater, open the main flow valve, and close both the idle and leakage flow valves. Select the correct pump rotation and operate the fuel pump at about 900 rpm. Move the throttle shaft back and forth to remove the air from

Name _____ Date _____ Class _____

the pump. If no air bubbles are present in the flow meter, adjust the fuel-inlet valve so that the vacuum valve shows 8 inHg [20.3 cmHg].

39. After the fuel pump is installed to the test stand and is ready for warm-up, what checks must you then make?
40. Outline how to check the gear-pump suction.

If the gear pump draws less than 28 inHg [71.12 cmHg], or if air enters the system, the gear pump must be rechecked. If there is an air leak, it must be corrected and then the gear pump must be retested.

41. Name five locations where air can enter the fuel pump.

After the gear-pump suction test has been completed, you must check (and adjust if necessary) the governor cutoff speed and the maximum calibration pressure.

42. Outline how to check and adjust governor cutoff speed (0.001-in shim is about 2 rpm).
43. Outline how you would bring the maximum calibration pressure to, for example, 320 psi [2206.4 kPa] when the tested pressure is 300 psi [2068.5 kPa].
44. Explain how you would test and adjust throttle leakage to specification.
45. Outline how to adjust the idle-speed pressure after having adjusted the throttle leakage.

46. Assume a rough maximum manifold pressure has been achieved and the fuel pressure is 15 psi [103.4 kPa] too high. Explain how you would now make the fine fuel-pressure adjustment using the internal throttle-shaft plunger.
47. Most fuel-injection shops first adjust the maximum fuel pressure about 10 psi [68.9 kPa] higher than specified and then reduce it to specification with the rear throttle screw. What is the reason for this procedure?
48. Explain how to use the rear throttle shaft to bring the maximum fuel pressure to specification.
49. Explain how to check the weight-assist pressure and, when necessary, how to make the pressure adjustment.
50. List 10 reasons why the gear pump may not pick up fuel at 450-rpm test stand speed.
51. List six problems which would prevent you from correctly adjusting the governor cutoff point.
52. List six reasons why the checkpoint pressure could be below or above specification.
53. What eight problems might you encounter, when checking maximum fuel pressure, which could cause an increase or decrease from specification?
54. List three purposes of the AFC valve.
55. At what boost pressure does the AFC control plunger begin to move? (Use example given in DM2, Unit 33.)
56. Outline the steps to adjust the AFC control plunger to the test code flow and pressure (73 psi, 247 pph, 1600 rpm, 8 inHg).

Name _____ Date _____ Class _____

ASSIGNMENT 33A
CUMMINS PTB, PTC, PTD, AND TOP STOP INJECTORS

1. What three factors control the beginning of injection?
2. Explain why the Cummins fuel injection is of the variable-beginning and constant-ending design.
3. Explain the purpose of each component numbered in DM2 Fig. 33-28.
4. List the major differences between the PTB and the PTC injectors.
5. In what way have these changes affected and improved the PTC injector performance?

PTD Injector

6. List the component design changes in the PTD injector in comparison to the PTC injector.
7. In what way have these changes improved performance and injector service longevity?
8. Outline the mechanical action and the fuel flow (with the engine at high idle) from the time the No. 1 piston starts its compression stroke to the time this piston returns to compression stroke.
9. Assuming that the engine speed (due to increased load on the engine) is reduced from high-idle (2300 rpm) to torque speed (1750 rpm), what changes will have taken place within the fuel system in regard to (a) fuel pressure, (b) fuel metering, (c) injection timing?
10. Assume that the code number on the adapter is 117A-8-6-2 and that the code number on the plunger coupling is A 75-2. (a) What do the three individual numbers on the adapter mean with regard to service and testing? (b) What does the last number on the plunger coupling mean with regard to service and testing?
11. If the engine is misfiring because of a faulty injector, how would you determine which injector is not operating satisfactorily?
12. Outline in detail the procedure to remove one injector from an engine in your shop.
13. Outline the steps to disassemble a PTD injector. (Use DM2 Figs. 33-38 and 33-43 as a guide.)
14. What is the first step you must take after removing the injector components from the cleaner?
15. Outline the checks you should make on each component listed below, and, where applicable, give the recommended service procedure: (a) spray cup, (b) barrel, (c) balance orifice, (d) adapter check valve and ball seat, (e) plunger, (f) plunger spring, (g) plunger length.
16. List the steps you must take in assembling a PTD injector.
17. Assume that either one injector is assembled without the check ball or that the check ball has a high leakage rate and the injector is installed into the No. 1 or No. 2 cylinder. What result would either of these conditions have on (a) engine torque and speed, (b) exhaust smoke, (c) acceleration, (d) engine shutdown?

After the retainer nut is finger-tightened snugly, loosen the retainer about ¼ in [6.35 mm]. Then dip the plunger in clean fuel and insert it into the barrel. Install the injector to the assembly fixture (Fig. 33A-1) and torque the hold-down stud to specification. Then torque the cup retainer to specification.

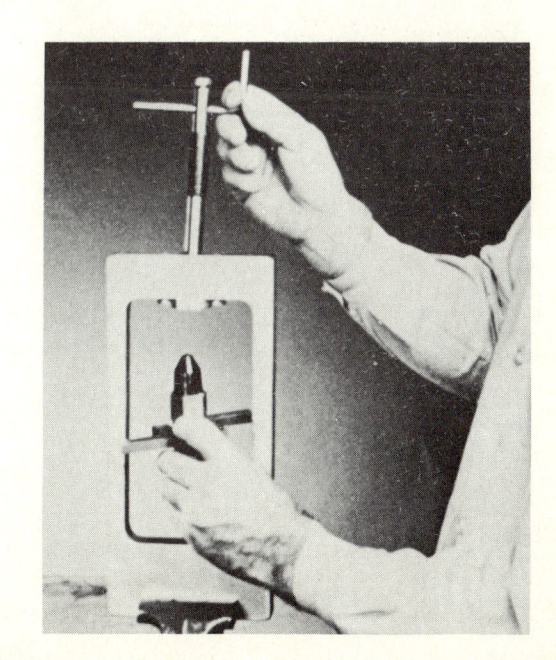

Fig. 33A-1 Installing the injector to the assembly fixture.

89

18. Why is the elaborate procedure outlined above necessary?
19. Explain how you would make the *(a)* drop test, *(b)* cup-spray-hole test.
20. Explain how you would lap the plunger to the spray cup, and outline the steps you must take after the lapping procedure.
21. From which source can you obtain the correct target ring?
22. When one stream of fuel sprays outside the large No. 1 window, what steps are necessary to correct the faulty spray?
23. How would you correct the fuel flow when it is *(a)* too high, *(b)* too low?
24. Explain how to adjust a top stop injector to a specification of 0.224 in.
25. Outline the remaining steps (after the injector is snapped into place and the hold-down clamp torqued to specification) to install the injector and make a valve adjustment.
26. Assume that the "A" or the "1-6 VS" mark aligns with the pointer. On what strokes are the other five cylinders when the No. 5 cylinder is on the compression stroke?
27. Explain how to install the dial indicator and list the steps you would take to measure and adjust one injector to 0.175 in.
28. What would result if the injector is adjusted *(a)* too loosely, *(b)* too tightly?
29. What advantage has the top stop injector over the standard PTD injector?
30. Explain how you would check the injector timing (when the injection timing should be fast), using the following specifications:

- Engine model: xxx
- Piston travel: 0.2032 in
- Pushrod travel:
    Normal: 0.0290 in
    Fast: 0.0280 in
    Slow: 0.0300 in

31. Write, using the specifications listed in the previous question, the timing specifications for the engine you are working on or for one of the engines in your shop.
32. Explain the steps required to change the timing from fast to slow on *(a)* an in-line engine, *(b)* a V-type engine.

ASSIGNMENT 34
DPA AND STANADYNE DISTRIBUTOR-TYPE FUEL-INJECTION PUMPS

1. A model DC fuel-injection pump is shown in Fig. 34-1. Explain the main purpose of each component.

2. Explain the action within the vane pump (model DM) which causes the fuel to flow into the automatic advance and to the metering valve. (Refer to Fig. 34-2.)

3. In what way does the fuel flow vary between the DM model and the DPA model shown in DM2 Figs. 34-1 and 34-2?

4. Explain the operation of the pressure regulator of a DM model and include how it is able to compensate for velocity changes.

5. All distributor-type injection pumps use some kind of pulsation device to reduce the pulsation between the drive shaft and the rotor. Explain how the pulsation device used on a DPA fuel-injection pump reduces pulsation to the governor weight assembly.

6. The amount of fuel metered per cycle depends on three conditions. The first two conditions are: (1) the extent to which the metering valve is open, (2) the psi of the fuel pressure. What is the third condition?

7. Assume that the metering valve is in full-fuel position and the pressure regulator is maintaining maximum fuel pressure. Explain the mechanical action and the fuel flow during the metering and charging cycle (model DM).

8. Under the same circumstances, explain the mechanical action and the fuel flow during the metering and charging cycle of a DPA model.

Depending upon the manufacturer, the maximum fuel quantity which is allowed to enter the opposed plunger is limited by one of two different mechanical devices.

9. Explain how the leaf springs limit the maximum metered-fuel quantity.

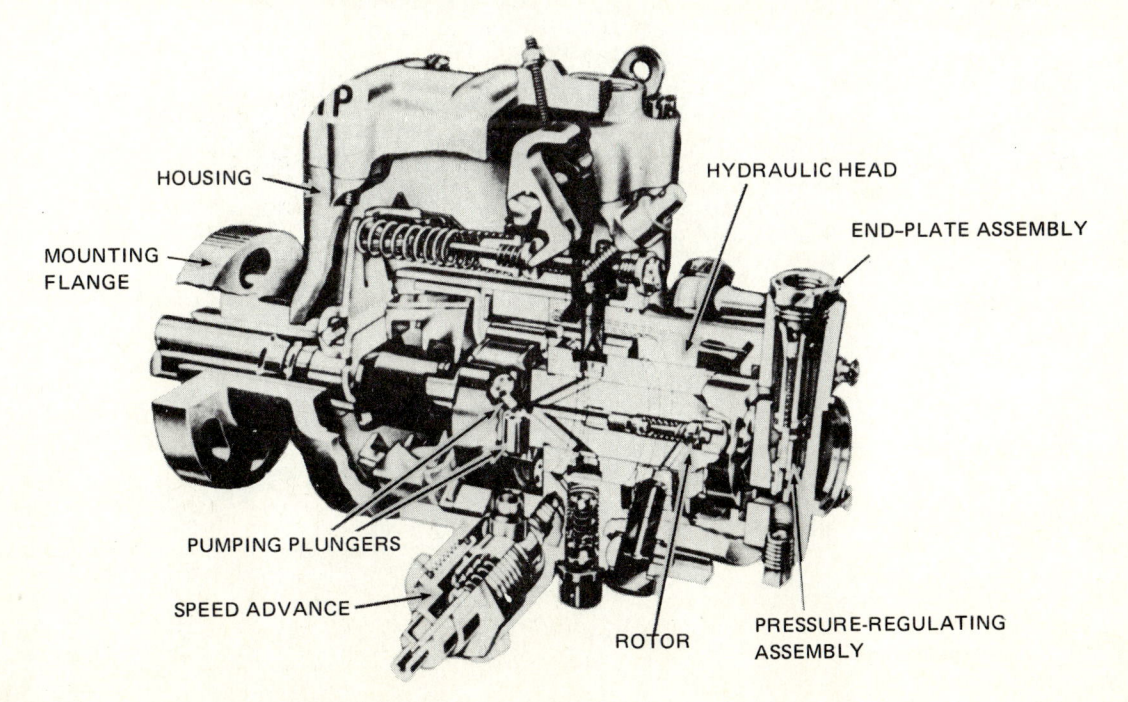

Fig. 34-1 Sectional view of a model DC Stanadyne fuel-injection pump. *(International Harvester Co.)*

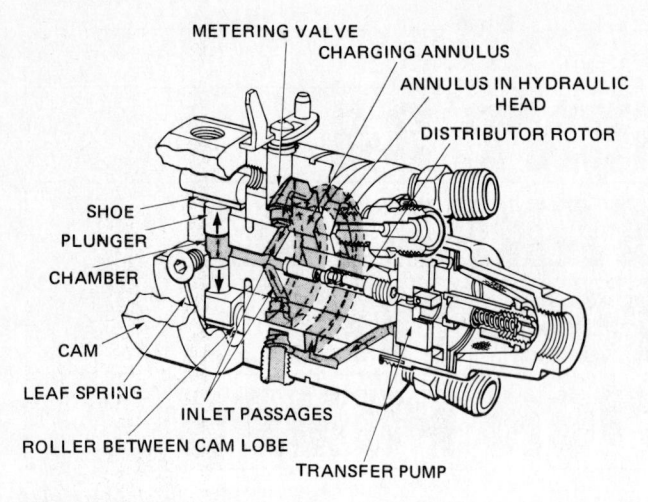

Fig. 34-2 Fuel flow in a model DM fuel-injection pump. *(Stanadyne Diesel Systems.)*

10. Explain how the adjusting plate is able to limit the maximum metered-fuel quantity.
11. Under which operating conditions are the opposed plungers so far separated that the roller shoes contact either the leaf springs or the adjusting plate?
12. Explain one pumping cycle and the distribution of fuel from the point where the charging ports come out of register to the point when they come in registration.
13. Explain why the distributor pumps have the inherent ability to change, automatically, the beginning of injection.
14. Refer to DM2 Fig. 34-1. Explain the fuel flow and the action resulting from the fuel flow, which moves the cam ring to (a) full advance position, (b) full retarded position.
15. Why is a ball check valve necessary in the advance mechanism?
16. Explain how the advance mechanism remains in the advance position when the engine load is reduced at any point in the speed range.
17. Explain the mechanical action of the model governor shown in Fig. 34-3 when the throttle is moved from idle-fuel to full-fuel position.
18. Explain the mechanical action of the DPA governor shown in DM2 Fig. 34-5 when the throttle is moved from the idle-fuel to full-fuel position.
19. When the engine operates at idle speed, the idle-speed adjusting screw fixes the position of the throttle shaft. Which components, and what forces, position the metering valve (DPA)?
20. Explain the component action (DPA) when the fuel-stop lever is moved to no-fuel position.

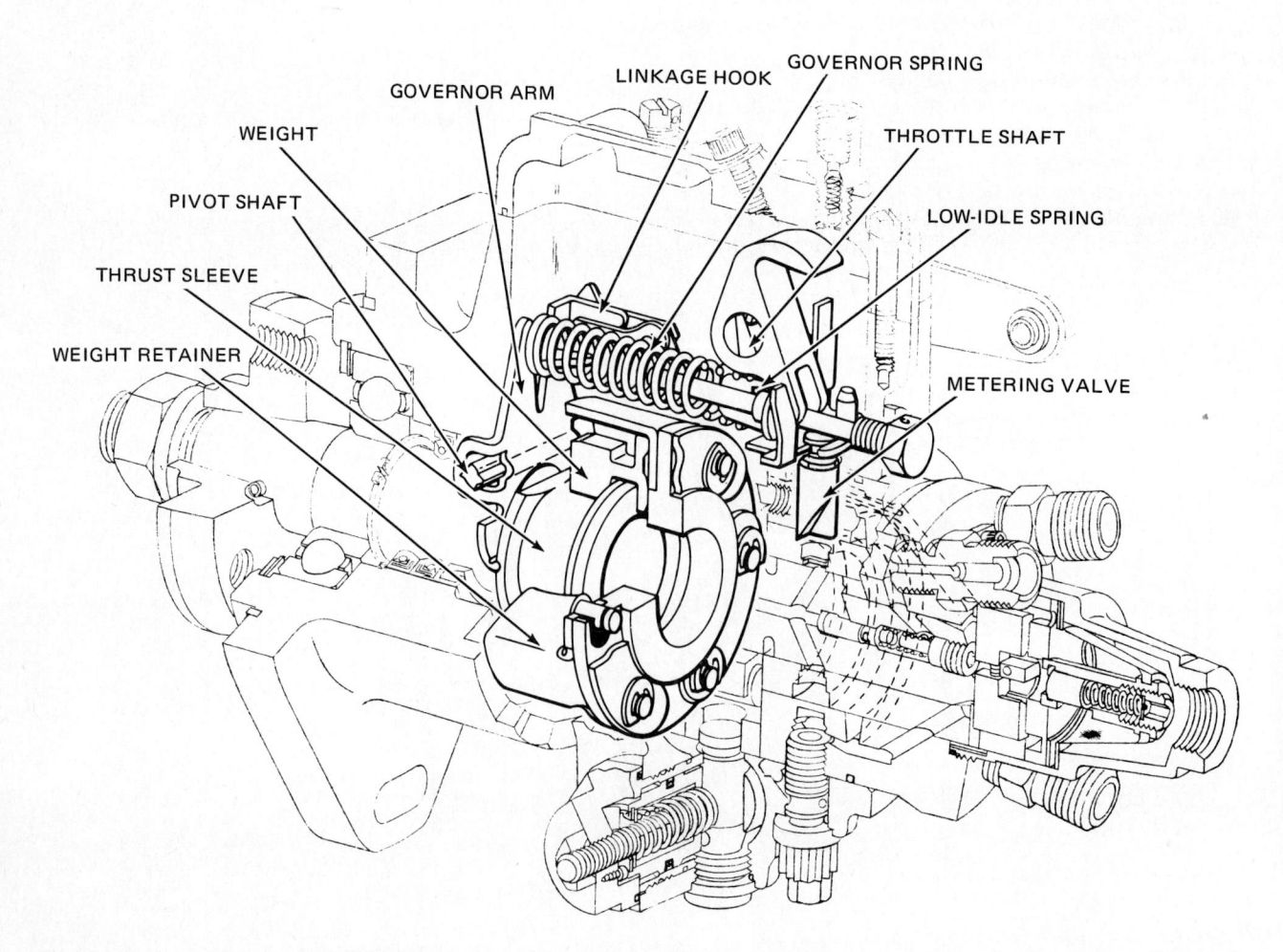

Fig. 34-3 Sectional view of a DM governor.

Name _____ Date _____ Class _____

21. In what way could steam cleaning damage the fuel-injection pump?
22. Outline the procedure to disassemble a model DM Stanadyne fuel-injection pump as far as the metering valve. Use DM2 Figs. 34-1 and 34-3 as a guide.
23. Outline the procedure to disassemble a DPA injection pump as far as the metering valve.
24. Outline the steps to remove the advance mechanism, the transfer pump, and the hydraulic head from a model DM fuel-injection pump.
25. Outline the steps to remove the advance mechanism, the transfer pump, and the hydraulic head from a DPA fuel-injection pump.
26. In which direction should the rotor be turned in order to loosen it?
27. Explain how the pressure-relief valve shown in DM2 Fig. 34-7 compensates for viscosity changes.
28. When checking the transfer pump for serviceability, which parts must be checked or measured?
29. Why are the liners of a vane transfer pump marked by "C" on one side and "CC" on the other?
30. Outline the steps to remove the opposed plunger from the (a) DPA fuel-injection pump, (b) DM fuel-injection pump.
31. Outline the steps to remove the delivery valve (model DM) from the rotor.
32. Outline the steps to remove the drive shaft from the model DM fuel-injection pump.
33. Explain how to remove the pressure regulator components from a (a) DPA fuel-injection pump, (b) DM fuel-injection pump.
34. Explain how to remove the weight retainer from a (a) DC injection pump, (b) DM injection pump, (c) DPA injection pump.
35. Eight common problems are listed below, followed by a list of parts which are to be inspected. For each part listed, write the number of the problem or problems which could occur to that part. Then briefly indicate what additional special checks or measurements should be made. One example is given.

PROBLEMS
1. Excessive wear
2. Foreign material or rust
3. Nicks or chipping
4. Scratches or scores
5. Thread damage
6. Cracks
7. Distortion
8. Freedom of movement

PARTS TO BE INSPECTED

Regulating sleeve *2, 3, 4, 6, 7, bypass ports for clogging*

Regulating piston _____

Thrust plate _____

End-plate adjusting plug _____

Inlet strainer _____

Liner _____

Blades _____

Hydraulic head _____

Vent wires _____

Plungers _____

Delivery valve _____

Distributor rotor _____

Cam rollers and shoes _____

Maximum fuel _____

Adjusting leaf springs and screws _____

Governor weights _____

Governor weight retainer _____

Thrust sleeve _____

Thrust washer _____

Pivot shaft _____

Linkage hook _____

Governor arm _____

Metering valve _____

Metering valve arm _____

Cam _____

Drive shaft _____

Housing _____

36. Explain the procedure for measuring and adjusting the roller-to-roller dimension to a specification of 1.960 in [49.784 mm], or to the specification for the pump you are working on.
37. What must you take into consideration when placing the cam ring in position?
38. List the steps you must take when reassembling a DPA transfer pump.
39. List the important points you must take into consideration when reassembling the (a) advance mechanism, (b) metering valve and governor linkage.
40. Explain the procedure you must follow when adjusting the throttle linkage to the recommended specification.
41. When you are pressure-testing a reassembled injection pump, you may find that air bubbles emerge from it. List the locations where you might find a leak.
42. Why must the mounting bracket of the fuel-injection pump be within the specified runout and alignment?
43. Why must you use only the specified test injectors and high-pressure fuel lines?
44. (a) What could cause the transfer pump pressure to be lower than specified? (b) Explain how to adjust the fuel pressure of the fuel-injection pump you are working on to the specification or to 50 psi ± 3 psi [344.74 kPa ± 20.68 kPa].
45. When the peak torque fuel delivery is below

specification, for example, 5 cm³, what step must you take in order to bring the fuel delivery to the recommended specification (Stanadyne)?

46. Explain how you would adjust the high-idle fuel delivery so that it is at the recommended cm³.

47. Assume that when checking the speed advance, you find it is 3° lower than specified. How would you change the advance mechanism of your fuel-injection pump, or that of a model DM fuel-injection pump, so that the speed advance is at the specified degree?

48. Explain how you would air-time or hydraulic-time the fuel-injection pump you have flow-tested and adjusted (or use another example).

49. Assume that the fuel-injection pump has a static time of 8° and a speed advance of 6°. Record the approximate beginning of injection at the following engine rpms: (a) low idle, (b) high idle, (c) peak torque speed.

50. List the steps you would take to install the injection pump you have serviced to the engine, or list the steps to install a model DM Stanadyne pump to an engine when the No. 1 piston is on compression and the engine timing marks are aligned.

ASSIGNMENT 35
AMERICAN BOSCH
DISTRIBUTOR-TYPE
FUEL-INJECTION PUMPS

1. Record the model number of the American Bosch distributor-type injection pump you are working on in your shop and interpret the nameplate; that is, explain what each part of the identification code stands for.

2. Using DM2 Figs. 35-6 and 35-7 as a guide, explain one pumping cycle. Begin and end with the tappet roller starting to move upward. (Omit discussion of the delivery valve, since its performance is the same as that of an in-line fuel-injection pump.)

3. Explain the movement or action of the control assembly and sleeve when the governor moves the control rod to (a) no-fuel position, (b) high-idle position.

4. Explain the oil flow and the action of the model 100 intravance unit as the engine speed continues to increase about 1000 rpm.

5. Outline the procedure to remove the (a) governor housing (include any precautions which should be taken during removal), (b) hydraulic head.

6. What checks and/or measurements must you make when inspecting the following: (a) pump housing, (b) camshaft, (c) drive shaft, (d) sleeve and tappet assembly?

7. Outline the procedure to disassemble the hydraulic head.

8. After washing the components in clean fuel, what checks would you then make on the (a) delivery-valve assembly, (b) hydraulic-head thrust washer, (c) plunger and sleeve, (d) control units, (e) two-piece gear and plunger drive guide?

9. Assume that the camshaft is installed and the end play is 0.05 mm above specification. How would you reduce the end play to the required specified limits?

10. Outline the steps you would take when measuring the clearance between the tappet guide and the roller.

11. Explain how to check the opening pressure of the delivery valve and how to adjust it to 1450 psi [9997.5 kPa].

12. Before installing the hydraulic head, you must first position the camshaft so that the keyway faces upward. Why must the keyway face upward before the head is installed?

13. What check must you make to determine if the pin is located correctly in the sleeve? (Refer to Fig. 35-1.)

14. List the vulnerable wear points of the governor components.

15. If the slipping torque were 30 to 40 lb·in [3.38 to 4.51 N·m] above specification, what steps would you take to reduce it to the correct specification?

16. List the alignment steps and checks to be made when installing the governor to the injection-pump housing.

17. List the checkpoints of the following components to ensure that the transfer pump is in sufficiently good condition to pump against a pressure of 40 psi [275.8 kPa]: (a) hand primer, (b) relief valve, (c) cover, (d) body, (e) gears.

18. What would occur in the operation or performance of the injection pump if the inner piston of the excess fuel device were seized in its retracted position?

Fig. 35-1 Sectional view of the hydraulic head.

19. How would you (a) measure the compression of the outer spring, (b) increase the compression rate by 1 mm?

20. List the steps and the precautions you must take when installing the transfer pump to the governor housing.

TEST SPECIFICATIONS
- Engine: DT-466
- Pump no.: 681237C91
- Rating: 150 hp at 2500 rpm
- Timing: Static 18° BTDC; Timing advance 14°
- Turbocharger no.: 674985C91 or 684237C91
- Shutoff control (type): Bowden wire
- Lift-to-port closure: 0.60–0.75 mm
- Delivery-valve opening pressure: 1150–1450 psi [7929.02–9997.46 kPa]
- Stop plate: Part no.: 681258C1; Code: −10/90°; Cam-nose angle: 60°
- Governor springs:
  Outer-spring precompression: 1.0–1.5 mm
  Inner-spring gap: 2.0–2.25 mm
  Spring nos.: Outer: 674945C1;
  Inner: 674929C1

TEST BENCH DATA			
	Rated speed	Torque check speed	Droop check speed
Pump speed, rpm	2500	1800	1200
Fuel delivery, cm³/1000 strokes	81.5	89.0	84.0
Transfer-pump pressure, psi [kPa]	40 Minimum 275.8		

21. Explain how you would proceed to spill-time the injection pump and how you would measure the plunger lift.

22. Assume the plunger-lift travel is 85 mm, but according to specifications it should be between 60 to 75 mm. What steps would you take to bring the plunger lift within specification?

23. When pressure-testing the injection pump, (a) where might you expect to find the occurrence of fuel leakage, (b) why would you find fuel leakage in this location?

24. Where would you expect to find leaks when testing the injection pump and the pressure drop is below 200 psi [1379 kPa] but there are no external leaks?

25. Explain how to adjust the cam nose to a 60° angle.

26. If the average fuel delivery were 6 cm³ lower than specified, what adjustment would you make to increase the delivery?

27. If, upon flow-testing "rated speed," you find fuel delivery 5 cm³ above average, what steps would you take to reduce the fuel delivery?

28. How would you adjust the high-idle adjusting screw?

29. If, upon checking the governor cutoff speed, you find that the fuel delivery is slightly higher than specified (say 6 cm³), what steps would you take to reduce delivery?

30. What adjustment must be made to increase or decrease the droop-speed fuel delivery?

31. How would you check the operation of the timing device?

32. Outline the steps to install the injection pump to an engine (DT466).

ASSIGNMENT 36
CATERPILLAR SLEEVE-METERING FUEL-INJECTION PUMPS

1. List six differences between the Caterpillar and the American Bosch fuel-injection pumps.

2. What are the main differences between the pumping elements of these two fuel-injection systems?

3. Trace the fuel flow within the pump housing and explain the method used to maintain a maximum fuel pressure (at high idle) of 32 psi [220 kPa].

4. Explain why the plunger cannot pressurize the fuel when the sleeve is in the no-fuel position.

5. Explain in detail the pumping cycle from the point when the lifter is on the base circle of the camshaft and then starts to move upward until it has returned to its base circle. (Assume that the control sleeve is in full-fuel position.)

6. Explain the position of the levers within the governor when the throttle is at high idle but the engine is not operating.

7. Explain the reaction of the levers within the governor from the time the engine starts until it is operating at high-idle speed.

8. When, because of increased load, the engine speed decreases from high-idle to droop speed, and then the load further increases, causing the engine to operate at maximum torque speed: *(a)* how does the governor respond to the reduction in engine speed, *(b)* what action occurs within the governor?

9. *(a)* What precautions must you take when removing the pumping element? *(b)* Why is it important not to remove the control sleeve or disassemble the element at this time?

10. What checks must you make on the components of a pumping element to ensure that they will be reusable?

11. What service must you give a pumping element that you are going to reuse?

12. On the Caterpillar transfer pump, why does the lip of the inner seal face inward and the lip of the outer seal face outward?

13. Why is the sleeve-metering injection pump automatically in phase?

14. Outline the procedure to adjust one pumping element. (Assume that the specification is 0.005 in. [0.127 mm])

15. List the steps you would take to install one pumping element.

16. Explain how you would adjust the governor when a torque screw is used.

17. Explain how to install an injection pump to one of your training engines.

18. Why is it necessary to bleed the sleeve-metering fuel-injection pump?

19. Why must the fuel-ratio control be adjusted after the fuel system setting?

20. Outline the procedure to adjust high and low idle to specification.

ASSIGNMENT 37
ELECTRICITY AND MAGNETISM

1. Define in your own words: *(a)* matter, *(b)* molecule, *(c)* atom.
2. Complete the following sentences by filling in the missing words: *(a)* An electron is a unit of an atom which is _____ charged. *(b)* A proton is a unit of an atom which is _____ charged. *(c)* A neutron is a unit of an atom which is _____ charged.
3. Briefly outline how like and unlike charges react to each other.
4. Explain why only certain types of matter have good conductivity.
5. Name three good and three poor conductors.

The next two questions are related to the characteristics of a conductor.

6. Explain how and why the conductivity of a conductor wire is affected when the conductor wire's *(a)* length is increased, *(b)* temperature is increased, *(c)* temperature is decreased, *(d)* area is increased, *(e)* area is decreased.
7. List four reasons why it is essential to insulate the conductor.
8. List the five most common causes of insulator failure which could damage electrical components or render an entire electrical system inoperable.
9. Define *resistance* with regard to electricity.

Complete the following sentences by filling in the missing words:

10. When using the current theory, the current flow is from the _____ terminal to the _____ terminal.
11. When using the electron theory, the electron flow is from the _____ terminal to the _____ terminal.
12. In your own words, define *(a)* direct current, *(b)* alternating current.

Volume (Amperes) and Pressure (Voltage)

The presence of electrons alone is not sufficient to produce work. You must also have pressure (voltage) to move the electrons. The combined effort produces work.

13. Define *voltage* (electromotive force).
14. Write the formula for *work*.
15. Give the abbreviations for the following: *(a)* volume, *(b)* pressure, *(c)* resistance.
16. Write the formula for calculating *(a)* pressure, *(b)* volume, *(c)* resistance.

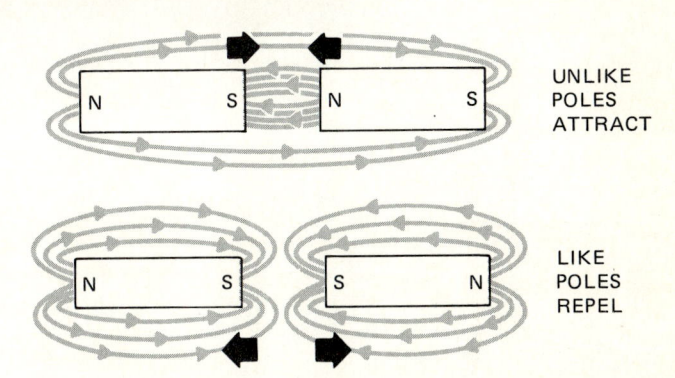

Fig. 37-1 Unlike poles attract and like poles repel. *(Delco Remy Division of General Motors.)*

17. What is a magnet?
18. How do the lines of force behave with regard to direction of travel and concentration?
19. What are magnetic poles?
20. How and why do two magnets behave when *(a)* two magnetic north poles are facing each other, *(b)* a south and a north pole are facing each other? (Refer to Fig. 37-1.)
21. List three methods you could use to make an unmagnetized material into a magnetized material.
22. Why is it that some materials retain their magnetism whereas others quickly lose it?
23. Why does a current-carrying conductor produce a circular magnetic field around itself?
24. Briefly explain how to change the direction of the magnetic field.
25. When equal current flows in the same direction through two parallel conductors, how do the conductors behave in relation to each other, and why? (Refer to Fig. 37-2.)

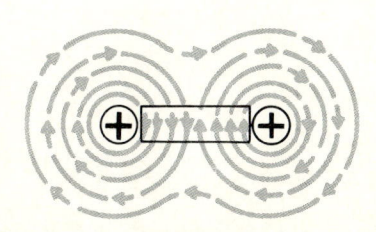

Fig. 37-2 Magnetic field of two parallel conductors. *(Delco Remy Division of General Motors.)*

26. In what electrical component would you find a conductor arrangement such as the one described in Prob. 25?

27. Why has the magnetic field both a north and a south pole once the conductor is formed into a loop? (See Fig. 37-3.)

28. Outline three ways to strengthen the magnetic lines of force to make an electromagnet useful.

29. If you know the direction of the electron flow, how would you determine the location of the magnetic north pole applying the rule of the electron theory?

30. Answer Prob. 29, applying the current theory rule.

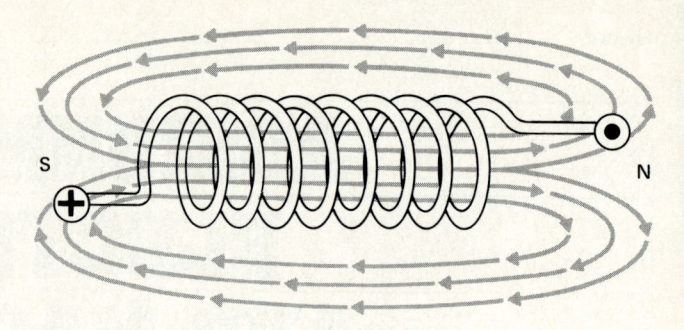

Fig. 37-3 Magnetic field conductor formed into a coil. *(Delco Remy Division of General Motors.)*

Name _____ Date _____ Class _____

ASSIGNMENTS 38 AND 39
ELECTRIC CIRCUITS AND TEST INSTRUMENTS

1. List the components needed to make up a simple electric circuit.

2. Explain the differences among the following circuit classifications: *(a)* series circuit, *(b)* parallel circuit, *(c)* series-parallel circuit.

3. Complete the following classifications to describe electrical failure with *(a)* an open circuit, *(b)* a shorted circuit, *(c)* a grounded circuit, *(d)* a circuit having a higher resistance than specified.

4. What could cause a circuit to have a higher resistance than that specified?

5. What is the specific purpose of *(a)* a voltmeter, *(b)* an ammeter, *(c)* an ohmmeter?

6. Assume that your vehicle has the electric circuit shown in Fig. 38-1, and that the headlights are burning dim. Assume also that the ammeter shows a current draw of only 20 A instead of 28 A. On Fig. 38-1, draw each voltmeter connection you would make in order to find the components which have high resistance.

7. What is the purpose of a carbon pile?

8. What is the purpose of a rheostat?

9. What is the difference between a carbon pile and a rheostat?

10. Calculate the current flow of a parallel circuit when the battery voltage is 14.5 V and the resistance of the components is *(a)* 0.5 Ω, *(b)* 3.5 Ω, *(c)* 4.0 Ω, *(d)* 5.5 Ω.

11. What is the main difference between a two-wire electrical system and a single-wire electrical system when the frame performs the function of the second wire?

12. In what way is the two-wire system more advantageous than the single-wire system?

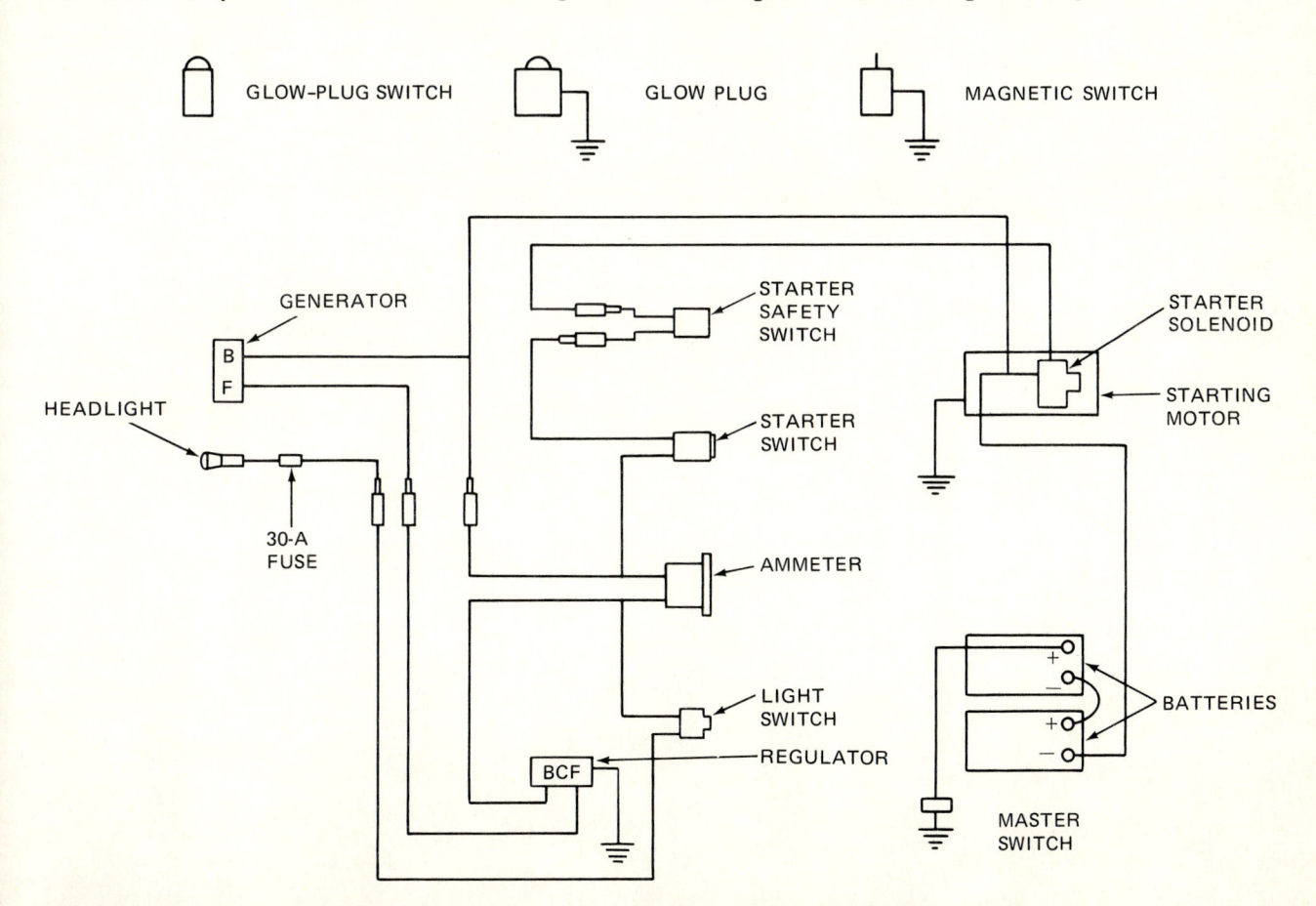

Fig. 38-1 Electrical system circuit diagram. *(Allis-Chalmers Corp. Engine Division.)*

101

13. Select and calculate, using the specifications for DM2 Fig. 39-2, the correct cable size for a cranking-motor circuit when cable length from battery to cranking motor is 115 in [292.1 cm], battery voltage is 24 V, and cranking-motor draw is 800 A.

14. What two factors govern the *wire size* of an accessory circuit?

15. What factor governs the *selection* of a terminal wire end?

16. Outline the steps to solder a closed-end battery terminal to a battery cable.

17. List the advantages of the new Delco 1200 battery-cable assembly (Fig. 38-2) over conventional battery cables.

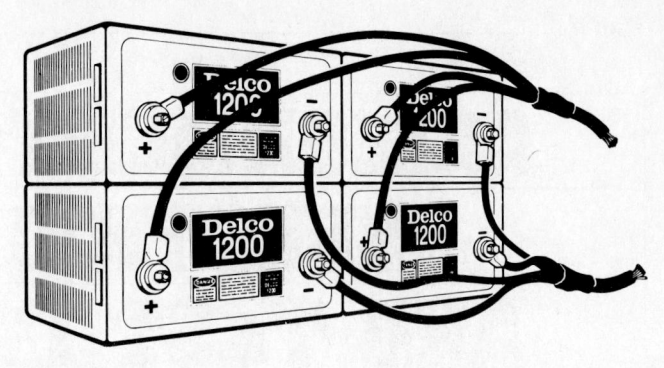

Fig. 38-2 Battery cable assembly used with Delco 1200 batteries. *(Delco Remy Division of General Motors.)*

Name _____ Date _____ Class _____

ASSIGNMENT 40
RELAYS, MAGNETIC SWITCHES, SOLENOIDS, AND SOLENOID SWITCHES

1. What is the difference between a relay and a magnetic switch?
2. What test or checks must you make in order to check the serviceability of a (a) relay, (b) magnetic switch?
3. Explain the difference in function between a solenoid and a solenoid switch.
4. Discuss the current flow through the solenoid switch shown in DM2 Fig. 40-5: when the (a) switch is turned to start position, (b) cranking motor is cranking the engine.
5. Explain why the pull-in winding loses its magnetism when the engine is cranked.

If the actuating circuit fails to engage the cranking motor, check and test the battery and all connections. If the connections and batteries are satisfactory, your next step is to check (using a voltmeter) the operating condition of the (1) master switch, (2) starter switch, (3) starter safety switch, (4) starter solenoid switch.

6. Using Fig. 40-1, draw in the voltmeter connections to check the (a) master switch, (b) starter switch, (c) safety switch, (d) pull-in winding, (e) hold-in winding, (f) contacts.
7. Outline the procedures to make all these connections.
8. Explain how to test the solenoid switch with an ohmmeter (Fig. 40-1) using the following specifications:

- Voltage: 12 V
- Current draw for both windings: 60 to 65 A
- Current draw for hold-in winding: 15 to 18 A

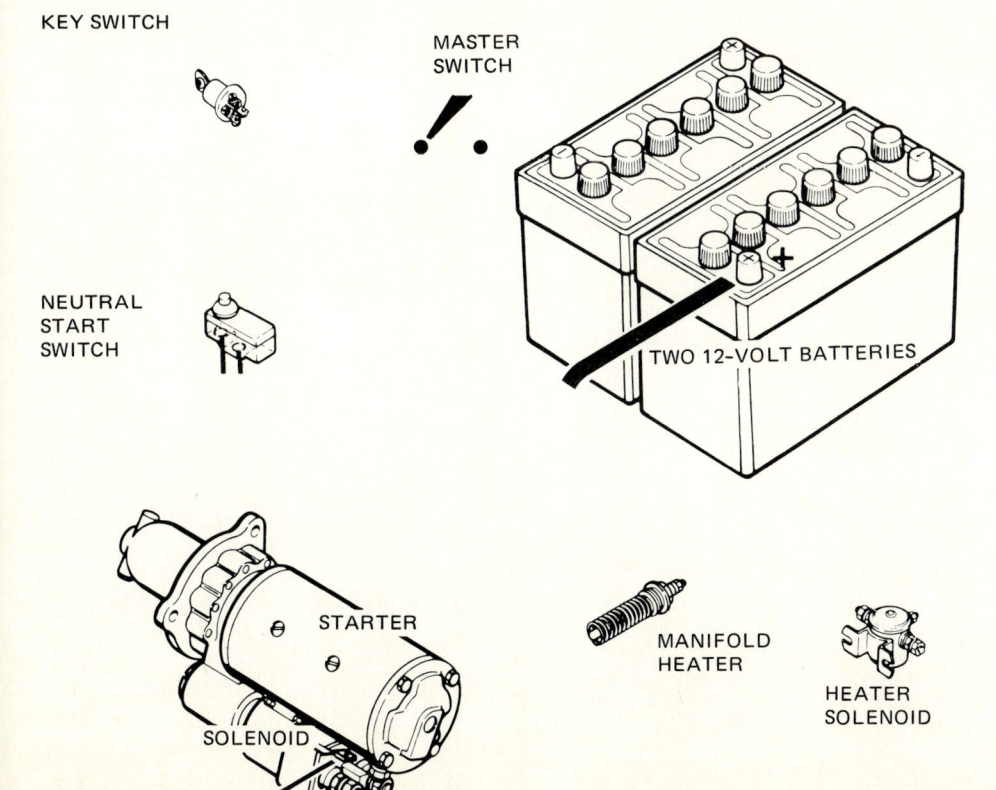

Fig. 40-1 Testing the solenoid switch.

103

Name _____ Date _____ Class _____

ASSIGNMENT 41
BATTERIES

The primary sources of energy which produce electricity are magnetism, heat, and chemical change.

1. Where are these three sources of energy found on a diesel engine?

The next eight questions relate to the lead-acid battery and its basic design, as well as to its construction.

2. What does the name *lead-acid battery* tell you?
3. What three functions must the lead-acid battery perform if the electrical system is to operate satisfactorily?
4. What is the purpose of the plate grid?
5. Define *plate group*.
6. Why does the negative plate group have one extra plate?
7. Why are separators placed between the negative and positive plates?
8. What does a battery element consist of?
9. How are the battery plates transformed (charged) into chemically active material?

After charging a battery, one plate group is then positively charged and the other plate group is negatively charged.

10. What color is a plate that is *(a)* positively charged, *(b)* negatively charged?
11. What is the chemical composition of the two plates?
12. What is the open battery voltage when the specific gravity of the electrolyte is 1.265?

The volume of power (watts) obtainable from a battery depends upon several factors.

13. What factors will increase the power output of a battery?
14. Why are the elements chemically separated from each other?
15. How are the elements electrically connected to each other?
16. What method is used to distinguish the negative from the positive battery post?
17. Discuss the differences (including advantages) between a battery having a one-piece battery cover and a battery having individual cell covers.
18. What is the percentage of water and sulfuric acid of the electrolyte?
19. Outline the steps you would take if you were to prepare your own electrolyte from pure sulfuric acid.

20. What immediate action must you take if electrolyte spills on your components or on you?
21. Why is it necessary to change the specific gravity of a battery when it is used in a *(a)* hot climate, *(b)* cold climate?
22. Describe how you would fill a dry-charged battery if the electrolyte were shipped in a 1-quart plastic container.
23. Briefly describe the construction and purpose of a hydrometer.
24. Why does a hydrometer contain a thermometer?
25. Assume two hydrometer measurements are made (on the same battery), one at 100°F [37.7°C] electrolyte temperature, and the other at 60°F [15.5°C] electrolyte temperature. What would be the difference, in specific gravity, between the two hydrometer readings?
26. When the temperature-compensated hydrometer reading is 1260, what is the open-circuit battery voltage?
27. What would it signify if a battery had a CCA rating of 900 A?
28. Why does a battery lose its power when the temperature is less than 80°F?
29. Discuss the possible reasons for the following: *(a)* a cracked battery case, *(b)* a buildup of grey deposit on the battery posts, *(c)* wetness on top of the battery cover, *(d)* loose battery posts, *(e)* bulged sealing compound of the individual cell covers.
30. Outline the steps to perform a battery leakage test.
31. List the causes of battery leakage.
32. Using different colored pencils, draw on Fig. 41-1 the battery connections which you might find when four 6-V batteries are used to produce a cranking voltage of *(a)* 12 V, *(b)* 24 V, *(c)* 24 V and, additionally, a series-parallel switch is used.
33. When removing batteries, which battery cable must be removed first, and when installing batteries, which is the last battery cable to be connected?
34. Why must the precautions referred to in Prob. 33 be taken?
35. Outline the procedure and the precautions you would take to clean a battery.

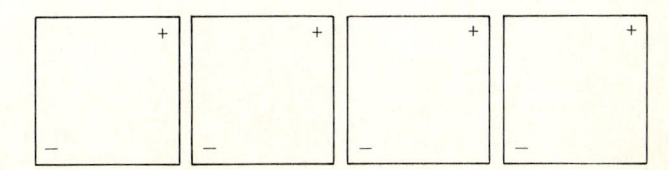

Fig. 41-1

105

36. Explain how to test (using a hydrometer) the chemical energy of the battery after the electrolyte level is checked and the surface charge is removed.
37. When testing a battery, what action would you take upon determining that one or more cells has insufficient energy?
38. Outline the procedure to measure the open circuit voltage using a *(a)* voltmeter, *(b)* cadmium probe tester.
39. If one battery cell reading is 1.95 V and the remaining cells show a voltage reading between 2.00 and 2.08 V, what would be your next course of action?
40. What is the purpose of the high-discharge test? Why should this test only be made when the battery voltage of the respective batteries is no less than the required 6 or 12 V?
41. On Fig. 41-2 draw in the lines to show the connections to the test instrument and battery when making a high-discharge test.
42. Outline the steps to perform a high-discharge test on a battery having a CCA rating of 475 A.
43. What test results would indicate that the battery being tested should be replaced?
44. Describe how to make a 3-minute charging test on a 6-V battery which has a CCA rating of 475 A.

45. How do you determine the correct charging-current setting?
46. If the 3-minute charging test reveals a voltage of 17.5 V, what would you judge the condition of the battery to be?
47. What is a *trickle charger*?
48. What is the difference between a constant-current charger and a constant-voltage charger?
49. What is the difference (effect on charging) between a fast charger and a slow charger?
50. Elaborate on the precautions which you must take while charging a battery, because of highly explosive escaped gases.
51. When would you be forced to charge the batteries with a constant-current charger?
52. Assume that you are servicing four batteries, of which one pair are 6-V and one pair are 12-V. Each battery has been cleaned and filled with water to the correct level. How are the two 6-V and the two 12-V batteries connected electrically to the charger?
53. What governs the selection of the charging rate?
54. Would you expect high or low charging voltage *(a)* at the beginning of the charging cycle, *(b)* near the end of the charging time?
55. Explain how to connect electrically four batteries of equal voltage to the charger.
56. Explain how to arrive at the correct charging rate for *(a)* a constant-voltage charger, *(b)* a constant-current charger.
57. What attention must you give to the batteries after they have been charged?
58. When using a booster battery or a set of batteries to start an engine, why is it important *(a)* to have the booster batteries and the batteries of the engine of the same voltage, *(b)* to have the booster batteries and the engine batteries of the same polarity, *(c)* to connect the ground cable of the booster battery to ground and not to the grounded battery post, *(d)* to disconnect the battery-booster ground cable before disconnecting the live battery cable, whether or not the engine is operating or has failed to start?

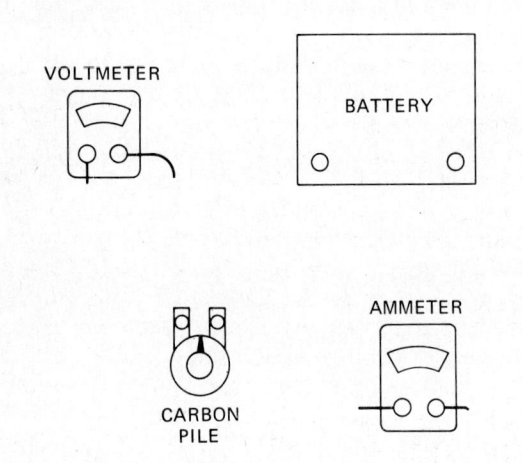

Fig. 41-2 Instruments used to make a high-discharge test.

Name _____ Date _____ Class _____

ASSIGNMENT 42
ELECTRIC STARTING
(CRANKING) MOTORS

1. Briefly describe an electric cranking motor.
2. A typical medium-duty cranking motor is shown in Fig. 42-1. Write the name and main purpose of each numbered component.
3. Why is the conductor shown in Fig. 42-2 forced to rotate in a counterclockwise direction and then stop when it is at an angle of 90° from the magnetic lines of force?
4. Why does the conductor loop rotate continuously as long as there is a current flow?
5. What principle is used in order to make one pole of north polarity and the other pole of south polarity?
6. Explain why the torque of the cranking motor is increased when all loops are connected to each other.
7. Why are the loops placed into the predesigned grooves of the armature core?
8. Why is the armature core made from laminated iron rather than from one piece of iron?
9. What three methods are used to increase the ampere turns of a field coil?
10. Why does a four-pole cranking-motor circuit with a series field-coil circuit have a higher cranking speed than a cranking motor having the same number of field coils, but with a series-parallel field-coil circuit?
11. Why do all cranking motors draw the maximum specified current when the armature is not turning, and draw less current as the armature increases in speed?
12. Why are one or two shunt coils in a field coil circuit able to limit the speed of the armature, say to 9000 rpm?
13. Explain why a pair of brushes or a set of field coils are connected to each other through a jumper wire.
14. Why do some cranking motors use an insulated grounded circuit?
15. Why are bronze bushings used to support the armature in the drive housing and commutator end frame instead of ball bearings?
16. Explain the purpose of the motor thermostat.
17. Outline the current flow to actuate the solenoid switch.
18. Explain how to test the motor thermostat.
19. What are the five major functions of a cranking-motor drive?
20. Outline the step-by-step disassembly procedure for the friction clutch cranking-motor drive.

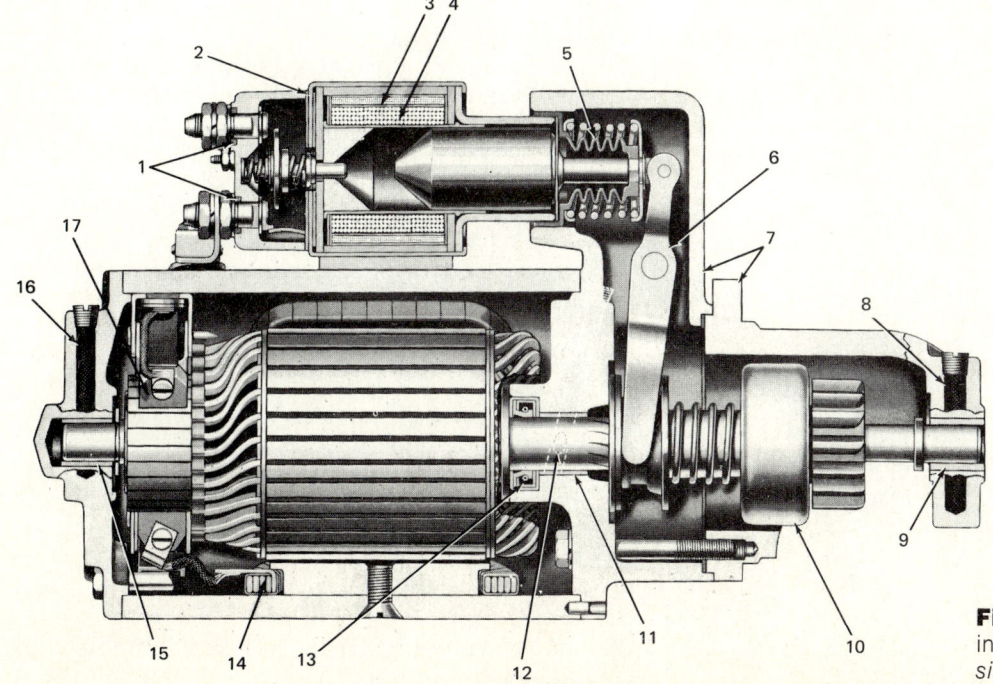

Fig. 42-1 Medium-duty cranking motor. *(Delco Remy Division of General Motors.)*

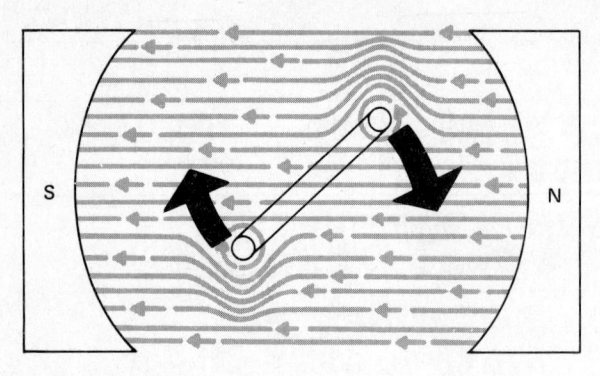

Fig. 42-2 Cranking-motor principle. *(Delco Remy Division of General Motors.)*

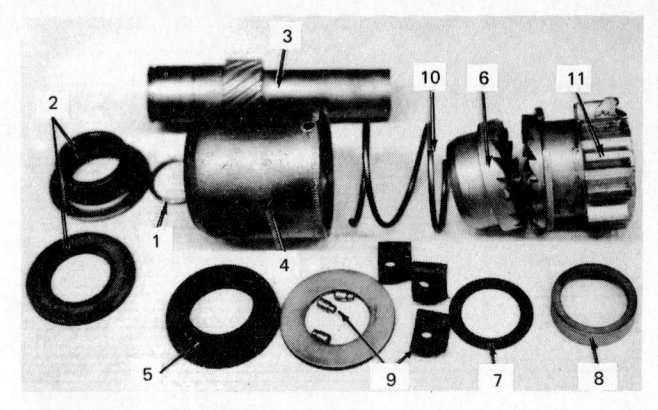

Fig. 42-4 Disassembled Positork drive components.

21. Explain how to adjust the friction clutch so that the drive is positive and yet the shock load can be absorbed. (Assume that the stall torque of the cranking motor is 40 lb·ft. [54.2 N·m])

22. List a number of differences between a cranking-motor roller overrunning clutch drive, and one with a sprag clutch drive.

23. Describe the movements of the components of a roller overrunning-clutch cranking-motor drive during engagement and disengagement.

24. List four reasons why a roller overrunning clutch could fail to stay in engagement with the ring gear.

25. List the modifications to the sprag clutch drive and describe how they have improved the drive assembly.

26. A disassembled sprag clutch drive is shown in Fig. 42-3. Which of the components illustrated require careful examination to determine if they are reusable?

27. During reassembly of the sprag clutch drive, what governs the direction in which you must install the sprags?

28. How would the engagement or disengagement be affected if the garter spring had lost its tension or if its installation were completely omitted?

29. List the circumstances under which a sprag clutch cranking-motor drive *(a)* will not engage at all or will not engage satisfactorily, *(b)* will not disengage or will only disengage slowly.

30. A disassembled Positork drive is shown in Fig. 42-4. Write the name and purpose of each component numbered in the illustration.

31. Explain the action within the drive assembly when the *(a)* pinion and ring gear butt together, *(b)* engine starts but the solenoid switch remains energized.

32. What would cause damage *(a)* to the pinion shown in Fig. 42-4, *(b)* to the lockouts?

33. List a number of maintenance requirements which will help extend the service life of the cranking motor.

34. Assume that you have a cranking motor which cranks the engine at about 80 rpm. You have tested the batteries and the engine appears to be in good mechanical condition. List the eight main sources of mechanical or electrical trouble that could be preventing the engine from increasing its cranking rpm.

35. Outline the steps you would take in order to remove the cranking motor from an engine in your shop. Do not omit the safety factors.

36. When examining the ring gear, you will notice that if wear or damage exists it is usually in one area only. When there is damage to the ring-gear teeth, why are only about 15 teeth affected?

37. Why is it a good work habit before disassembling the cranking motor to *(a)* identify the location of the cranking-motor end frame and the drive housing with respect to the field-frame assembly, *(b)* lift the brushes from the commutator and hold them in place with the brush springs?

38. Assume, after the cranking motor is disassembled, that you have found the following problems: *(a)* thrown armature windings, *(b)* armature polished at one end, *(c)* one or more burned commutator bars, *(d)* thrown solder inside the field-frame assembly, *(e)* high commutator micas, *(f)* worn commutator bars, *(g)* burned insulating washers of the insulated brushes and of the main terminal, *(h)* excessive wear of the armature shaft splines, *(i)* indication of burned field-coil insulation. How would you remedy each problem?

39. What type of cleaning fluid should be used to clean electrical components?

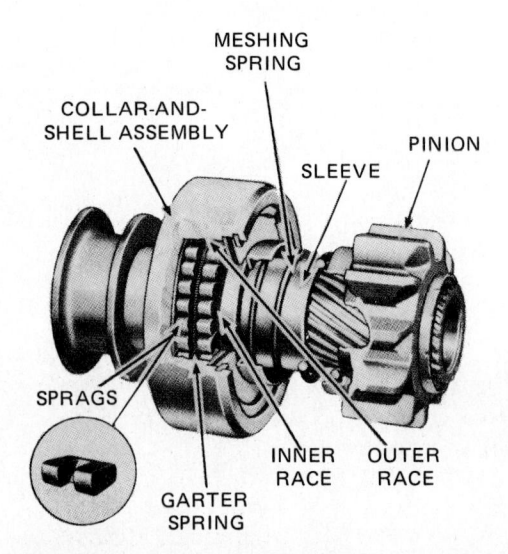

Fig. 42-3 Sectional view of the sprag clutch.

Name _____ Date _____ Class _____

40. Under what conditions must a cranking-motor brush be replaced?
41. Explain how to remove and to install the commutator end-frame bushing when the bushing bore has a blind hole.
42. List the checks and measurements you must make on the end frame (excluding brush wear and spring tension).
43. How is the cranking-motor performance affected when the (a) armature-shaft runout is greater than that allowed in the specifications, (b) commutator runout is greater than the allowable runout?
44. Outline the procedure for testing the armature for an open circuit.
45. During testing of the armature for a shorted circuit, why does the steel blade vibrate 60 times per second when one armature loop is shorted?
46. Why do some cranking motors require the mica to be undercut whereas others do not?
47. What are the three methods used to remove the mica in order to conform to specified width and depth?
48. What could cause the insulation from one or more field coils to burn?
49. Describe how to test the field coils for a grounded circuit when two shunt coils are used.
50. When installing a new set of field coils, or when replacing only one coil, what must you first consider before placing the coil onto the pole-shoe pieces?
51. How would the cranking-motor speed and the torque be affected if the (a) cranking-motor brushes were only one-half the original length, (b) brush spring tension was only one-half of its original strength?
52. When the cranking-motor brushes are reusable, what service would you give them before installing them into the holders?
53. Why must the seating area make up at least 25 percent of the total brush area, and why must it be restricted to the center of the brush area? (Refer to Fig. 42-5.)
54. What is the importance of the following procedure? When installing the brushes, first hold them in the up position in their holders without tightening the screws. When the cranking motor is assembled, lower the brushes onto the commutator and then, while holding the brushes on the commutator, tighten the screws.
55. On Fig. 42-6, draw the connections from the test instruments to the cranking motor and the battery you would use to make a cranking-motor no-load test.
56. Assume that the test results of the no-load tests of five serviced cranking motors having the same model number were as follows:

- Motor A: current draw—95 A, 26 V, 7500 rpm, battery—27 V
- Motor B: current draw—110 A, 24.2 V, 8700 rpm, battery—27 V
- Motor C: current draw—160 A, 19 V, 6000 rpm, battery—27 V
- Motor D: current draw—60 A, 25 V, 5000 rpm, battery—27 V
- Motor E: current draw—110 A, 26.3 V, 6500 rpm, battery—27 V

The specifications for the cranking motor are:

- Current draw maximum no-load: 115 A
- Voltage draw maximum no-load: 23.3 V
- Minimum rpm: 8750

What could bring about the differences in the test results of cranking motors A, B, C, D, and E?

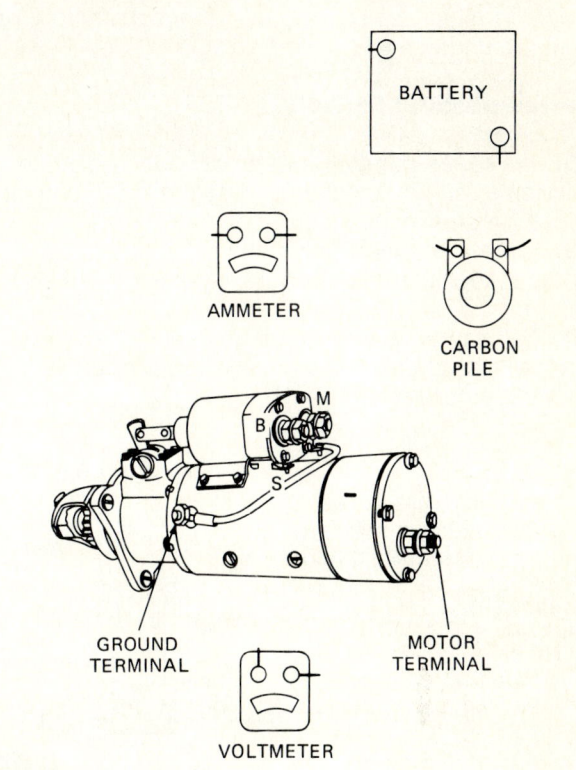

Fig. 42-6 Testing instruments required to make a no-load cranking-motor test.

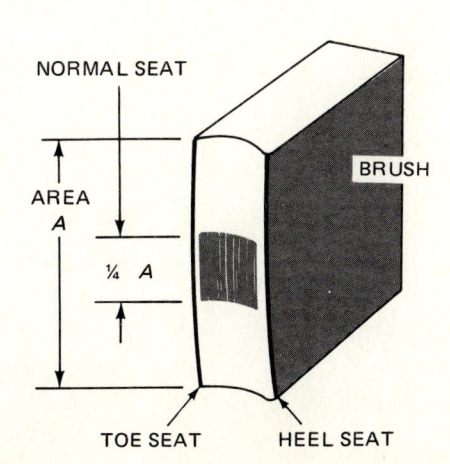

Fig. 42-5 Brush seating area. *(Delco Remy Division of General Motors.)*

109

57. From the test results listed in Prob. 56, which cranking motor would you say is in satisfactory operating condition?

Series-parallel Switch

58. A series-parallel switch can be a source of problems for any mechanic. List the most common series-parallel switch failures.

59. Describe the maintenance procedures you would follow in order to reduce series-parallel switch failure.

60. When using a series-parallel switch, why does one set of batteries usually have lower open voltage than the other set?

61. On Fig. 42-7, draw the voltmeter connections you would use in order to check the series-parallel switch as well as the remaining connections of the charging system.

62. Assume that a series-parallel switch is used, the batteries are fully charged, the cranking motor was tested before installation, and the connections from the batteries to the series-parallel switch and to the cranking motor have been tested and found to be satisfactory. Again on Fig. 42-7, draw the voltmeter connection(s) you would use (and provide a written explanation of your choice) in order to test the cause of the (a) cranking motor not being actuated, (b) engine being cranked at a reduced speed, (c) series-parallel switch not engaging.

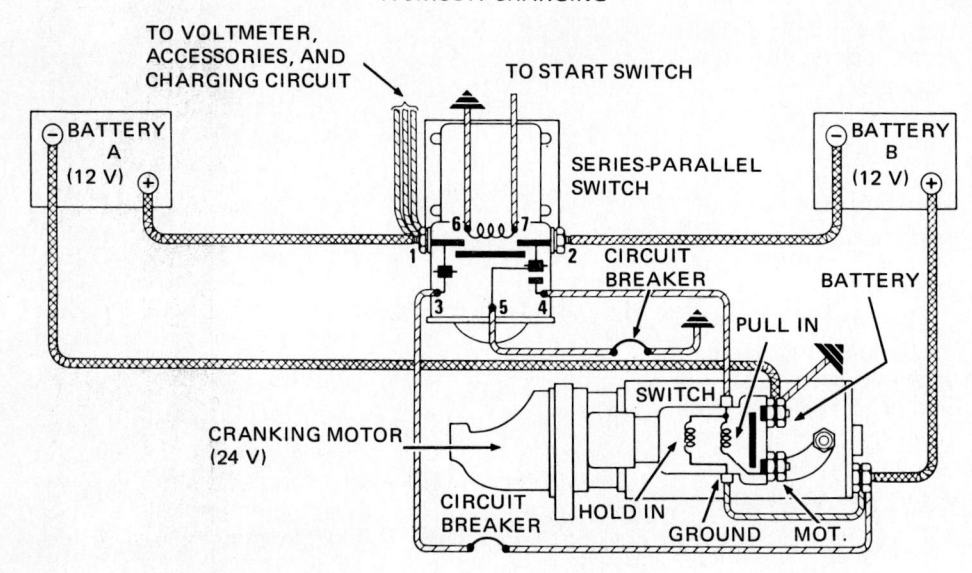

Fig. 42-7 Schematic illustration of a series-parallel switch during charging. *(Delco Remy Division of General Motors.)*

ASSIGNMENT 43
AIR AND HYDRAULIC STARTING SYSTEMS

1. What advantage has the air starting system over the hydraulic starting system in regard to (a) simplicity, (b) reliability, (c) testing, (d) service, (e) maintenance?

2. What advantages have both the air and hydraulic starting systems over the electric starting system?

3. How can you prevent the entry of contaminants (water, oil, dust, and dirt) into the air system?

4. What check would you make to ensure that the air cranking motor is supplied with lubricant?

Failure of the relay valve is usually due to contamination and very rarely to mechanical failure.

5. Which air-starting-system components are worn or damaged when the relay valve is (a) not supplying full reservoir pressure to the air motor, (b) actuated and air is escaping from the exhaust port, (c) in the release position and air is escaping from the exhaust port?

6. What could cause push-button valve failure?

7. Why is a one-way check valve used on the inlet of the air-starting-system reservoir?

8. List the main reasons why the air starter shown in Fig. 43-1 would have reduced efficiency when the following four types of damage are present: (1) bearing failure, (2) a worn or damaged end plate, (3) a worn or damaged vane, (4) a worn or damaged cylinder.

9. What conditions will increase the wear rate of the reduction gear teeth?

10. What checks or adjustments must you make when the drive-gear teeth or driven-gear teeth are broken?

11. Explain the airflow and the mechanical action of each component within the air starting system from the point where the operator actuates the push-button valve to the point where the pinion engages with the ring gear.

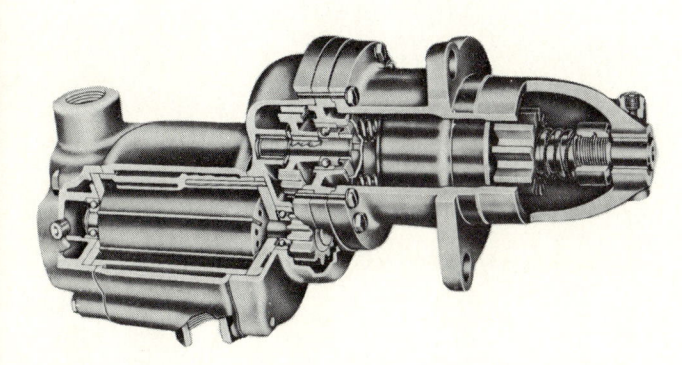

Fig. 43-1 Sectional view of an air starter. *(Ingersoll-Rand.)*

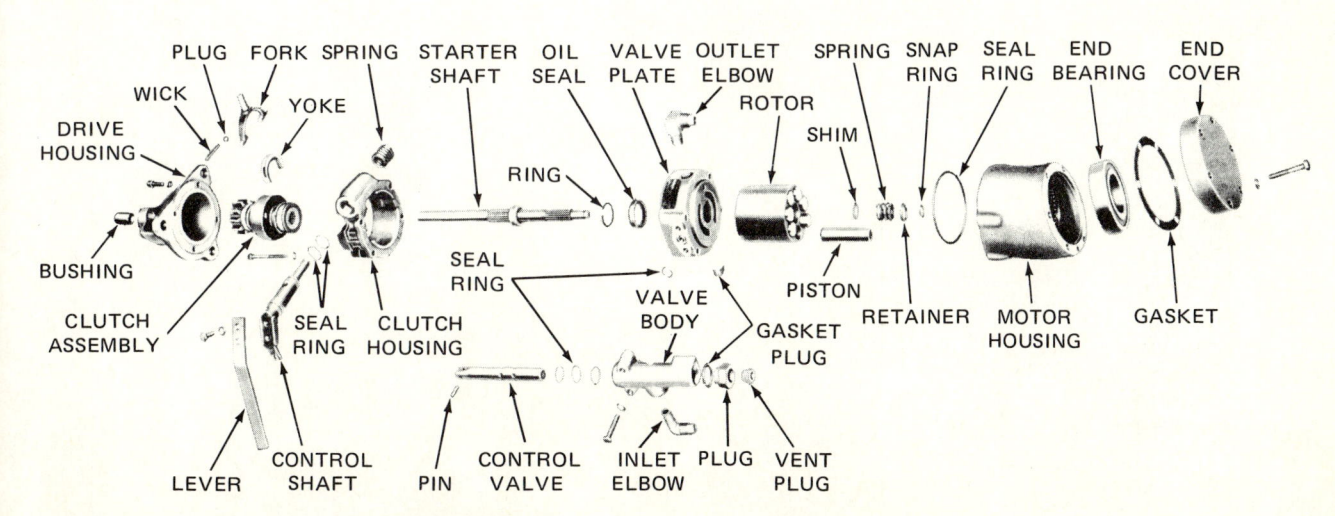

Fig. 43-2 Exploded view of hydraulic starting motor. *(Detroit Diesel Allison, Division of General Motors Corporation.)*

12. It sometimes, though not often, happens that the air starting motor remains in operation (until all air from the reservoir is exhausted) after the operator has already released the push-button valve. Why would this condition cause a continuous air supply to the air motor?

13. What maintenance procedures will prevent the oil from becoming contaminated?

14. List five causes for low or absent accumulator pressure when the engine is operating.

15. List the reasons why there might be no cranking pressure but the system pressure could still show 1500 psi [10,342 kPa].

16. Why are the following safety precautions mandatory? *(a)* When removing any component from the hydraulic starting system for service, first make certain that the hydraulic pressure is released. *(b)* When servicing the accumulator, release the nitrogen pressure before disassembling the accumulator.

17. When servicing the vane-type engine-driven hydraulic pump, what checks must you make to determine the serviceability of the components?

18. Using the disassembled components shown in Fig. 43-2 (see p. 111) as a guide, outline why the following components could reduce the cranking speed of the motor: *(a)* end bearing, *(b)* motor housing bearing, *(c)* bushing and drive housing, *(d)* rotor, *(e)* valve plate, *(f)* starter shaft, *(g)* control valve.

19. Assuming that the accumulator is serviced, the reservoir cleaned, and the components reconnected, you are now ready to prepare the system before cranking the engine. List the steps you must follow in order to make the hydraulic starting system operational.

ASSIGNMENT 44
COLD-WEATHER STARTING AIDS

1. Briefly outline the operating principle behind a block heater and an oil heater.
2. Why should you use extreme caution when using an ether aerosol can to start an engine?
3. Outline the step-by-step procedure in using a hand pump as a starting aid.
4. What problems might you encounter when using the hand pump?
5. Why is "Quick Start" considered to be safer than ether aerosol or a hand pump?
6. What is the glow plug's greatest disadvantage as a cold-weather starting aid?
7. Using Fig. 44-1, complete the starting system by drawing in the missing cables and wires needed for the glow-plug circuit.
8. Again on Fig. 44-1, draw the voltmeter connection you would make in order to check the (a) actuating circuits of the glow-plug solenoid, (b) resistance of the solenoid when engaged, (c) voltage drop at the glow plug.
9. What could cause a 12.1-V reading at the positive side of the glow plug solenoid when the battery open voltage is 12.8 V?
10. When more than one glow plug is used, why are they connected in parallel?
11. If the specifications for the glow plug were 4-Ω resistance with a battery voltage of 12 V, how many amperes will the glow plug draw and how much power will it develop?
12. Give two advantages to the "Quick Start" cold-weather starting aid over the glow plug.

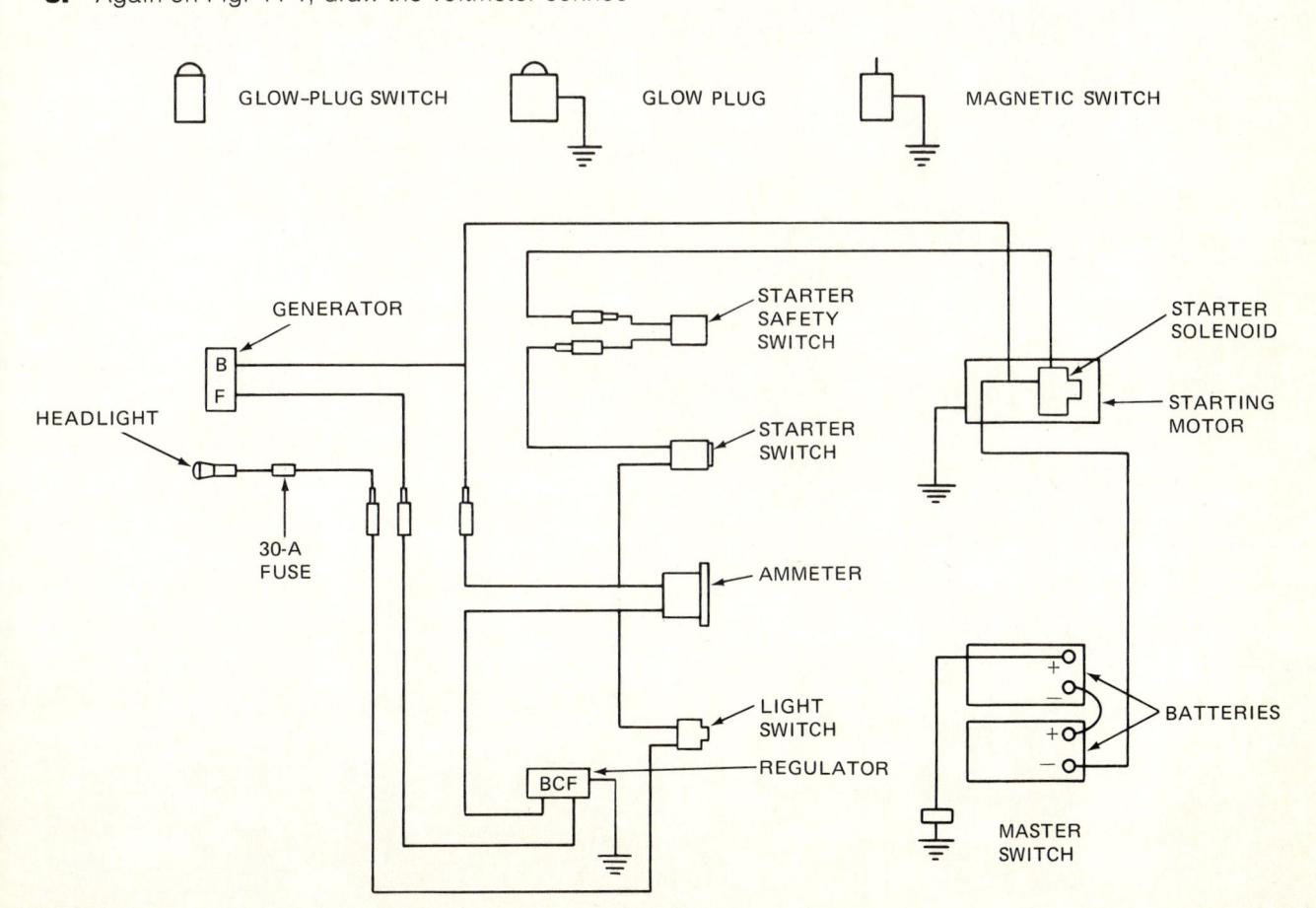

Fig. 44-1 Electrical system circuit diagram. *(Allis-Chalmers Corp. Engine Division.)*

ASSIGNMENT 45
CHARGING SYSTEM

1. Define *ac generator (alternator)*.
2. Define *rectification*.
3. Define *alternating current* and *direct current*.
4. List a number of reasons why direct current is used on truck, tractor, and marine installations.
5. List the major advantages of an alternator over the dc generator.
6. Explain why alternating electromagnetic induction occurs when the conductor is moved into the magnetic field and then moved out of the magnetic field, or when the magnetic field is rotated within the conductor. (Refer to Fig. 45-1.)
7. How can you determine the polarity and therefore the direction of current flow?

Three factors which will increase the induced voltage (current flow) are (1) the speed with which the conductor cuts across the magnetic lines of force or vice versa (that is, where the magnetic lines of force cut across the conductor), (2) the number of conductors that cut across the lines of force, and (3) the strength of the magnetic field.

8. Explain why each of these three factors will increase induced voltage.
9. How is the maximum current output in an alternator controlled?

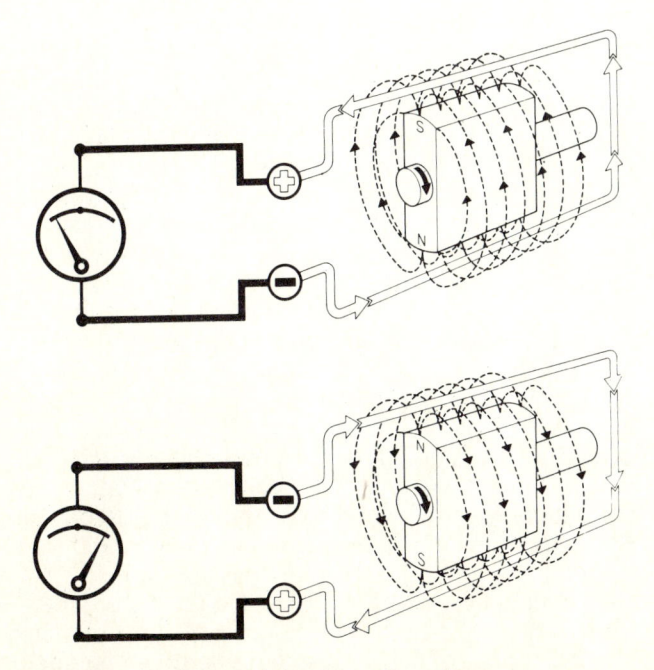

Fig. 45-1 Basic principle of an alternator.

10. Discuss the electrical connections of an A field circuit and of a B field circuit. What advantage has one over the other?
11. Discuss the construction of a rotor which uses brushes to excite the field.
12. When there is a current flow in the circuit, why does one pole piece become a north pole and the other a south pole?
13. What are the electrical differences between a Y- and a delta-wound stator?
14. Why are three-phase stators used instead of single-phase stators?
15. Why do some stators have a different number of poles and coils than others?
16. Define the following terms: (a) phase, (b) cycle, (c) frequency.
17. Give a brief outline on the atomic structure of (a) P material, and (b) N material.
18. Explain why P or N material, placed in a circuit, will cause electrons to flow from the negative to the positive terminal but there will be only a movement of holes within the P material.
19. What prevents the free electrons and/or the remaining holes from crossing the junction?
20. Which type of material (N or P) is connected to the negative terminal of the battery when the diode is connected in forward bias?
21. Why does the diode block the electron flow when it is connected in reverse bias?
22. How do manufacturers identify and discern between positive and negative diodes?
23. As mentioned previously, three-stator phases are used in all alternators; therefore, a minimum of three negative and three positive diodes are required. Why are at least three negative and three positive diodes needed?
24. Why is the cooling fan designed to draw air from the diode or regulator side of the alternator toward the drive side of the alternator?
25. Why do some alternators have separate heat sinks for the negative diode set and for the positive diode set?
26. Why is it important for you to know which diode is in the insulated heated sink that is connected to the output terminal (B terminal)?
27. On a battery with negative-ground polarity, what type of diode must be in the heat sink which is connected to the battery terminal of the alternator?
28. Explain your answer to Prob. 27.
29. Assume that you originally have two alternators of the same design, both using a Y stator connection, and that you change one to a delta stator connection.

115

You then test both alternators on the test stand, using the following specifications: 12-V, 3.5-A field current; 3500-rpm, 15-V, 80-A output. Assume that the actual testing shows that the alternator with the delta stator connection produces a current output of 140 A and the alternator having a Y connection produces 80 A. Why does the alternator having the delta-wound stator connection produce a higher current output?

30. What checks or tests should be made before testing the alternator and regulator?

When the procedure just mentioned has not revealed the cause of the undercharged battery condition, connect the test instruments to check the voltage-regulator setting and the alternator-specified maximum (current) output.

31. On Fig. 45-2, draw in the test-instrument connections you would use in order to check the output voltage of the alternator.
32. Why should you operate the engine for at least 10 minutes before taking the final voltage reading?
33. Explain how, with the aid of an ohmmeter, you would determine which type of field current is used on the alternator.
34. On Fig. 45-2, draw in the necessary connection changes to perform an alternator output test.
35. Describe how you would make an output test using the following specifications: 80-A, 15-V, 1200-W, 12-V field current (3.2 to 3.5 A), 3200 rpm.
36. Why must the batteries have a counterelectromotive force (cemf) of at least 12 V before making an alternator output test?
37. Outline the procedure and discuss the precautions you must take to remove an alternator from one of your shop engines.
38. Disassemble a training alternator or the alternator you have removed from one of your shop engines. Outline your disassembly procedure.
39. What parts, if damaged or worn, would necessitate the replacement of the rotor assembly?
40. When testing the rotor for a shorted circuit, how is the ohmmeter connected?

41. How do you know if the field-coil resistance is correct? (Use the specifications given for the output test in Prob. 35.)
42. What test for checking the rotor for a shorted field coil is more reliable than an ohmmeter?
43. Why must the runout of the slip ring be within specification?
44. Why must the slip-ring surface have a mirror finish?
45. List the tests you must make to ensure that the brush holder is correctly installed.
46. Why is it unnecessary to seat the brushes to the slip ring on an ac alternator?
47. List the checks you must make after the brushes are inserted into or screwed to the brush holders.
48. Upon examining the stator, what damage or malfunctions would you look for (apart from one or more discolored phase coils) to determine if the stator assembly should be replaced?

The stator should always be tested with an ohmmeter or test light for an open or grounded circuit.

49. Why is it not possible to test the stator for a shorted circuit?
50. Outline the steps to check a delta-wound stator for an open circuit.
51. Why cannot diodes, rectifiers, or heat sinks be properly checked when the stator leads are connected?
52. If you were testing diodes, how would you classify the problem in each of the following: (a) equally high resistance in both directions, (b) equally low resistance in both directions, (c) high resistance in one direction and, say, about 7-Ω resistance in the other direction?
53. Describe your installation procedure for installing one diode (from an alternator in your shop) into the heat sink.
54. Why must you hold the stem of the diode with a pair of pliers when resoldering the stator connection?
55. How could the following defects affect the current output of the alternator: (a) bolts holding the heat sink in position but the heat sink is broken, (b) partly destroyed insulation between the heat sink and the slip-ring end frame, (c) partly shorted, grounded, or open battery terminal.
56. How would the alternator output be affected when the (a) transit condenser is open, shorted, or has high leakage, (b) transit diode is open, grounded, or shorted?
57. How would you support the rotor when pressing a new bearing onto the rotor shaft?
58. By what method can you determine which heat sink (a) must be insulated, (b) is to be connected to the battery terminal when both require insulation?
59. At what time during the assembly would you install the fan and the drive pulley?
60. Outline the steps you would follow before reassembling a shop alternator, in order to prevent damage occurring to the brushes and the brush holder.

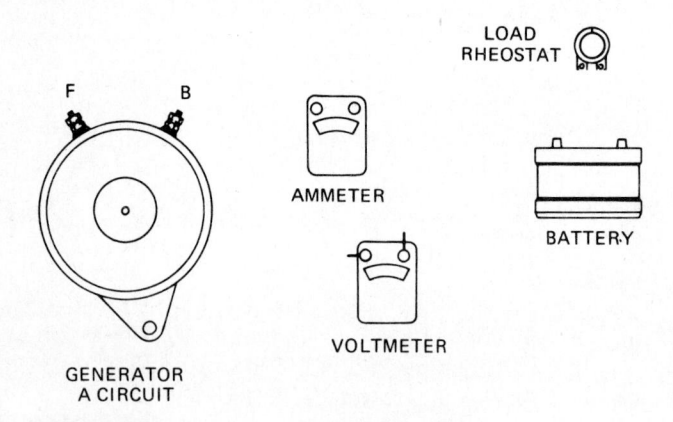

Fig. 45-2 Components required to perform an alternator output test.

ASSIGNMENT 46
REGULATORS

1. Why must the alternator voltage be within a specified value, for example, 14.6 to 15.0 V?

2. How can you determine if the alternator voltage is adjusted (a) too high, (b) too low?

3. List five reasons why transistor regulators are used instead of vibrating voltage regulators or transistorized regulators.

4. What purpose do resistors and capacitors serve within a transistor regulator?

5. Draw the symbol for a zener diode and explain how the zener diode reacts to system voltage in regard to its conductivity.

6. What is the difference between an NPN and a PNP transistor?

7. How does the manufacturer change the current-flow ratio between the emitter to the collector circuit and the emitter to the base circuit?

8. A transistor can be tested by using a test light or an ohmmeter. List the precautions you must exercise when using a test light to check the serviceability of a transistor.

9. Describe how to test a NPN transistor using an ohmmeter. Include in the explanation which ohmmeter test lead (positive or negative) is connected to the emitter, to the collector, or to the base when testing.

10. Why have manufacturers changed their alternator design to an (a) A-type field circuit, (b) integral charging system?

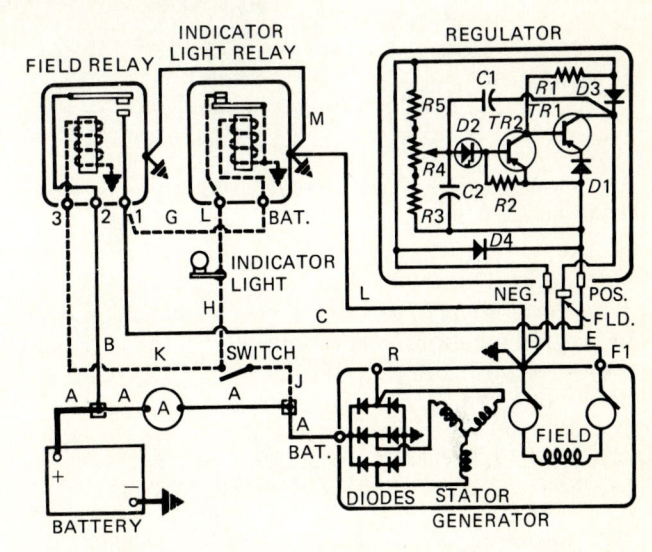

Fig. 46-2 Typical older-type wiring diagram showing internal circuits using a field relay and light relay. *(Delco Remy Division of General Motors.)*

An integral charging system of the 27/SI series type 200 is shown in Fig. 46-1, and a different type of charging system is shown in Fig. 46-2. There are some minor differences between these two systems.

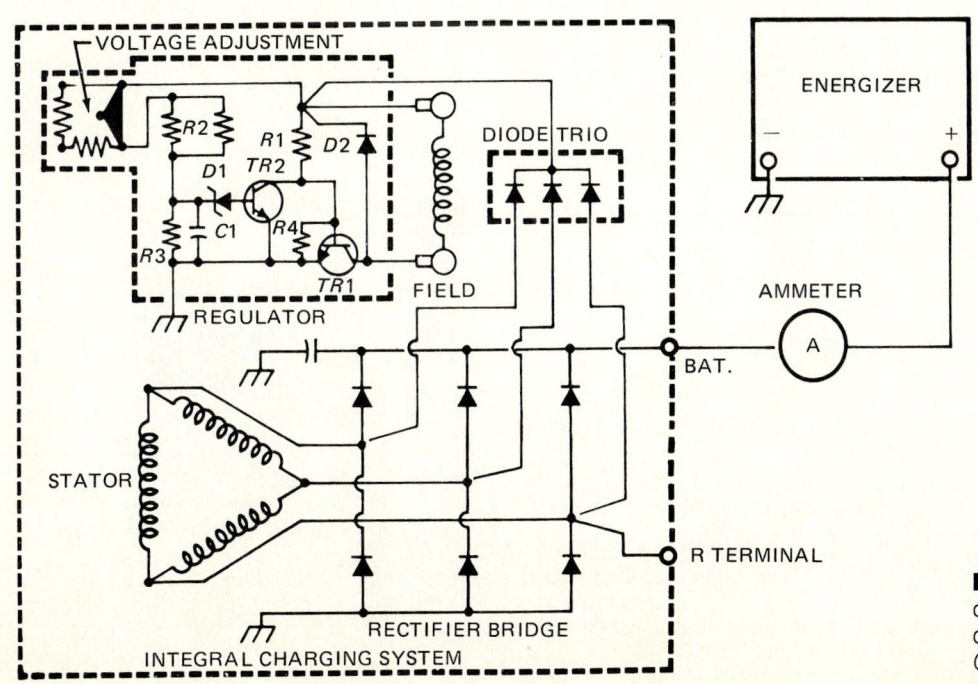

Fig. 46-1 Typical 27/SI wiring diagram showing internal circuits. *(Delco Remy Division of General Motors.)*

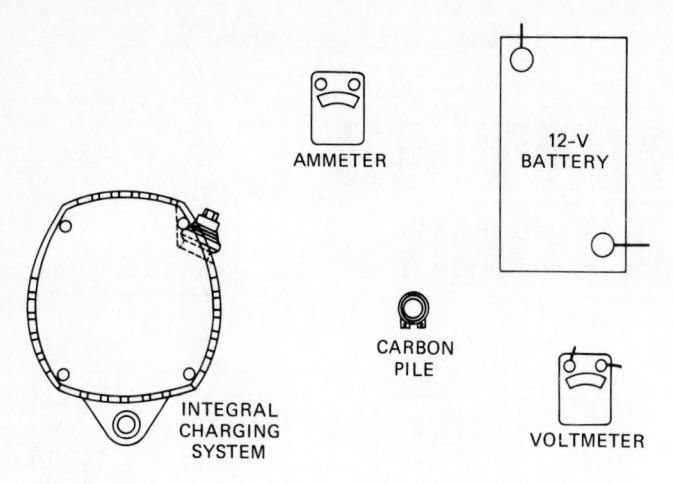

Fig. 46-3 Components required to perform alternator output test.

11. List the major electrical differences which exist between the integral charging system (Fig. 46-1) and the older-type charging system (Fig. 46-2). One example is given.

INTEGRAL CHARGING SYSTEM	OLDER-TYPE CHARGING SYSTEM
stator has delta connection	stator has Y connection

12. What advantage, in regard to alternator voltage control, has the integral charging system by having the alternator output voltage directed over the voltage adjustment and over the two parallel resistors (R2) onto the zener diode?

13. When the voltage adjustment is in the position shown in Fig. 46-1, why is the regulator adjusted to its highest voltage control?

14. Describe (when the alternator is operating) the current flow of the field circuit when the output voltage is (a) below regulator adjustment, (b) at the (adjusted voltage) regulator setting.

15. Using different colored pencils, draw, on Fig. 46-1, the field-circuit current flow under both conditions mentioned in Prob. 14.

16. On Fig. 46-3, draw in the necessary connections to check the (a) regulated alternator voltage, (b) alternator current output.

17. Explain how you would adjust the regulator in order to reduce the alternator voltage to its minimum voltage control. (Refer to Fig. 46-4.)

When the alternator is not within 10 percent of its specified current output, insert a screwdriver into the test hole. (Refer to Fig. 46-1.) If the current subsequently increases to the rated specification, this indicates that the alternator is operating satisfactorily. In this case, the cause of the reduced or zero output must lie in the regulator.

18. What purpose does the screwdriver serve when you insert it into the test hole?

19. On Fig. 46-1, indicate the point where the screwdriver makes contact within the regulator.

20. What advantages does a brushless alternator have over a slip-ring-type alternator?

21. Why do some manufacturers recommend remagnetizing the rotor after the alternator is reassembled?

22. Describe how to remagnetize a brushless rotor.

23. What is the purpose of the 12/24-V charging system?

24. (a) How are the TR transformer coils connected (series, parallel, delta, or Y)? (b) To which points are the primary coil leads connected? (c) To which points are the secondary coil leads connected?

25. Which method is used to rectify the transformer voltage?

26. What voltage is used to energize the magnetic switch?

27. What voltage is used to energize the cranking-motor solenoid switch?

28. (a) What test will determine if the alternator or the TR unit is not performing satisfactorily? (b) Outline the instrument connections for answer (a) above.

29. List the checks you should make before installing the alternator to the engine.

30. Why are the pulley alignment and the belt tension so important to the alternator life and the belt life?

31. Why should newly installed drive belts be rechecked after about 8 hours of operation?

32. Why should the charging voltage be rechecked after a new or rebuilt alternator is installed to the equipment?

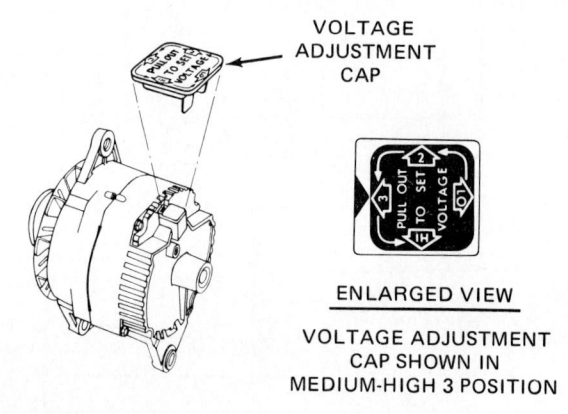

Fig. 46-4 Enlarged view of the voltage adjustment cap shown in medium-high (3) position. *(Delco Remy Division of General Motors.)*

ASSIGNMENT 47
INSTRUMENTS
AND THEIR CIRCUITS

1. List the four instrument gauges essential to a diesel engine.
2. Using a school training engine, record the location of the oil-pressure and coolant-temperature sensors.
3. What is the main difference between an oil-pressure sensor and a fuel-level sensor?
4. List four gauges or warning lights that could be used on motor vehicles in addition to those which are standard.
5. Outline how to check the oil-pressure sensor.
6. Why are some engines equipped with an engine shutdown system?
7. How is the shutdown on (a) Cummins, (b) International Harvester, and (c) Detroit Diesel engines accomplished?
8. When attempting to start the engine shown in DM2 Fig. 47-5, why must the keyswitch be in the "S" position?

Name _____ Date _____ Class _____

ASSIGNMENT 48
HAND TOOLS

1. If you were to buy an entire set of new hand tools, what five factors should you take into consideration?

2. Elaborate on, or give the reason for, the following general precautions: (a) Clean and store tools which are not being used. (b) Keep the tools sharp and properly ground, and the handles securely fastened. (c) Use a clamp to hold the work. (d) Pull a wrench; do not push it. (e) Keep proper footing and balance at all times. (f) Do not use a chisel or a punch without using safety glasses. (g) Use the right tools.

3. Compare the major differences in the design and the purpose of a (a) center punch, (b) starter punch, (c) pin punch, (d) alignment punch, (e) flat cold chisel, (f) cap chisel.

4. Discuss why the chisels in Fig. 48-1a and b are not cutting satisfactorily.

5. Why should the chisel edge be ground to a slightly convex shape?

6. A file can easily be ruined if it is stored improperly. How would you store a file?

7. On Fig. 48-2 draw the fundamental characteristics of a (a) bastard-cut file, (b) single-cut file, (c) double-cut file, (d) smooth-cut file.

8. What are the differences between (a) a mill file and a flat file, (b) a round file and a half-round file?

9. Explain how you would use a double-cut flat file to (a) resurface a flat mounting flange, (b) draw-file the surface.

10. Name six common types of screwdrivers.

11. List four tasks for which a screwdriver often is, but should *not* be, used.

12. Why is it important that a screwdriver fit properly in the screw slot?

13. Draw a properly ground and dressed screwdriver.

14. Discuss the four factors you must take into consideration when selecting a hacksaw blade for cutting metal. (Refer to Fig. 48-3.)

15. How would you determine if you could use a hacksaw to cut a specific metal?

16. What method could you apply to increase the number of cutting teeth which contact the surface to be cut?

17. Explain why the cutting speed and pressure are important with regard to blade cutting action and blade line.

18. Why must you start a new cut if you break the hacksaw blade while cutting?

19. Name the general purpose of each of the following pliers: (a) combination pliers, (b) grip pliers

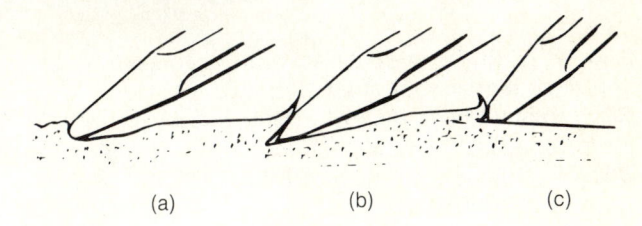

Fig. 48-1 (a), (b), (c) Cutting results.

(water-pump pliers), (c) diagonal pliers, (d) needle-nose pliers, (e) snap-ring pliers, (f) vise grips.

20. By what methods can the force of a hammer blow be increased?

21. List some tasks for which a hammer should *not* be used.

22. Outline the major differences between a box-end and a combination wrench.

23. Why does the combination wrench have an advantage over the box-end and open-end wrenches?

24. Why should you use a flare-nut wrench instead of an open-end wrench to loosen or tighten a fitting?

25. If, because of circumstances, you are forced to use an open-end wrench to loosen or tighten a bolt, in which way must you place the wrench onto the bolt head?

26. Why, in your opinion, is a socket-drive wrench set the most used and the safest type of wrench?

27. When using a hex bolt which is torqued, say to 200 lb·ft, which type of socket wrench and handle would you select to loosen the bolt?

28. When would you use a (a) flex-socket wrench, (b) deep-socket wrench, (c) speeder handle, (d) crow-foot wrench?

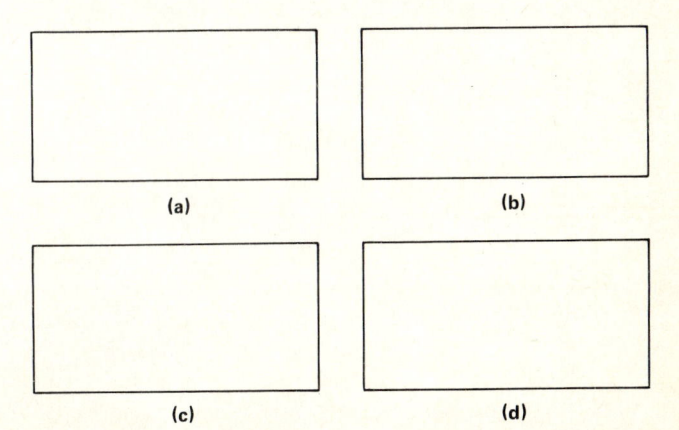

Fig. 48-2

121

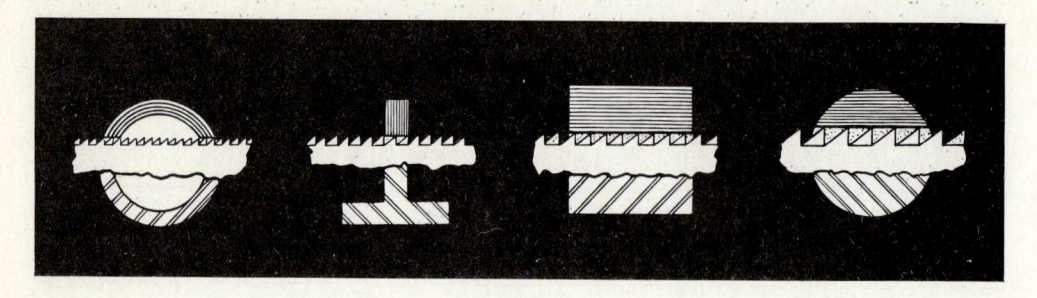

Fig. 48-3 Correctly selected hacksaw blades. *(Owatonna Tool Company, Tools and Equipment Div.)*

29. Outline the precaution you would take to prevent a socket wrench from slipping.
30. Explain how you would check a torque wrench for accuracy.
31. Explain the principle of Hooke's law as it applies to a torque wrench.
32. Why is it important, when pulling on the torque-wrench handle, that your *(a)* direction of pull is 90° to the measure element, *(b)* pulling grip is exactly in the middle of the torque-wrench handle?
33. Assume that you have to torque a bolt to 250 lb·ft [338.75 N·m] but that you only have a torque wrench which measures up to 150 lb·ft [203.2 N·m]. Explain how you would calculate the desired torque reading in pound-feet when using a 6-in [152.4-mm] extension.
34. When using a torque wrench with an adapter, what precaution must you take to achieve a precise torque reading?
35. How do you determine if a bolt is torqued to specification?
36. Explain why you must *(a)* follow the recommended torque sequence, *(b)* torque the bolts or nut in three passes.
37. What is the designed purpose of *(a)* an adjustable wrench, *(b)* a pipe wrench?
38. Why should you not use a pipe wrench or a vise grip to remove a stud?
39. Explain how you would remove a stud using a wedge-type stud remover.
40. List the five methods used to remove a broken stud.
41. List the preparations you should take before drilling the pilot hole.
42. If the chips or spiral resulting from drilling are not even, what is wrong with the drill?
43. Why is it necessary to *(a)* use a soft, medium-grain grinding wheel to sharpen a drill, *(b)* have a sharp and flat grinding-wheel surface?

Before sharpening a drill, you have to determine the point angle and the lip clearance angle required.

44. What point angle and lip clearance angle are appropriate when the drill will be used to drill a hole in *(a)* cast iron, *(b)* tool steel, *(c)* brass?
45. Why should you try to have the dead-center line 120° to 135° from the cutting lip (drill point) when grinding a drill for general purposes?
46. When is it necessary to drill a pilot hole?
47. What safety precautions will ensure that the hand drill will not twist out of your hand when drilling a 5/8-in hole?
48. Assume that you have to drill a hole (either small or large) using a drill press with a variable drill speed. How would you calculate the drill speed when drilling a 3/4-in hole?
49. What precautionary measurement must you take when enlarging a hole with a drill?
50. Explain the purpose of a reamer.
51. Explain how you would use an adjustable reamer to bring the bushing diameter to 1.500 in [38.1 mm] when the existing bore is 1.495 in [37.973 mm].
52. Why should you never turn the reamer counterclockwise?
53. List the precautions you must take when using a *(a)* chisel-edge scraper, *(b)* flexible carbon scraper, *(c)* standard wire brush, *(d)* carbon brush.

ASSIGNMENT 49
SHOP TOOLS

1. Explain how you would prepare and adjust the steam cleaner in your shop so that you could properly steam-clean components.

2. Explain why you should (a) shut off the electric switch only when the water that leaves the nozzle is cool, (b) place the components to be steam-cleaned on a wooden pallet, (c) not apply cold water to the components after you have steam-cleaned them, (d) apply a lubricant to the machine surfaces after they are steam-cleaned.

3. Explain why it is important to always follow the manufacturer's instructions.

4. List the steps and precautions you must take (a) when inserting and removing the components from the hot tank, (b) after you have removed the components.

5. List the preparations you must make before you glass-bead a component.

6. List the precautions you must take while glass-beading the components.

7. List seven lifting or pressing tools that you may find in your workshop and state the purpose of each.

8. List five general safety precautions you must take or consider when lifting, pulling, or pushing an object.

9. Assume that you have to press the coolant pump impeller onto the shaft (see Fig. 49-1). Explain in detail the precautions you would take before and while pressing the bearing onto the shaft.

10. When pressing or pulling a bearing or gear from a shaft, which safety precautions must you take to protect yourself and others as well as the components?

11. When working on an engine, you may find that sometimes you cannot locate the suitable puller and/or attachment for a particular task. What three main factors must you take into consideration when selecting the puller and the attachment?

12. List the safety rules you must obey when performing the tasks shown in DM2 Fig. 49-6.

13. Outline seven safety precautions when using an electric drill.

14. List the protective steps you would take to prevent an accident and to protect the engine components from contamination when using a grinder.

15. Name the type of material used and its respective purpose, when the grinding wheel has an identification color of (a) red, (b) white, (c) green.

16. Explain how you would check a grinding wheel for damage.

17. List the mandatory tasks to be completed during and after installation of a grinding wheel.

18. A bench vise is by far the most universal tool in any shop. List the purposes a vise (a) should be used for, (b) should never be used for.

19. Which type of protective devices are used to (a) extend the service life of an air or impact wrench, (b) prevent the components from being overtorqued?

20. For what reason should you use only impact sockets and adapters and not standard socket wrenches or adapters?

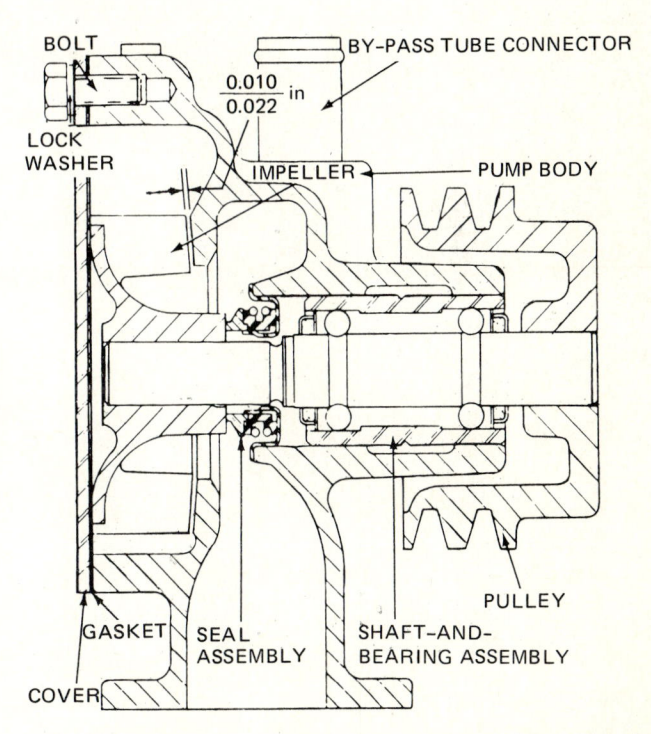

Fig. 49-1 Sectional view of coolant pump. *(International Harvester Co.)*

ASSIGNMENT 50
MEASURING TOOLS

1. How would you protect the measuring tools from damage during storage?

2. Three steel rulers with different graduations are shown in Fig. 50-1. What is the smallest measurement you can make with each of these steel rulers?

3. What are the measurements indicated by the letters A to L on Fig. 50-1?

4. Convert the fractional measurements (J, K, L) indicated on Fig. 50-1c to decimals.

5. Explain the method you would use to measure a distance using a thickness gauge (feeler gauge), for example, when measuring the backlash of the timing gears.

6. What information is relayed by the number stamped on the gauge blade?

7. What is the main difference between a caliper and a divider?

8. Explain how you would find the correct diameter of the bore shown in Fig. 50-2, using an outside caliper.

9. List the various methods you could use to measure the distance of the outside caliper.

10. What precaution must you take when taking the measurement from the outside caliper?

11. A combination set with a square head, center head, and protractor head is a versatile tool suitable for repair work. List the functions of the (a) square head, (b) center head, (c) protractor head.

12. Assume that you have to adjust the preload of an idler gear which has a specification of 30 lb·in [3.4 N·m]. If the gear has a diameter of 6 in [152.4 mm], explain the method you would use to measure the rolling torque of the idler gear. (Refer to Fig. 50-3.)

13. What would the spring scale reading be in pounds and in kilograms when the rolling torque is 30 lb·in [3.4 N·m]?

14. Name the three most common micrometers and give the designed purpose of each.

15. Regardless of the type of micrometer you use, the first thing you must check is that it is adjusted correctly. Explain how to check the accuracy of an inside micrometer.

16. Give the reason for each of the following pre-

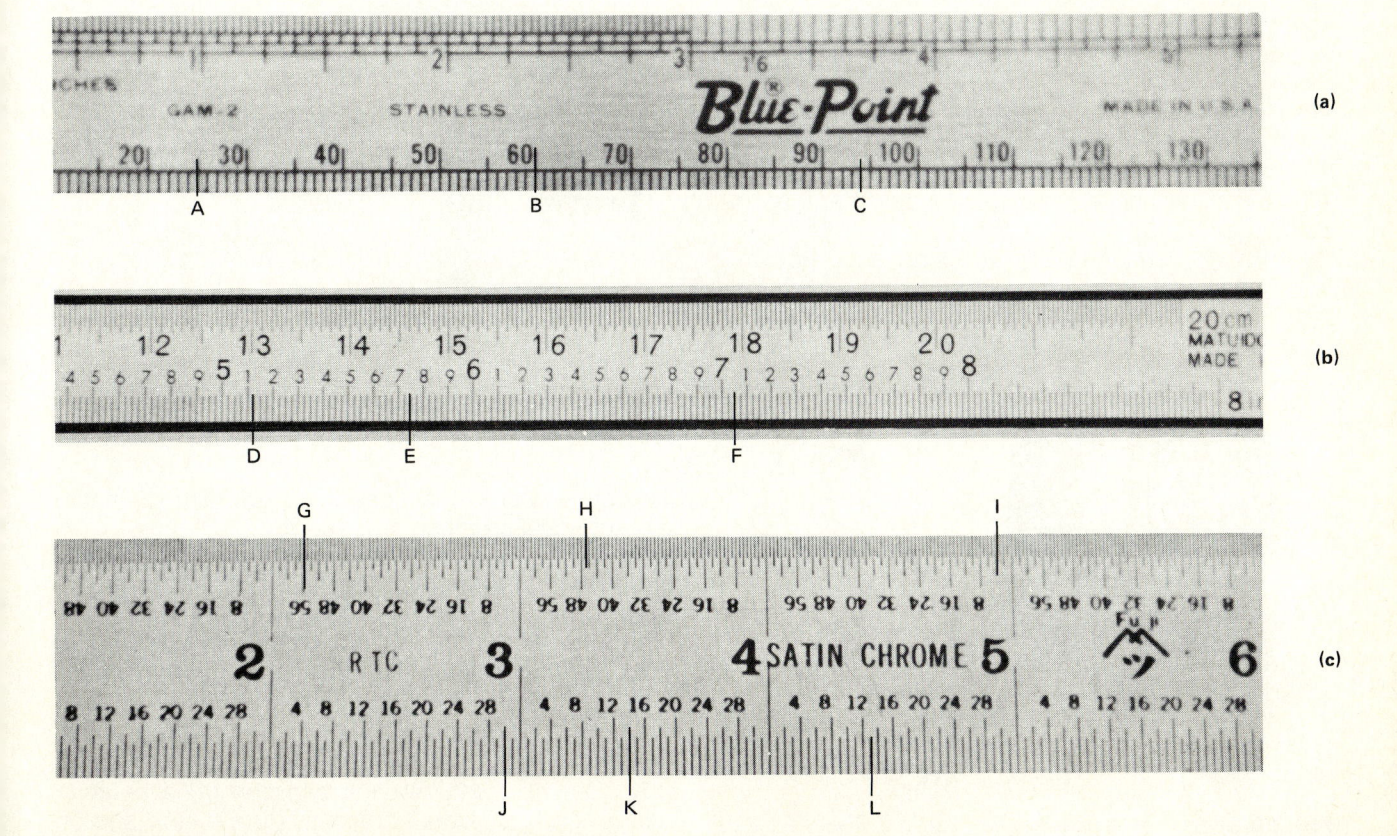

Fig. 50-1 Steel rulers.

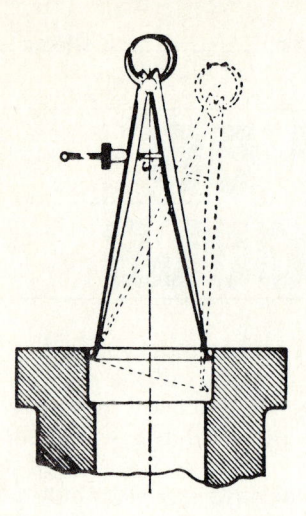

Fig. 50-2 Measuring the bore diameter using an outside caliper.

cautions: *(a)* Do not hold the micrometer too long in your hands or place it where it will become heated. *(b)* Hold the frame with one hand while turning the thimble with the other hand. *(c)* Turn the thimble lightly between the thumb and first finger until the face of the anvil and thimble contact the work. *(d)* When a ratchet is attached, turn it until at least two ticks can be heard. *(e)* Do not slide the micrometer excessively back and forth across the object. *(f)* Take the reading before removing the micrometer from the object. *(g)* Do not spin the micrometer.

17. What are the main differences between *(a)* a micrometer and a vernier micrometer, *(b)* a micrometer graduated in hundredths of a millimeter and a micrometer graduated in thousandths of a millimeter?

18. How much, in thousandths of an inch and in hundredths of a millimeter, is the spindle moved when the thimble is turned one complete turn?

19. What are the precise micrometer readings indicated in Fig. 50-4*a*, *b*, *c*, and *d*?

20. When measuring a bore using an inside micrometer, what precautions must you take to ensure that the measurement is correct?

21. Explain the main difference between a micrometer and a depth micrometer.

22. Explain how you would measure the lifter height shown in Fig. 50-5, using a depth micrometer.

23. What are the precise depth-micrometer readings indicated in Fig. 50-6*a*, *b*, and *c*?

24. How do you obtain a dial-indictor measurement?

25. Outline the difference between *(a)* a balance and a continuous dial indicator, *(b)* a metric and an English dial indicator, *(c)* a dial indicator graduated

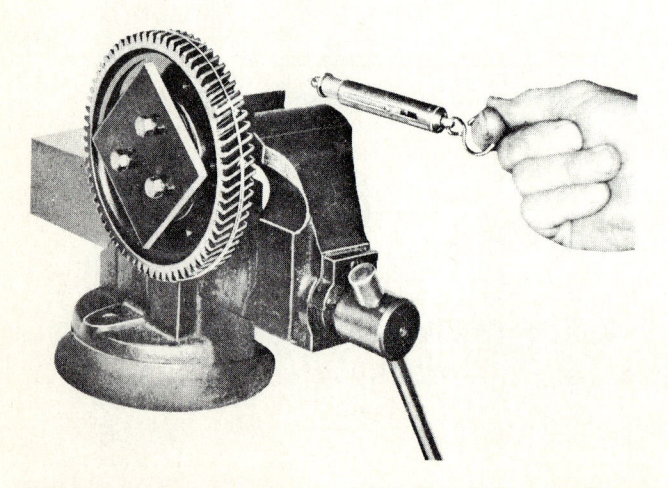

Fig. 50-3 Measuring gear preload. *(Detroit Diesel Allison, Division of General Motors Corporation.)*

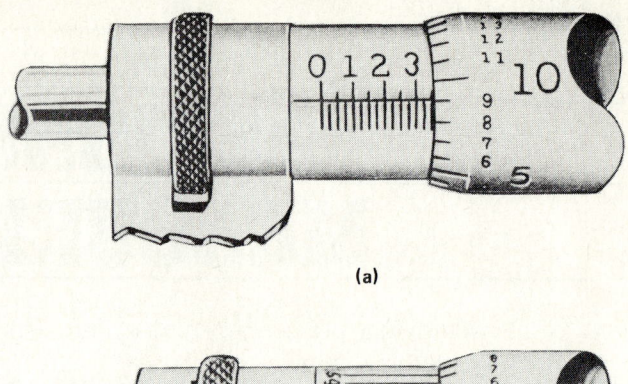

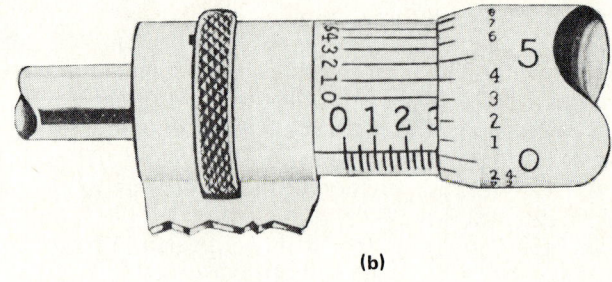

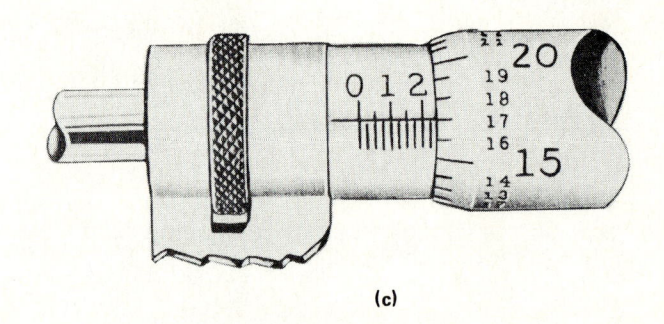

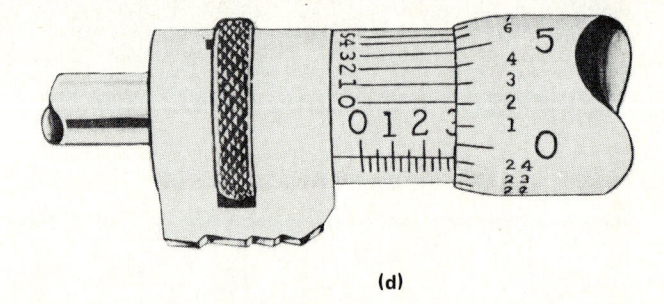

Fig. 50-4 Reading micrometers.

Name _____ Date _____ Class _____

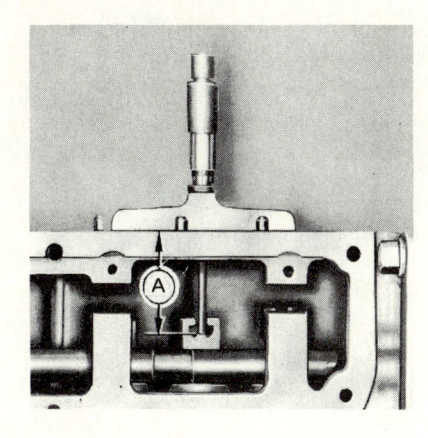

Fig. 50-5 Measuring lifter height. *(Caterpillar Tractor Co.)*

of a fuel-injection-pump camshaft, and include your method of setting up the dial indicator.

28. Explain how you would set the dial bore gauge to 5.160 in [131.064 mm] using a master micrometer or an outside micrometer.

29. Outline the procedure to measure one diameter of a cylinder sleeve using the dial bore gauge.

30. Assume that you have taken several outside measurements with a vernier caliper, and that the measurements are locked in as shown in Fig. 50-7.

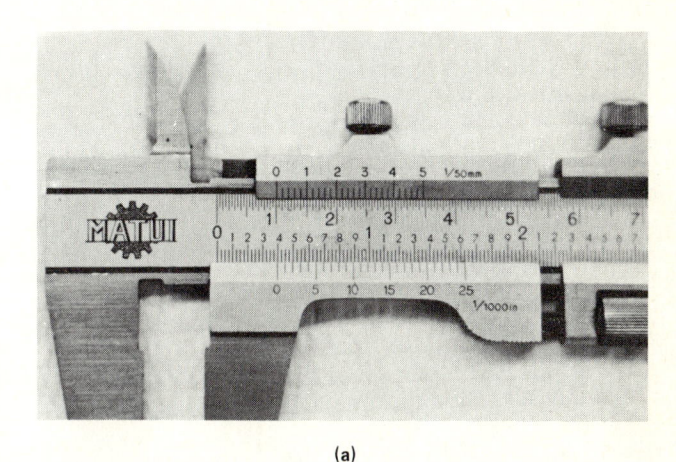

in 0.001 mm and one graduated in 0.0005 mm, *(d)* a dial indicator graduated in 0.01 mm and one graduated in 0.002 mm.

26. "You can only expect a precise dial-indicator reading when the attachment and/or holder is well fastened and the contact point is 90° to the contact surface." Give the reasoning behind the above statement (that is, why, under other circumstances, is the dial-indicator reading incorrect).

27. Outline the procedure to measure the end play

(a)

(b)

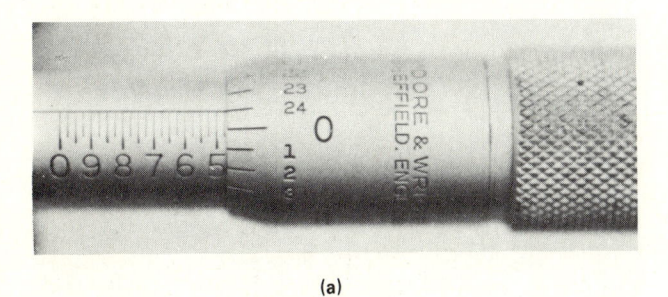

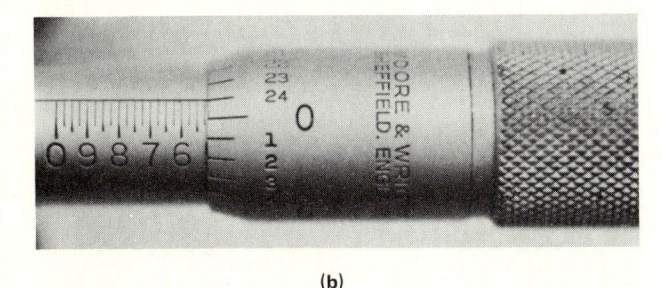

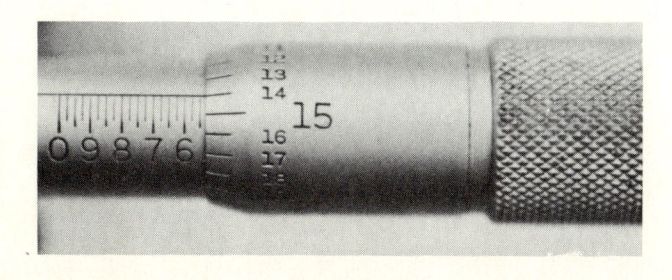

(c)

Fig. 50-6 Reading depth micrometers.

(a)

(b)

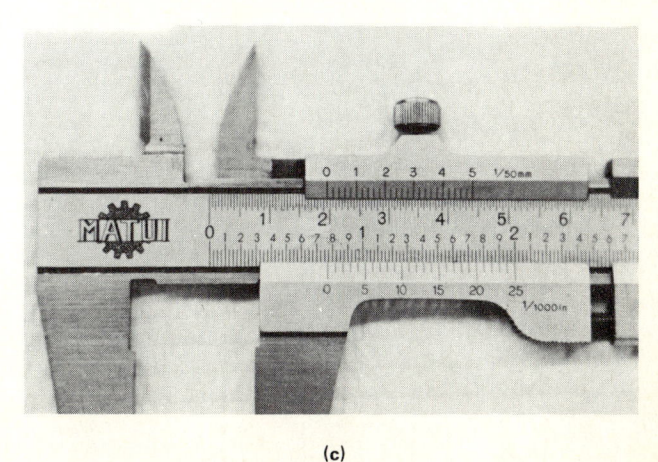

(c)

Fig. 50-7 Reading vernier calipers.

127

Give the exact reading of each measurement illustrated.

31. Explain the major difference between metric and English vernier calipers.

32. Outline the required steps you must take before and while making an outside measurement using a vernier caliper.

33. Give the exact reading of the dial-indicator vernier caliper shown in Fig. 50-8.

34. Give several situations in which you would use a *(a)* hole gauge, *(b)* telescopic gauge.

35. Why is the following statement of such importance with regard to precise measurement? "To achieve a precise measurement with either measuring tool, you must have a fine sense of feel."

36. Explain how you would adjust a hole gauge to 9.85 mm.

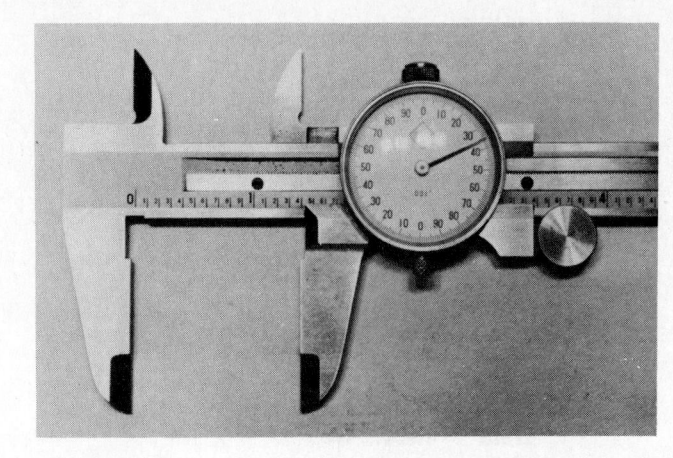

Fig. 50-8 Reading a dial-indicator vernier caliper.

ASSIGNMENT 51
FASTENERS, TAPS, AND DIES

1. Name the five methods used to join two metals together.
2. What is the main difference between (a) a bolt and a screw, (b) a screw and a setscrew, (c) a round-head and a flat-head screw, (d) a stud and a screw, (e) a 12-point head and a square-head screw, (f) a head-locking bolt and a hex-head screw?
3. On Fig. 51-1, indicate what is meant by the following (with respect to bolts or screws): (a) bolt size, (b) thread length (shank), (c) head design, (d) head size, (e) minor diameter, (f) major diameter, (g) pitch, (h) threads per inch (thread series), (i) body.
4. Define the following: (a) thread class, (b) NF, NC, N.
5. Any type of fastening can become loose or fail entirely. Name at least eight causes or reasons why a thread fastener could lose its holding power.
6. Name the two devices besides a thread file which are used to restore a damaged thread.
7. Assume that you have a damaged thread on a cylinder head stud which is ½-in NF. Explain how you would restore the damaged thread using a thread file.
8. When you are forced to make a ½-in NC puller bolt, what preparation must you make on the round stock?
9. Outline the steps for (a) installing the dies into the collet, (b) adjusting the dies.
10. Why should you turn the die stock slowly in a clockwise direction until the turning effort signifies poor cutting, and then turn only one land in reverse direction?
11. Explain the adjustment and checks to be made when preparing to make the second thread cut, to ensure that the thread is not too loose or too tight.
12. State the purpose of a nut.
13. What is meant by nut (a) grade, (b) size, (c) thread series?
14. List the common applications of the following nuts: (a) palnut, (b) jam nut, (c) self-locking nut, (d) castle nut.
15. When should you use (a) a flat washer, (b) an internal lock washer, (d) an external lock washer?

Hand Tapping Drilling a hole in the right place and of the right size is especially important if hand-tapping is to be done.

16. List some reasons why you may have to drill a hole and then hand-tap it.
17. If you do not have a drill-size chart for selecting the correct drill size, how would you determine the drill size if, for example, you have a ½-in NC thread to tap?
18. Explain why you could have a poor or damaged thread when (a) the drill is not properly sharpened, (b) the drill is dull, (c) cutting oil is not used when drilling the hole?
19. Assume that you have drilled a blind hole which requires tapping. Explain the procedure for hand-tapping this blind hole.
20. Which type of cutting oil is best when drilling or tapping a hole in (a) steel, (b) brass, (c) cast iron?
21. Name the three most common riveting methods used.

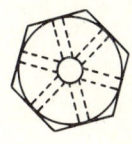

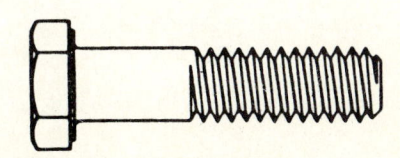

Fig. 51-1 Hex bolt.

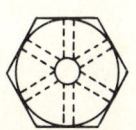

Fig. 51-2 Safety-wiring a hex bolt.

129

22. Regardless of the riveting method you choose, what five additional factors must you consider if you wish to achieve a good bond?

Locking Devices Palnuts, jam nuts, locknuts, etc., are locking devices; however, they cannot be used for all locking needs.

23. List the locking devices used to hold or position a *(a)* gear, *(b)* pulley (to a shaft), *(c)* shaft, *(d)* nut, *(e)* bolt, *(f)* screw.

24. On Fig. 51-2 (see p. 129), draw the correct way to safety-wire the hex bolt.

Name _____ Date _____ Class _____

ASSIGNMENT 52
CHECKS AND ADJUSTMENTS BEFORE STARTING THE ENGINE

1. Explain in detail how you would *(a)* bleed the coolant system (also describe why this is important), *(b)* prime the fuel-injection system of the engine, *(c)* prelubricate the turbocharger, *(d)* prelubricate the engine, *(e)* connect the battery to the engine.

2. Why should you disconnect the turbocharger return oil line before the engine is cranked over for the first time?

3. Under what circumstances will an engine fail to start even though it is correctly assembled, timed, and adjusted, and has a cranking speed of 200 rpm?

4. Once the engine has started, what instruments, including the dynamometer, must you watch closely during the warm-up period and why?

5. Why do some engine manufacturers recommend retorquing the cylinder head bolts and adjusting the valves (injectors) before beginning the engine run-in?

6. Perform a break-in run on an engine in your shop. Follow the manufacturer's recommended specification and procedure as well as the dynamometer report (Fig. 52-1). Record your test results.

7. Assume that the blowby of a phase run-in (that is, under a particular rpm and load condition) is higher than specified. Why must you backstep and repeat the last satisfactory run-in phase until the blowby is within specification?

8. Why must the engine be cooled down before it is shut off?

DYNAMOMETER REPORT

Date: _____ Customer: _____

WO # _____ Model _____ S/N _____

FP s/n _____ FP code _____ RPM _____ PSI _____ FLOW _____

Time	RPM	BHP	Oil psi	Water In	Temp. Out	Oil Temp.	Blow-by	Blk. PSI	Int. PSI	Fuel PSI	Fuel Cons.	Remarks

HP	RPM	% Power	Oil PSI	Block PSI	Blow-by	Int. PSI	Fuel PSI	Fuel Cons.	Smoke	Cooling System Inlet	Outlet	PSI

Engine Running Time: Hours _____ Minutes _____ Sight Glass Upper _____

	RPM	Oil
High Idle		
Idle		

Operator _____

Supervisor _____

Fig. 52-1 Dynamometer report.

Name _____ Date _____ Class _____

ASSIGNMENT 53
TROUBLESHOOTING, TESTING, AND ADJUSTING

1. List 10 questions you should ask the operator that could reveal the cause of the engine trouble.

2. What type of information would you look for in the engine log book and service record sheet?

3. Before beginning diagnosis of any alleged engine trouble, there are a number of superficial checks which should be made. List six.

Troubleshooting Chart It cannot be overemphasized that over 90 percent of all engine trouble can be prevented by periodic inspection and good maintenance. Furthermore, the time needed to do this is only a fraction of the downtime caused by the engine failure (Table 53-1).

4. Read carefully the following list of complaints. Then write the matching complaint *number* next to the appropriate cause and write what you would do to correct the complaint. One example is given.

COMPLAINTS
1. Engine will not turn
2. Engine will not start
3. Engine hard to start
4. Engine stops frequently
5. Engine stops suddenly
6. Engine overheats
7. Engine shows loss of power
8. Engine runs unevenly and vibrates excessively
9. Engine knocks
10. Engine parts show rapid wear
11. Insufficient air supply to cylinders
12. Engine temperature too high
13. Engine temperature too low
14. Overheating of lubricating oil
15. Excessive oil consumption
16. Engine misses
17. Excessive smoke under load
18. Excessive fuel consumption

CAUSES
1. Weak battery *1 Check batteries, starter, generator, and connections*
2. Restricted air intake _____
3. High exhaust back pressure _____
4. Thin air in hot weather or high altitude _____
5. Air leaks between cleaner and engine _____
6. Dirty crankcase breather _____
7. Out of fuel or short on fuel _____
8. Poor-quality fuel _____
9. Air leaks in suction line _____
10. Restricted fuel lines _____
11. Incorrect fuel pressure _____
12. External or internal fuel leaks _____
13. Plugged injector spray holes _____
14. Broken fuel pump drive shaft _____
15. Scored gear pump or worn gears _____
16. Loose injector inlet or drain connection _____
17. Wrong injector _____
18. Cracked injector body or cup _____
19. Mutilated injector-cup O ring _____
20. Faulty throttle linkage _____
21. Incorrectly assembled governor weights _____

133

Maintenance Schedule

TABLE 53-1 MAINTENANCE SCHEDULE

EQUIPMENT NO. _____ ENGINE SERIAL NO. _____
MECHANIC _____ MILEAGE, HOURS _____
TIME SPENT _____ CHECK PERFORMED _____
PARTS ORDER NO. _____ DATE _____

Cummins Automotive Engines

Check each operation as performed.

A—Daily	B—Check	C—Check	D—Check	E—Check	Seasonal
☐ Check Operator Report	☐ Repeat "A"	☐ Repeat "A" and "B"	☐ Repeat "A, B and C"	☐ Repeat "A, B, C and D"	☐ Spring and Fall
☐ Check Leaks and Correct	☐ Change Engine Oil	☐ Clean Engine	☐ Clean and Calibrate Injectors	☐ "In Chassis Inspection"	☐ Clean Cooling System
☐ Check Engine Oil Level	☐ Change Full-Flow Filter Elements	☐ Check Alternator and Cranking Motor Brushes and Commutators	☐ Replace Fuel Pump Screen and Magnet	☐ Check Engine Blow-By	☐ Check Hose
☐ Check Oil Bath Cleaner Oil Level	☐ Change By-Pass Filter Element	☐ Adjust Injectors, Crossheads and Valves	☐ Check Fuel Pump Calibration		☐ Clean Electrical Connections
☐ Check Completely for Damage	☐ Record Oil Pressure	☐ Check Exhaust Back Pressure	☐ Clean Turbocharger/Check Clearance		☐ Check Cold Starting Aid
	☐ Change Fuel Filter(s)	☐ Check Vibration Damper	☐ Inspect/Install Rebuilt Units as Necessary		☐ Check Thermal Controls
	☐ Check Air Piping and Mountings	☐ Check Fuel Manifold Pressure	☐ Replace Bellows and Calibrate Aneroid		☐ Check Mountings
	☐ Check Air Cleaner Restriction — Service Element(s)/Oil Level as Required	☐ Change Aneroid Oil and Replace Aneroid Breather	☐ Clean Oil Bath Air Cleaner		☐ Check Fan Mountings
	☐ Clean Crankcase Breather	☐ Check Aneroid Adjustment	☐ Rebuild or Replace Water Pump		☐ Check Crankshaft End Clearance
	☐ Check Throttle Linkage	☐ Inspect Water Pump, Idler Pulley and Fan Hub			
	☐ Change Water Filter [2]				
	☐ Check Engine Coolant				
	☐ Check and Adjust Belt Tension				
	☐ Adjust Injectors, Crossheads and Valves[3]				

Engine Series	Interval Basis[1]	B	C	D	E	
V6, V8 (470, 504, 555) VT-555	Miles	6000	30,000	90,000	180,000	Stop and Go or Shorthaul
	Hours	200	1,000	3,000	6,000	
	Calendar	3 Mos.	1 Year	2 Years	4 Years	
Super-250, NH, NT, V-903, VT-903	Miles	10,000	50,000	150,000	300,000	Line haul
	Hours	250	1,250	3,750	7,500	
	Calendar	3 Mos.	1 Year	2 Years	4 Years	

Notes:
1. Perform checks on operating basis of interval that occurs first. Normally calendar period is used only when mileage is less than 1/3 that suggested during the three (3) month period.
2. At any time cooling system is completely drained and/or flushed, use DCA pre-charge element until next "B" Check.
3. At first oil change or initial inspection, adjust injectors and valves, thereafter at "C" Check.

Name _____ Date _____ Class _____

22. High-speed governor set too low _____

23. Inoperative cranking motor or cranking-motor switch _____

24. Locked or seized engine _____

25. Engine control out of adjustment _____

26. Insufficient supply of fuel to injector nozzle _____

27. Improperly timed fuel-injection pump _____

28. Fuel transfer pump not operating properly _____

29. Insufficient air supply to cylinder _____

30. Incorrect valve lash _____

31. Poor compression _____

32. Worn parts in blower or turbocharger _____

To verify the correctness of your analysis you must test, measure, and adjust or service the components which you believe caused the trouble.

The following problems refer to testing and measuring.

5. Explain how to check for a restricted air-intake system (naturally aspirated engine).
6. Which visual checks may determine that an air-intake leak exists?
7. Explain how to test for a suspected air-intake leak between the engine and the air cleaner. (See Unit 18, Air-intake System.)
8. Explain the procedure to test (a) blower pressure, (b) turbocharger boost pressure.
9. Explain the procedure to check the mechanical condition of a turbocharger. (Refer to Fig. 53-1.)
10. Explain how to check (a) cylinder compression pressure, (b) blowby. (Refer to Fig. 53-2.)
11. Explain how to check and analyze the exhaust back pressure.
12. What could result if the exhaust back pressure were double the maximum allowable restriction?
13. List the factors which would indicate high oil consumption.
14. Why can excessive oil pressure (above specification) cause high oil consumption?

Fig. 53-1 Measuring blowby. (Cummins Engine Company, Inc.)

15. List five points where fuel could enter and dilute the engine oil.
16. List five points where coolant can enter and dilute the engine oil.
17. How would you pinpoint the location where coolant has entered the lubrication system?
18. List 10 checks or tests which would determine why an engine overheats.
19. How would you check the coolant system for aeration?
20. Outline the procedure to check the coolant system's pressure and temperature.
21. When excessive engine temperature is caused by the fuel-injection system, which checks or tests will reveal the part of the system at fault?
22. Explain how to check the (a) transfer pump, (b) manifold pressure, (c) volume of the transfer pump.
23. List eight reasons why an engine emits grey to white exhaust smoke.

Fig. 53-2 Checking the turbocharger. (Cummins Engine Company, Inc.)

135

24. List eight reasons why an engine emits 20 to 100 percent hot, dense exhaust smoke.
25. An engine will emit blue exhaust smoke when oil is present in the combustion chamber. List six reasons why oil could be present in the combustion chamber.
26. Explain how to locate a misfiring cylinder when using (a) an in-line injection pump, (b) a PT or GM fuel-injection system.
27. Explain how to check the operating condition or serviceability of a (a) rubber vibrating damper, (b) viscous vibrating damper.
28. List four problems which cause engine vibration.